I0892235

# EDGAR AND BRIGITTE

JEWS AND JUDAISM: HISTORY AND CULTURE

*Series Editors*
Mark K. Bauman
Adam D. Mendelsohn

*Founding Editor*
Leon J. Weinberger

*Advisory Board*
Tobias Brinkmann
Ellen Eisenberg
David Feldman
Kirsten Fermaglich
Jeffrey S. Gurock
Nahum Karlinsky
Richard Menkis
Riv-Ellen Prell
Raanan Rein
Jonathan Schorsch
Stephen J. Whitfield
Marcin Wodzinski

# EDGAR AND BRIGITTE

## A German Jewish Passage to America

Rosemarie
Bodenheimer

THE UNIVERSITY OF ALABAMA PRESS
*Tuscaloosa*

The University of Alabama Press
Tuscaloosa, Alabama 35487–0380
uapress.ua.edu

Copyright © 2016 by the University of Alabama Press
All rights reserved.

Inquiries about reproducing material from this work should be addressed to the University of Alabama Press.

Typeface: Caslon

Manufactured in the United States of America
Cover image: Brigitte and Edgar in their Davis living room, 1978; background image, family naturalization document; courtesy of Bodenheimer family collection
Cover design: Erin Bradley Dangar / Dangar Design

∞

The paper on which this book is printed meets the minimum requirements of American National Standard for Information Sciences—Permanence of Paper for Printed Library Materials, ANSI Z39.48-1984.

Cataloging-in-Publication data is available from the Library of Congress.
ISBN: 978-0-8173-1925-0
E-ISBN: 978-0-8173-9022-8

For my family

# Contents

List of Illustrations ix
Acknowledgments xi
Preface xiii
1. Coming of Age in the Weimar Republic 1
2. Emigration 24
3. Brigitte Levy 45
4. Seattle 72
5. Back East, Out West 94
6. Returns 112
7. Family Law, Natural Law 137
8. Gray Lady 156
9. Family Life in Salt Lake City 176
Afterword 190
Notes 197
Works Cited 205
Index 209

# Illustrations

1. Bodenheimer family tree xix
2. Levy family tree xx
3. Sachs family tree xxi
4. Edgar Bodenheimer at eighteen, 1926 3
5. Edgar with Rosi and Siegmund, ca. 1911 6
6. Edgar skating with his sister Bebs, ca. 1919 10
7. Siegmund Bodenheimer in 1944 34
8. Rosi Maass Bodenheimer in 1948 40
9. Ernst Levy with his unit in World War I 48
10. Wolfgang, Marie, and Brigitte Levy in 1915 51
11. A Levy family portrait, 1924 52
12. Marie with eighteen-year-old Brigitte, 1931 54
13. Edgar and Brigitte's wedding at the Hotel Alden 68
14. Ernst Levy in 1944 78
15. Marie Wolff Levy in 1942 79
16. Nuremberg in 1945 116
17. The Bodenheimer children in 1951 138
18. Brigitte in 1965 143
19. Edgar in his office during the 1960s 149
20. Brigitte and Edgar in their Davis living room, 1978 154
21. Kaethe Sachs 159
22. Kaethe, Rosemarie, Brigitte in the yard, Salt Lake City, ca. 1950 174
23. Edgar in 1985 193

# Acknowledgments

Without the support of my brothers, Peter and Tom Bodenheimer, I could not have started or finished this book. Both of them read draft chapters, gave me astute suggestions, and cheered me on. My nephew Dan Bodenheimer, the family genealogist, manages a vast and sprawling family tree on the Geni website, which has been an indispensable tool in my attempts to figure out the lives and relationships of family members. He solved several puzzles that came up in the course of my research and prepared many of the photographs.

Others have contributed stories and documents that filled out aspects of family history I could not have found in my father's files. My cousin Edna Levy Lowe sent me a transcript of our grandmother's diary about her young children, translated by her father Wolfgang Levy. Her brother Ralph Levy supplied information about their parents' lives and moves in the United States. On my father's side, cousin Ron Blau gave me transcripts of interviews he did with his parents, Gerda (Bebs) and Teddy Blau. His imaginative collage films, based on family footage from the 1930s, have made him an inspiring co-conspirator in the business of family history. His brother, Fred Blau, who masterminded a family translation of our grandfather Siegmund Bodenheimer's memoir *Mein Leben*, made it possible for me to draw on that document in readable English and German. Fred has also helped me along with memories and facts about our grandparents' lives in Berlin and New York. For her proficiency in turning some letters written in Gothic script into readable German, I thank Karin Vanderspeck.

In the course of his work on the Marianne Weber circle in Heidelberg, the sociologist Guenther Roth got in touch with me, and supplied letters and information that shed important new light on my mother's young life in Max Weber's ancestral home. In my quest for knowledge about the life of Kaethe Sachs, I turned to Charles A. Miller, who has kept the flame of Vera Lachmann's life and writing alive for decades. He provided a letter that settled at least one of my questions, and got me in touch with Beate Frankfurther Planskoy. Beate, the stepdaughter of Vera's sister Nina Frankfurther, remembered Kaethe from her youth in Berlin. The few hours I spent talking with her in London, learning about her family life and their last-minute emigration to England, remain among the most cherished memories this research has brought in its wake. Without her contributions and suggestions, my account of Kaethe's life could not have fulfilled its purpose.

I would like to thank the many friends and colleagues who read draft chapters and let me know that they wanted to hear more. Remarkably, each of my readers found different moments in the text to question or correct, so I have been well served by a community of keen eyes. I owe special thanks to Ilona Bell, who brought her mother's Hungarian Holocaust history along with her sympathetic readings and smart editorial suggestions. The Boston Victorian reading group, led by Martha Vicinus, gave me their collective commentary on "Returns" in a session that sped me toward completion of the book. I have also benefited from the attention, knowledge, and advice of colleagues who brought different kinds of professional expertise to their reading of the entire manuscript: Matilda Bruckner, Elizabeth Graver, Lisa Rodensky, Jonathan Strong, and Peter Weiler.

I am very grateful to Dan Waterman of the University of Alabama Press for seeing the potential in this material, and for his clear guidance in charting the path from manuscript to book. My anonymous press readers provided historical perspectives and suggestions for revision from which I profited a great deal.

Always last and best, I thank my beloved husband and in-house reader, Andrew Von Hendy. He was the one who knew it was time for me to get going on this project.

# Preface

When the *List or Manifest of Alien Passengers for the United States* was filled out for the German vessel MS *St. Louis*, departing Hamburg on September 3, 1933, one page carried a single name: Brigitte Levy. She is twenty years old, born in Berlin, last residence Heidelberg. Yes, she can read and write. Occupation: student. Under "Race or People" the word "German" is typed in, but it has been crossed out and "Hebrew" written above it in neat capital letters. The *St. Louis* would become notorious in May 1939, when nearly a thousand Jews fleeing Hitler were barred from entry into Cuba and the United States, and the ship was forced to carry its desperate refugees back to Europe. Brigitte Levy, an early emigrant, was one of the lucky ones. She was soon to meet Edgar Bodenheimer in the Columbia Law School Library, to marry, have children, and build an American legal career alongside her husband's. Had it not been for that substitution of "Hebrew" for "German," none of it would have happened.

*Edgar and Brigitte* is the story of my parents, Edgar Bodenheimer (1908–1991) and Brigitte Marianne Levy Bodenheimer (1912–1981). It is a narrative of assimilation, emigration, and reassimilation. It is also a record of two families who were deeply at home in a culture that now exists only in fragments of memory, objects handed down, and half-conscious, inherited habits of being. In many ways these families, the Bodenheimers and the Levys, were perfect case studies for the peculiar class of assimilated Jews that developed in Germany during the later part of the nineteenth century: more German than Jewish, highly educated, and saturated to the core in German Enlightenment ideals. As so many studies tell us, such families assumed that their *Bildung*—their embrace of German culture, their reverence for Goethe and Schiller, their love of German music, and their enormous success in German business, finance, arts, letters, and scholarship—had wiped out any traces of "primitive" Jewishness that might trigger anti-Semitic feelings in their fellow Germans. It was just this infatuation with *Bildung*, we are told, that made it so difficult for German Jews to realize what was happening when Hitler came to power. There is surely a good deal of truth in this analysis, but its generalities cannot comprehend the varieties of response and the individual experiences of living through such a period. This book is an attempt to get an angle on that history through biographies of a few particular lives and careers.

There is a wide literature of Holocaust testimony and survival, but this is not a Holocaust story. Nor is it a study of well-known German émigré artists and intellectuals who created communities in the boroughs of New York City, the hills of Los Angeles, and major academic centers such as Harvard, Yale, Chicago, or Berkeley. The Bodenheimers contributed to American public life in their modest ways as lawyers, scholars, teachers, and writers. They are readily traceable in public documents and legal bibliographies. But they pursued their American lives in places like Seattle, Salt Lake City, and Davis, California. If they are to be representative at all, they might stand for those emigrants who fled Nazi Germany to become American citizens in cities and towns where they shared their heritage with very few others.

When Hitler became Chancellor of Germany on January 30, 1933, there were 525,000 Jews living in Germany. By the end of that year 37,000 had left the country—my mother and father among them. They were not yet connected with each other, but they both faced the same barrier in their homeland: as apprentice lawyers or law students, they were no longer employable. Edgar was twenty-five, Brigitte twenty. Their parents pushed them, and they went, doubtless with hopes of returning when sanity reigned again in the German state. Unlike so many Jewish Germans, who stuck out Nazi policies of exclusion and humiliation for the next five or six years before they could or would try to escape, they had easy emigrations—in my father's case, you could call it downright luxurious. But emigration is never easy, and its effects last a lifetime.

My father made and kept a record of that trajectory. After he died in May 1991 my two brothers and I packed up boxes of files and papers he had left behind, all carefully organized and labeled in his characteristic fashion. The family archive then went to rest for twenty years in one brother's basement. I began working on this book when I was sixty-five, nearing retirement from an academic life as a professor of Victorian literature. As the youngest child of the family and the one most interested in the past, I had been putting family papers that came my way into folders, vaguely thinking that someday I would make use of them. But when my brother shipped over a hundred pounds of handwritten and printed material, I was astonished at what I found. I had expected the professional papers, but Edgar had kept everything: school grade sheets, high school essays, private journals starting in 1925, family poems, and, most of all, letters: his own, my mother's, a few written by his father, father-in-law, and other relatives, professional correspondence, and, surprisingly, two small groups from former girlfriends in Germany. All had been sifted and sorted into sets and filed by place or correspondent. A few had little explanatory notes penciled on them, while the occasional gap revealed that some had been discarded. It looked as if Edgar had been preparing to write a record of his lifelong quest to discover a philosophical basis for hope in civilized society, after suffering from the collapse of the Weimar Republic and the breakdown of law in Nazi Germany. He wanted, at least, to save the material that attested to his personal and intellectual struggles with principles of law, with Judaism, and with the experience of exile.

To me, the carefully preserved evidence of Edgar's life felt like a posthumous invitation to make a story from the assembled documents. Because they are records of moments as they pass, letters and journals have a historical beauty that cannot be matched by retrospective memory or oral histories. They are unmarked by knowledge of what was to come, or by the inevitable unconscious distortions that occur in the processing and reprocessing of memory over time. And, though letters are addressed to a particular audience of one or two people, they are free of the omissions and additions that arise when an older teller is shaping a story for a younger listening audience.

Edgar had had time to think of his past during retirement, after his full-time employment as professor of law at the University of Utah and the University of California at Davis had come to a close. Brigitte died at sixty-eight, in the thick of her late-blooming career in family law. Cancer interrupted her mission as the US delegate to the Hague Conference on Private International Law, where her work on a uniform code regulating child custody would be ratified. Less inclined to save up the evidence of her own life, she left a box of childhood letters from family and friends in Germany and a few small daily diaries. Immersed in the practicalities of managing her family and her work, Brigitte had little time for the big questions, though she listened patiently to Edgar's ideas and helped him negotiate the changing circumstances of their lives. Edgar preserved a good many of her letters, and one of Brigitte's students taped an autobiographical interview with her when she retired from teaching at the UC Davis Law School. The tape script shows that Brigitte was quite conscious of what her young American interviewer would be likely to assume in 1979. Nonetheless, her recollections are the most vivid evidence I have of my mother's life before I knew her, and I make full use of them in telling her story.

One of the difficult aspects of emigration is the forced abandonment of a native language, especially for a natural writer like Edgar. He wrote with beautiful clarity in both German and English, but he retained his German accent and worked hard to get his mind around the strange manners of American speech. Throughout his American life he kept a small binder called Idioms and Phrases, numbering as he went. #1: "To give countenance to an interpretation." #1581: "He is all screwed up." As so often happens, my mother was the more readily adaptable of the two. Our family language was English, with the occasional German word or sentence thrown in. When my parents spoke and wrote to each other or to their own parents, German or English, or both, might be the language of choice on a particular occasion. The language of Edgar's journal writing also varies, depending on the context in which he was writing. When he returned to Germany in 1945 as a researcher for the American prosecution team at the Nuremberg war-crimes trial, he kept his journal in English, though his usual practice was to record his private intellectual life in German.

I picked up enough German to understand its syntax intuitively; the translations in this book are my own. For a biographer of my generation, the challenge is German handwriting, especially the old-style Gothic script. The debate about whether Gothic or Roman script should be practiced in Germany went back at least to the eighteenth century, but Gothic seems to have prevailed until early in the twentieth century, when the more liberal schools began to teach children to write in Roman script. Various mixtures ensued; happily for me, by the 1920s both Edgar and Brigitte wrote intelligible modern hands. The handwriting of the older generation was more difficult, but I was fortunate enough to find a transcriber who opened up some key letters written by my grandfathers.

As it happened, I was prepared to write a narrative drawing from letters, journals, published work, and historical accounts. I had done it twice before, in biographical-critical studies of George Eliot and Charles Dickens. When I began to work on this book, my father had been dead for twenty years, my mother for thirty. I had put in my time thinking about Edgar and Brigitte in their roles as my parents. I wanted to see them as they represented themselves: as two resourceful individuals who had emerged from their own powerful culture and restarted their lives in the face of a historical crisis that pulled all the rugs from under their feet. Calling my parents and grandparents by their given names, which I did not do while they were alive, has been one way to create that historical perspective.

Of course it was not like writing about a long-dead Victorian novelist I had never met, since I was constantly reexperiencing or discovering aspects of family experience that I had not previously understood. As I read, translated, and took notes on each set of materials, I would have strong emotional reactions to what I was learning, and would sometimes find myself shying away from my desk for several days or weeks. Meanwhile, some accommodating magic would go on in the back rooms of my consciousness. By the time I had set my parents more firmly in their cultural contexts and arrived at the point of writing, the task had been transformed into the familiar process of finding an order and getting the sentences to do what I wanted.

The bar of personal privacy was set high in my family. Like other Europeans of their class, Edgar and Brigitte disapproved of Americans who lived their private lives in public. For them, it was natural to maintain discreet and cordial distances, and to leave personal matters largely unspoken. In writing this narrative I have violated that privacy—both my parents' and my own—while also attempting to honor it. My alternations between daughterly familiarity and biographical distance stem from that tension, and from the way I encountered the details of my parents' lives so long after their deaths. With their American children, Edgar and Brigitte were quite reticent about their own experiences and rarely indulged in the reminiscing that binds generations in many families. Busy with our lives, my brothers and I did not ask many questions about our German Jewish heritage before our parents died, though we had lived in its atmosphere throughout our childhoods. (I do not use the hyphenated adjective "German-Jewish" in this book, because the Nazis forced a division between those identities that I would like to signal.) My own memories of family life, beginning in the 1950s, do come into play in the later chapters. But most of this book is written through the lens of a biographer who is newly learning about the lives of her parents through the writing they left behind.

That perspective, along with my desire to maintain a vestige of the respectful distances our parents modeled, means that this narrative is, for the most part, less intimate than memoir. The privacy of the living is important to me, so I write about my own generation primarily when we appear as children through the eyes of our parents. My older brothers have verified or corrected facts they recall, but I have not interviewed them about our parents, nor did I think it appropriate to say much about the psychological effects of growing up in my family. However, I am fully present in my roles of interpreter, participant, and carrier of memory, as well as in nuances of tone and style that could emerge only from emotional engagement with my subjects.

As a child, I assumed that Edgar's idealist philosophizing and Brigitte's zeal for legal reform stemmed from their idiosyncratic characters. In the process of preparing this narrative, I have discovered how deeply their distinctive visions were rooted in German Jewish culture, as it flourished during the late nineteenth and early twentieth centuries, reaching its peak during the Weimar Republic of the 1920s. The specific circumstances of my parents' experiences were naturally determined by the lives of their own parents, who play important supporting roles in this story. The Berlin banker Siegmund Bodenheimer and the Roman law scholar Ernst Levy had very different reactions to the Nazi takeover, which caught them both at the height of significant careers. Their wives, Rosi Bodenheimer and Marie Levy, sounded early warning signals, though each was ignored until the Nazi facts on the ground proved irrefutable. Still, both families were among the fortunate who got out well in time, carrying subtle scars of exile that were partially obscured by successful lives in the United States. A sadder story occupies chapter 8, which pieces together the life of Rosi Bodenheimer's cousin Kaethe Sachs. A last-minute refugee, Kaethe ended up as a member of our household, playing a rather lonely and ambiguous role as relative and housekeeper. Her evident losses, and those of the people close to her, serve as a reminder of some darker shades in the histories of bourgeois German Jews who got "safely" out of Germany.

Despite my inherited reservations about making private matters public, it seemed important to tell these stories in order to provide an everyday window onto some aspects of German Jewish thought and culture that have, understandably, been overshadowed by the devastating events we now call the Holocaust. The experiences of child refugees and the children of survivors have been quite well documented, but I have read little that echoes my own experience in a family of early emigrants from the Third Reich who created satisfying lives in the United States. I wanted to make my family's history available to the many others who share my heritage and to readers still fascinated by the extraordinary complexity, tragedy, and resilience of those whose lives were upended by Hitler. Like every biographer, I also hoped to bring my subjects to life in a narrative that reveals a good deal about them, and something of the history that determined the course of their lives.

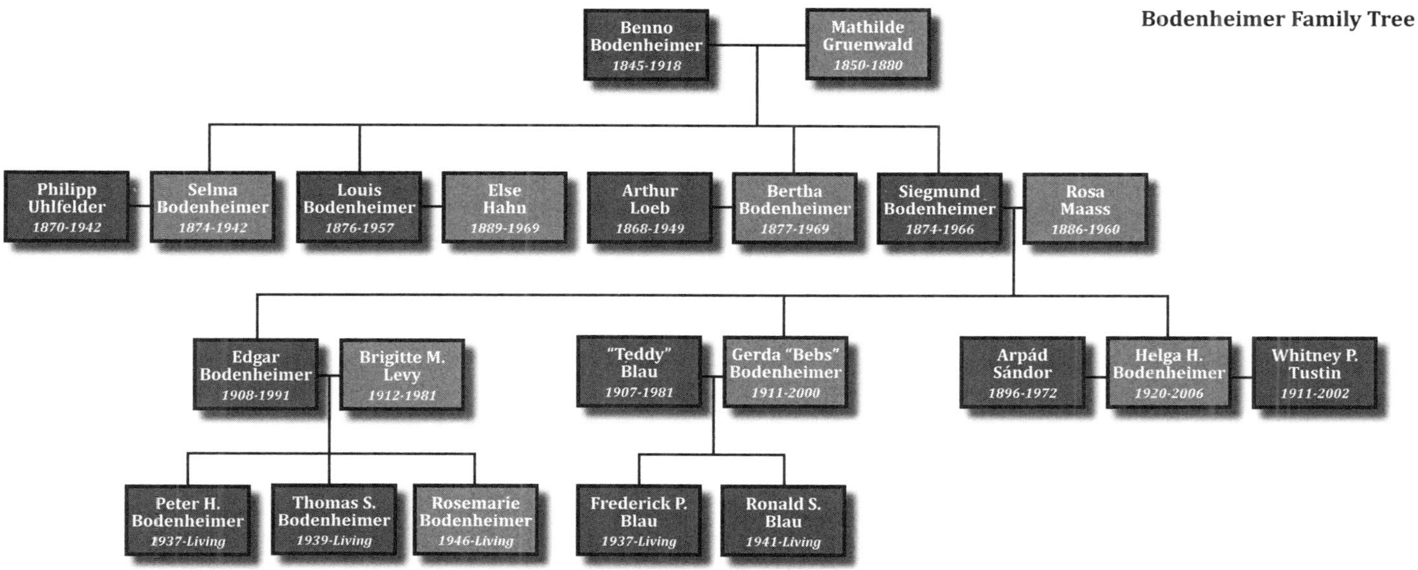


Figure 1. Bodenheimer Family Tree

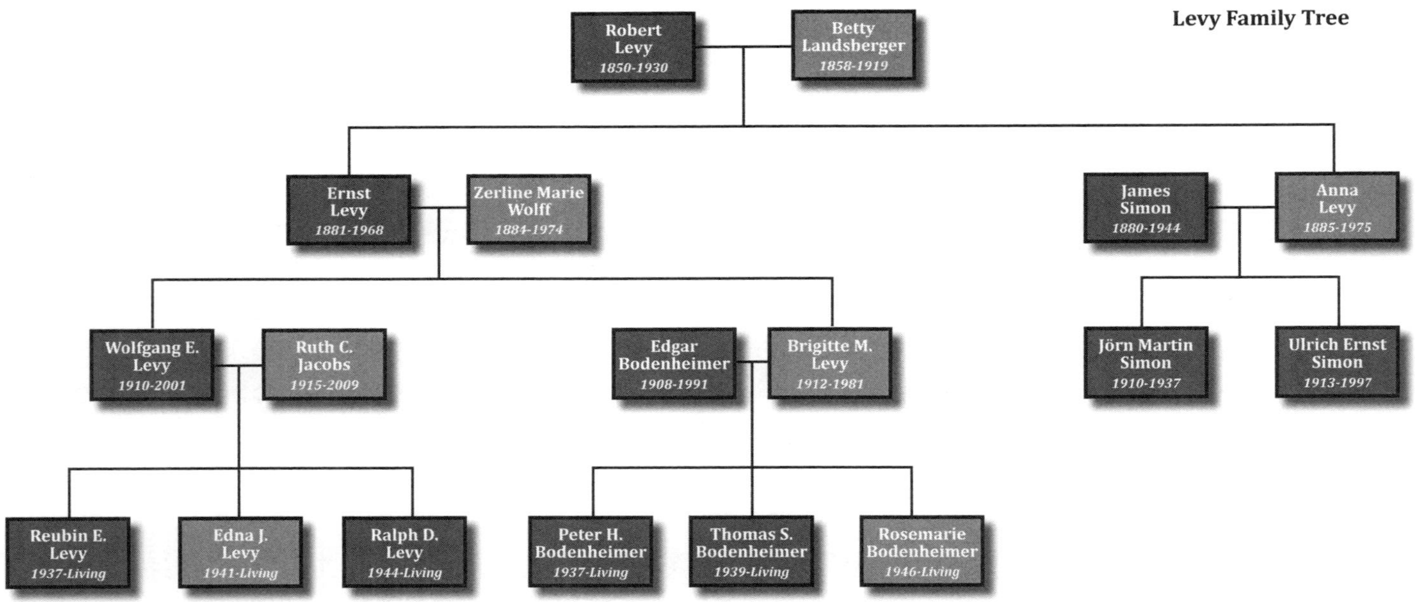


Figure 2: Levy Family Tree

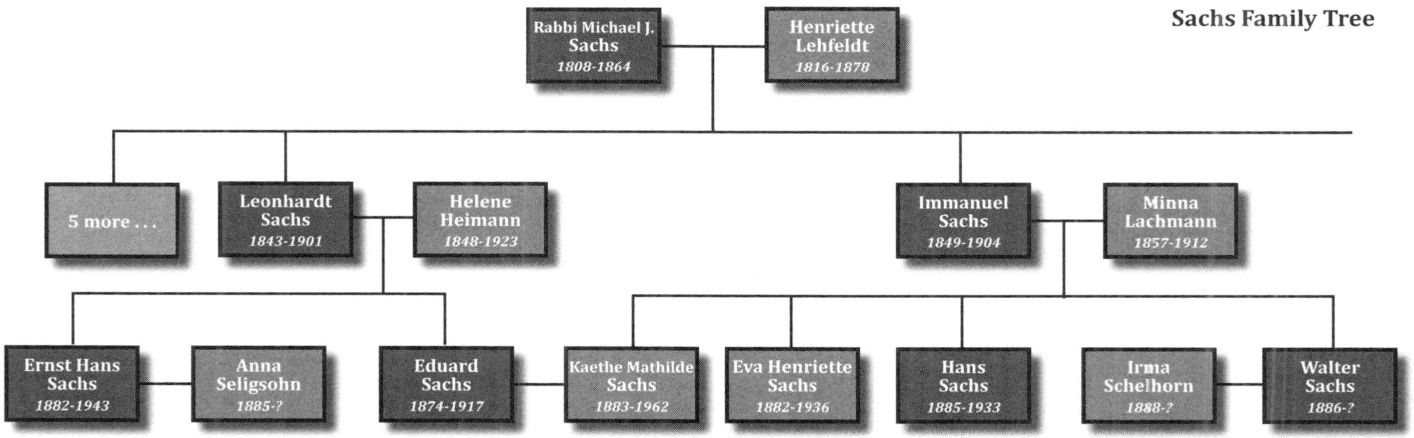

Figure 3. Sachs Family Tree

# EDGAR AND BRIGITTE

# I
# Coming of Age in the Weimar Republic

My father on his seventeenth birthday emerges from the first page of a soft black oilskin-covered journal, labeled with his name, Edgar Bodenheimer, and the date, 1925. That morning of March 14, he had *eine höchst angenehme Geburstagsüberraschung*, a delightful birthday surprise: school was *schneefrei*, declared a snow day. It didn't take him long to take advantage of this pleasant situation. With three of his closest school friends, Herbert, Robert, and Hilde, he took off for the morning to ski in the Grunewald woods, meeting two other companions on the way. More merriment and horsing around than serious sport, he noted conscientiously. In the afternoon two friends came over to his family's house in Grunewald; later they drove together to a dinner-dance at the Seligsohns, where they all had a wonderful time eating, dancing, and smirking at the awkward antics of an affected, foolish classmate. There was a *Blumenwaltz*, and Elli, a girl Edgar admired, got the most flowers. She was at the top of her form as he most liked to see her, fresh, merry, and high-spirited.

He, too, was at the top of his form at this moment: sociable, full of hopes for himself, interested in everything. He was in his last year at the Grunewald Gymnasium, preparing to make his *Abitur*—the qualifying exam for university—the following February. About three years earlier his banker father, Siegmund Bodenheimer, had moved the family from their central Berlin apartment to a large villa with an extensive garden in the leafy, lake-filled suburb of Grunewald. At fourteen Edgar had switched schools, moving from the traditional humanist Joachim Friedrich Gymnasium in Berlin-Wilmersdorf, where he had been since he was six, to the famously progressive Grunewald Gymnasium, a short walk from the family's new house. This school had taken the very unusual step of allowing boys and girls to study together; it was also known for its liberal student-teacher relationships and for its mission to widen students' cultural horizons and build their characters. The student body was about equally divided between

Jewish and Christian children.[1] A handful of girls who wanted to study Greek, normally not taught in girls' schools, were in Edgar's class. Among them, Hilde was special; she had become the sole female member of his small band of friends.

One day in May Edgar listed what had been discussed in his classes. The school day began with a distinction between static classical art and dynamic northern art: Aeschylus and Goethe; Raphael and Rembrandt. In Latin class, Catullus. In Greek class, how the Greeks had established that the Being of the cosmos is repeated in the Being of the soul, another cosmos eternally in motion. (Edgar would remain enamored of such universal analogies for the rest of his life.) The Greek instructor, Dr. Walther Kranz, was their class advisor that year. He was an inspired instructor who poured out his own enthusiasms, engaging his students' idealism as well as their artistic capacities. Even Kranz's signature on Edgar's grade sheet, more calligraphy than handwriting, announces his bold, self-conscious cultivation of beauty. That year he directed his class in Euripides' *Heracles*, performed in Greek with incidental piano music composed and played by Edgar, and Hilde playing the heroine's role.

In that era of German Hellenism, Kranz filled his students with a sense of Germany as the new Greece, encouraging individual self-development through the cultivation of reason and aesthetic taste. He embodied the ideal of *Bildung* that had emerged from the German Enlightenment in the work of Wilhelm von Humboldt, Goethe, and Schiller. Greek ideals of harmonious and well-proportioned beauty were revered; the gradual emergence of each person's special character was to take place through the internal cultivation of rational balance, discipline, and self-control. Tolerance, friendship, and equality based on self-cultivation rather than class or religion were central values. As George Mosse writes, "Surely here was an ideal ready-made for Jewish assimilation, because it transcended all differences of nationality and religion through the unfolding of the individual personality." Mosse argues that this "noble illusion," embraced wholeheartedly by middle-class German Jews, had already begun to change its character for Germans by the end of the nineteenth century, when culture gradually became associated with nationalism, romantic myth making, outward discipline, and conformity. Failing to take notice, German Jews continued to practice the older form of *Bildung* as their highest claim to German citizenship.[2] Kranz, who was half Jewish, seems to have enthralled many of his seventeen-year-old students with all the facets of that "noble illusion."

The emphasis on sport and physical training at the Grunewald Gymnasium also reflected the ethos of the period. Partly because the Treaty of Versailles in 1919 had stripped Germany of its military capacity after World

Figure 4. Edgar Bodenheimer at eighteen, 1926

War I, the physical training of young bodies was consigned to schools, where it became an important focus during the Weimar Republic. Edgar devoted himself with all his native good health and enthusiasm to gymnastics, skiing, mountain climbing, and tennis, recording his wins and losses when tennis reigned supreme during school vacations. He noted with satisfaction that his bodily development over the past two years had made him more comfortable at the dances his circle enjoyed almost every Saturday night at one of their families' homes; now he was more inclined to assume that others (meaning girls) would care for him. (He doesn't mention how good-looking he was, though he was always very aware of attractiveness or its absence in others.) In July 1925 he wrote, "My ideal is a god-like body and a strong soul, deliberately free of sentimentality, loving all things forceful and beautiful. . . . Also in music I hate mushiness: Mendelssohn, Grieg, Saint-Saëns I am averse to." He was never averse to emphatic ways of phrasing his likes and dislikes.

Most prominent in the journal of 1925 was his devotion to music and his conscious cultivation of musical taste. He worked intermittently at the piano and went to concerts once or twice a week, using his journal to assess what he had heard. He loved a Scriabin piece he was practicing for its simplicity and its powerfully sad minor ending. He puzzled over Richard Strauss, the leading German neo-Romantic composer, praising the *Rosenkavalier* waltzes but opining that Strauss fails when he tries to search inwardly. *Tod und Verklärung* is absolute kitsch, but it might be otherwise with the songs, which he doesn't know very well. He hears Beethoven's Ninth Symphony for the fourth time, conducted by Furtwängler. The impression of the piece strengthens each time he hears it, but Furtwängler's affected style of conducting is not appropriate for this piece. And then for a fifth time: only now can he really let the great symphony work in him. Is he practicing for a career in music criticism? Probably not, but he is intent on making himself a cultured, a truly *gebildete*, listener. As for modernist experiment—there's no room for that. He hears Schoenberg for the first time in concert and hates it. Without form, rhythm, or harmony, it is the product of a sick mind and makes him want to weep. He turns with relief from this conventional reaction to praise the *kraftvolle*, powerful *Macbeth* of Strauss.

Where do these judgments come from? Edgar represents them as his own, though his father was a lifelong music and opera lover of strong opinions and probably accompanied Edgar to at least some of the concerts he attended during this period. But *die Eltern*, the parents, make only rare appearances in Edgar's journals of this time. Nor does his fourteen-year-old sister Gerda, called Bebs, who had been a close companion during their childhoods. The postwar baby, Helga, was only four. Like seventeen-year-olds in general, Edgar was not much interested in thinking about how his inner life was shaped by the family, or how his cultural self-making was an inheritance from his father's financial acumen and social ascent. Siegmund Bodenheimer was a very German father: obsessed with his work, anxious and demanding, he exacted deference and expected success from his children. The journal, on the other hand, was a private place for the thoughts of a new generation—one less devoted to materialist success. Edgar used it to develop his intellectual life, to comment on his reading, to record impressions of people, conversations, and new places, and, quite consciously, to hone his opinions into a coherent worldview. It was important to have clear opinions, to separate the cultural wheat from the kitschy chaff; he wanted to make himself into a fair-minded man of many talents, ready for whatever the future might bring. Like every German schoolchild he had been thoroughly drenched in the greatness of Goethe, whose cultivation of many-sidedness was legendary. To be *einseitig* (one-sided), unbalanced, or stuck in a partisan point of view, was in Edgar's mind the worst of sins.

*Einseitig* was his father's word of disapproval as well, though Papa used it in the context of banking practices. In November 1944, his parents safely established on Central Park West in New York City, Edgar gave Siegmund a blank notebook for his seventieth birthday. The inevitable quotation from Goethe was inscribed on its first page, along with a request that his father compose a memoir. When it was finished, Siegmund Bodenheimer's unpublished *Mein Leben* (My Life) proved to be a detailed record of a banking career in the context of German history and politics, with a rare formal nod to the importance of matters like marriage and family. By 1944 the defeat of Hitler looked probable, but this German Jewish banker was still concerned to produce a document that would attest to his personal and professional integrity, especially in the face of repeated Nazi claims that Jewish bankers had been guilty of infiltrating and destroying the German economy.

For two or three years after his required military training, Siegmund writes, he worked for a small bank in Mannheim run by his stepmother's two brothers. He disliked their *einseitige* devotion to stock speculation, for which—as he tactfully put it—he had no inclination or talent. So, at twenty-four, he picked up and went to Berlin, to seek his fortune in the banking industry that he had served in low-paying jobs since the age of sixteen. (He would later joke that he spent his youth as an office boy licking stamps.) And his fortunes rose: Through a combination of diligence and a fortunate merger he became, at thirty-five, a director of the important Darmstädter Bank für Handel und Industrie, second among German credit institutions. He joined the bank in 1902, enjoying the prewar period of economic and industrial expansion, which he attributed to the best aspects of German character: hard work, a talent for organization, and a spirit of invention. Phrased in the ubiquitous turn-of-the-century language of the nerves, a rare sentence also admits to the personal cost: "It has been my lifelong tendency to push my strength to the limit, even though I had a highly nervous sensibility, which it has often taken all my energy to fight." Coming from a person who was always ready to see his life as an exemplary tale of the self-made man, the sentence was a reminder to his children that any sign of personal weakness was there to be overcome.

By 1907 he was well enough established to support a wife. He married Rosa (Rosi) Maass; on the honeymoon she conceived their son. It was all just as it should have been: he provided the serious business, she the charm and sociability of the household. As their daughter Bebs recalled in an interview with her son, "My father was a very serious man, and a very . . . extremely energetic, self-made, goal-directed person, who tended to worry quite a bit, even at times when, probably objectively, there was not that much to worry about. My mother, on the other hand was . . . well, I would call it a sunny nature. She had a beautiful smile, and she did not let the

Figure 5. Edgar with Rosi and Siegmund, ca. 1911

heaviness of her husband be contagious for her. . . . I'm sure she would cheer him up often and give the house kind of a lighter atmosphere. She was extremely hospitable. We always had friends or relatives around, and she was generally loved."[3]

In his younger years Siegmund had moved frequently from one German town to another in pursuit of better positions, always judging places by their cultural offerings. For him, Berlin was packed with the pleasures of opera, concerts, theater (he admired the controversial Ibsen), water sports, and bicycle trips. He became the proud owner of a motorboat, named Rosi 2 after his wife. Siegmund would later look back on life in prewar Berlin as a golden age: money was tied to gold bullion, people saved for their children and grandchildren, marriages were holy and indissoluble, inflation was merely a word in a textbook. Only the unbalanced, impulsive militarism of Kaiser Wilhelm II threatened his sense of achievement and enjoyment.

Siegmund's war was the Kaiser's folly, World War I. Like so many others, he described the summer of 1914 as the death of an era: "With the declaration of war a curtain fell over the world I was born into; a new and a worse age broke forth, in which people forgot elementary things they had learned, and were forced to learn new concepts under shattering conditions." The shock and fear of instability remained with him; in the event, however, the war provided yet another lucky break for him. At thirty-nine, he was immediately called up and sent to the eastern front to secure the border with Russia. The Darmstädter Bank went into high gear to have him released, arguing that, as a loan officer, he was essential to the national effort to finance the war. Their arguments worked, and Siegmund returned to Berlin, while most of his regiment was quickly wiped out in combat with the Russians.

Wartime banking was presumably good business. Writing his own history, however, Siegmund was not about to admit to any wartime profits that might fan the flames of prejudice against Jewish bankers. The years 1914–1918 exist in his memoir as a general history of military campaigns and strategy. Once the Kaiser had fled to Holland and the Social Democrats had taken over the state, Siegmund swerved back to his own experience: "Before the door stood the darkest future, perhaps chaos, and in the soul of a German bank director the future looked threatening and hopeless." He feared anarchism or Communist revolution but was able to report only on occasional shots fired in central Berlin when he went to work in the mornings.

His anxious sense of a hopeless future would prove true for many Germans in the 1920s, but not for him. Although financial practices had, in his view, lost their prewar integrity, the Socialist revolution he feared was averted. The fledgling Weimar Republic, Germany's first experiment in democracy, seemed to take at least tentative hold. The postwar inflation of the early 1920s decimated middle-class lives in ways that would never be forgotten in later years—but not his.[4] In 1922, as the crazed period of hyperinflation set in, the Darmstädter Bank finalized its merger with the Nationalbank für Deutschland, becoming the Danat-Bank. Siegmund was promoted again, becoming one of the bank's seven owner-partners. The merger allowed him to invest his increasingly worthless cash in real property, the large villa in Grunewald where his children could grow up in security, sheltered from the poverty and desperation that prevailed in other sections of Berlin. The house signaled his arrival in upper-middle-class Jewish life; for some time Grunewald had been a preserve of the cultured Jewish families who formed a special subgroup within the German middle class.[5] By 1924, after the currency stabilization and the apparent restoration of normal economic life, the Bodenheimers enjoyed a very good life in the house at 29/33 Jagowstrasse, supported by a staff of servants, surrounded by a garden the children loved, and regularly filled with family and friends.

Siegmund's upward mobility was grounded in the need to help his father, Benno Bodenheimer, support a growing family. Born in 1874, Siegmund had entered the world just as Otto von Bismarck was consolidating the unification of Germany under Prussian rule. At sixteen, he left school reluctantly: his father, who ran a men's haberdashery in Heidelberg, required money to provide for the children of three successive wives. Siegmund had a brother and two sisters, along with four stepsisters; all of those young women would need funding before they married. Throughout the lives of his siblings, and crucially during the Nazi period, he would act as their patron and financier and guarantee the affidavits required for emigration. During the 1920s Siegmund expanded his philanthropic efforts beyond the family, becoming a member of the *Gesellschaft der Freunde* (Society of Friends), a Jewish welfare society that traced its roots to the late eighteenth century. By Siegmund's time it had evolved into an elite association of banking and business leaders who were active in social causes.

Siegmund did not attempt to obscure his Jewishness, nor did he pretend that Germany was an easy place for Jews. His memoir acknowledges that "anti-Semitism was always present in Germany" and takes note of the virulent scapegoating of Jews that was triggered by the recession following the German stock market crash of 1873. The beginning of his work life in 1890 coincided with another brief anti-Semitic flare-up, though it had calmed down by the time he began his professional ascent at the turn of the century.[6] He was also clear about restrictions on Jewish professional life that led so many into careers in banking and finance—restrictions that had remained in place long after official policies of emancipation were installed by the German-speaking states early in the nineteenth century. The majority of his colleagues and friends were Jewish and tended to marry other Jews of their class; everyone seemed to be at least distantly related to everyone else.[7] Judaism itself was assumed but often left unpracticed; there was no need to emphasize what fellow Germans seemed willing to forget.

As the acknowledged center of his extended family, Siegmund was dutifully respected, admired, and sometimes feared. When he summoned, people came. His fiftieth birthday celebration, on November 22, 1924, brought the entire family of siblings and stepsisters, spouses, relatives, and friends to Berlin, from as far away as Brussels. For their father's fiftieth, the Bodenheimer children somehow managed to publish a special edition of the local newsletter, the *Grunewald Echo*, beautifully printed on shiny paper in Gothic typeface. Each section of the paper, including the ads, contained invented news about members of the extended family. The lead article, certainly written by Edgar, praised their father while teasing him about some of his habits and activities, including his severity as a theater critic. Had that been his actual profession, Edgar joked, the theaters of Berlin would soon be empty.

According to Siegmund's custom, the company was regaled with a long poem in rhyming tetrameter quatrains, one of the many he composed and delivered on birthdays and major anniversaries throughout his life. Long meditated, these verses were perhaps the vestiges of Siegmund's frustrated early ambition to excel in a learned or artistic vocation, though they were also common practice among the German bourgeoisie. His children and grandchildren would be taught to reciprocate with performed rhymes or little plays of their own on family occasions. Edgar produced a number of verse dramas imitating Goethe or Schiller during his childhood. An envelope containing miscellaneous family papers coughed up two forgotten little poems that I recited in German at large events on the Upper West Side when I was six and ten.

A fiftieth birthday was a major event to be commemorated, and Siegmund's poem articulates the pride of an eminently successful man at a high point of achievement. It begins with jokes about the travails of being fifty: the acquisition of embonpoint that's rapidly becoming—oh horror!—a belly, the beginnings of grey hair. The long last section enumerates all the family members, colleagues, and friends who were present, saluting each of them with a couplet or two. But Siegmund's central concern was autobiographical, a look back at his own ascent. He recalls his Heidelberg childhood, his yearning for "Poesie," his awakening to realism, the struggle to rise, his fortunate marriage to a wife who wasn't jealous of her namesake (the motorboat), the recovery from inflation. It is charming, funny, sharp, and immensely satisfied with its own proper sentiments. Like the reams of verse written to celebrate Rosi's birthdays, it is centrally devoted to recent political and family history, as if the poems were Siegmund's semipublic form of journal keeping. Edgar could not help but learn from his father's annual poems that a life was something to be kept and recorded. Its trajectory was important, and it was not to be sullied by dwelling on unpleasant elements. Only when painful events occurred in the political realm were expressions of outrage or despair permissible.

Edgar at seventeen was attempting to forge his soul in the sheltered, luxurious world his parents had made. He had been a child during the war, but his father had stayed at home. Overt anti-Semitism, urban unrest, the famous Weimar Berlin of cabarets, jazz, modernism, and mass culture—all of this was temporarily kept at bay. Only Bebs, who thought she was the only family member who looked Jewish, could recall being harassed by anti-Semitic remarks on the street. But the beginnings of Edgar's political

Figure 6. Edgar skating with his sister Bebs, ca. 1919

attentiveness are evident enough. A school friend called Rathenau was a close acquaintance; could he have been somehow connected with Walther Rathenau, the Jewish Foreign Secretary of the Weimar Republic who had been assassinated by right-wing terrorists on June 22, 1922? The shooting had taken place just a few blocks from the Grunewald Gymnasium as the foreign secretary was being driven to work. Rathenau, who had masterminded the wartime economy in which Siegmund had participated, was hated for his highly cultured, assimilated Jewishness as well as for his liberal policies.[8] Edgar doesn't mention him, nor does he sound his schoolmate's first name, but the event itself had come dangerously close to home for his own family. (After the war, the school was renamed the Walther Rathenau Gymnasium.)

In 1925, the presidential election was a more immediate concern. Edgar discussed his enthusiasm for the Social Democratic Party candidate Otto Braun with his friend Herbert, until Herbert turned the conversation from liberalism to questions of unrequited love. Between 1919 and 1925 the political arena had shifted strongly to the right, and the long tradition of Prussian militarism on which Bismarck's nineteenth-century German Empire had been built was reasserting its opposition to the new republic. Otto Braun withdrew from the second round of voting to throw his support to a centrist candidate, but the move did not prevent Field Marshal Paul von Hindenburg, the iconic Prussian leader of the German army during World War I, from winning the election. Although Hindenburg maintained the republic for a few years, his administration would ultimately pave the way for Hitler's ascent and the reestablishment of an authoritarian state.

On May 12, 1925, Edgar wrote, "A big day. Hindenburg's swearing in." Together with Rathenau, Herbert, and Hilde, he cut out of a boring speech at a school celebration and went into the city. Pretending to be staff members of the Darmstädter Bank, the little group pushed their way through barriers and crowds into the bank, and landed in the office of a Herr Wolfson. From there they could watch the departure of Hindenburg in a Mercedes, leaving at exactly 11:45 for the ceremony in the nearby Reichstag and returning forty minutes later accompanied by mounted police and looking very solemn. *Grosse Begeisterung* (great enthusiasm), Edgar notes dryly. On the way home Edgar, Hilde, and Rathenau played a *Scherz* (prank) in honor of the new regime. At Berlin's central square, the Potsdamer Platz, each of them bought both the black-red-gold flag of the Weimar Republic and a black-white-red flag displaying the old imperial colors, which Hindenburg would restore for foreign diplomatic use. Placing the flags together in their buttonholes, they marched through the streets watching people's reactions. Some approved, some laughed, some muttered about the decklessness of youth. Whoever dreamed up this prank, it's Edgar's mind I hear in the motto that sums up their attitude: "We set ourselves against the nationalists as a club of rationalists."

The flag play had an odd sequel. A few days later, on the Bismarckallee Bridge between their Grunewald homes, Hilde confronted Edgar in a mock duel, and a *Hakenkreuz* (swastika) was ceremonially transferred. Herbert and Rathenau served as seconds. By this time Hitler had reshaped the black-white-red imperial colors into a Nazi Party flag with the swastika emblem at its center. I cannot tell exactly what this little drama was supposed to mean, what Edgar thought of it, whose idea it was, or what kind of political consciousness lay behind the shenanigans of these privileged teenagers. Clearly, the Nazis were still a matter for jest.

In more serious frames of mind, Edgar was well aware of Hitler and his effect on the populace. A year earlier he had composed a school essay on an assigned subject, "My Newspaper," in which he was asked to consider three questions: Why is the newspaper necessary? What do I expect from my newspaper? What requirements doesn't my newspaper fulfill? "The newspaper is for a modern person a necessity he can't do without," he begins. It is especially necessary in case of war or revolution; we have experienced the *fieberhafte Unruh*—the feverish agitation—that overcomes the city when the papers don't print and unbelievable rumors circulate. It is the duty of a paper, he writes, to be precise and thorough, but this, unfortunately, is not always the case. As an example, he cites the recent trial of Hitler after his failed attempt at revolution, the Beer Hall Putsch of November 8–9, 1923. Edgar had followed the trial, which had begun in February 1924, and knew that Hitler had used it as a forum to elicit sympathy from the populace; the newspapers had reported everything he said. The trial had been painted in a different color in almost every newspaper, he writes, depending on its political affiliation. But that was a failing: newspapers should be separate from official party organs. Most people, who don't have what it takes to form an individual opinion, blindly trust what they read in the paper: "What's in black and white they can safely take home." In this way papers have done a lot of mischief, when they should be dedicated to reporting the many-sidedness of events in the world, leaving readers to form their own opinions. As he wrote, Hitler was living comfortably in a posh prison, beginning to compose *Mein Kampf.*

Edgar's essay, mixing liberal idealism with a patrician distrust of "most people" and a well-earned fear of right-wing propaganda, was predictive. He would continue throughout his life both to be deeply troubled by any sign of right-wing agitation and to stake his belief in the ideal possibility that well-informed public servants could make rational, unbiased judgments for the common good. It was an Enlightenment legacy that would never leave him, even after the worst had happened. At sixteen, however, he ended his essay with a bow to postwar national feeling, wishing that more German newspapers were read in foreign countries, so that appreciation for German life and culture would rise again in the rest of the world. His patriotism was not in doubt. The punitive judgments and heavy reparations demanded by the Allied victors in the 1919 Treaty of Versailles were on everyone's minds, including his.

For the moment, however, social life was in the foreground, and the antics of the little band of friends were primarily attempts to test the boundaries of proper behavior. One May morning they went to Dr. Kranz's house, hung their coats on his fence, recited a poem he had been teaching them, whistled the Tristan motif, and belted out the school song. Their teacher did not emerge. Disappointed—and perhaps relieved—they went home in high spirits. At the end of the month Kranz took his class on a school excursion to the Plauer See, a lake resort west of Berlin near Brandenburg. As they walked from the train to the hotel, Edgar, Herbert, and Hilde ran ahead and tacked off into the woods, where they lay on the leafy ground in a makeshift wigwam and watched excitedly as their schoolmates trekked by and strangers on the road reacted to the red glow of their flashlight in the dark forest. When the trio caught up with the rest at the hotel, Kranz made no comment and continued to enthuse about a poem. For him, the class retreat was an opportunity to infuse his students with the spirit of nature and poetry through walks and talks in a beautiful place, to chide them gently for slacking in their commitment to class debate, and to urge them to experience every passing moment to the fullest. But his patience had a limit.

Edgar described that limit as a *Katastrophe*. Gearing up to record it, he wrote that he had hardly experienced anything in his life that had made so deep an impression on him. He'd gained as an insight into the psychology of a certain person (Kranz)—perhaps his judgment was wrong, but he didn't think so, and his friends and parents supported him. His version of the terrible event runs like this: before going to bed on the second night, he and Herbert invited Hilde and another girl into their room to share some chocolate. Rathenau and two other classmates joined them, bringing in a bottle of wine and some cigarettes, which they passed out to everyone. The room filled with cigarette smoke. One boy, sent out to fetch a second bottle of wine, roused Kranz as he tried to sneak back. Kranz followed him down the hall, just as someone opened the door to the smoke-filled room. At this point Edgar becomes quite novelistic. Kranz appeared in the doorway. "'Dear friends, haven't you yet—' he began, but as he spoke he saw the two young girls. Instantly his character changed: 'We depart tomorrow. Leave the room. Forward!' The 'Forward!' was shouted loud enough to wake the whole house. He added, 'It is over between us, and for good.'"

What follows for pages of Edgar's journal is a hot, detailed account of the moment's long aftermath, in which he tries to deal with the revered teacher who had apparently turned into an irrational monster. Next morning, the boys endure a lecture in which Edgar and Herbert are singled out for their teacher's fury because they invited the girls to their room with, Kranz implies, the shameless intention of getting them drunk and necking. Kranz doesn't at all like the way they have been treating Hilde, either during the trip or earlier in Berlin: if they love her, they must honor her and put her on a pedestal. As it is, they all deserve to be thrown out of school. The guiltier parties, who brought in the wine, seem to be getting less attention. Edgar works out why that might be: perhaps Kranz was home after all when they serenaded his house; perhaps he was especially upset when the trio huddled secretly in the woods. No one seems to consider the panic that might strike a teacher responsible for the well-being of his charges away from home, especially in an unusual coed situation.

Then, the trip is not going to be cancelled after all. They stay for their last day, Kranz silent and sulking while the boys energetically stick to their schedule and pretend they are having a wonderful time. The morning before departure, Kranz retreats further. He tells them that the matter will have to be forgotten; otherwise they cannot stay together. They take the train journey to Berlin, during which Edgar beats four of his classmates in chess, he's concentrating so hard. Back at school, Kranz summons Edgar and Herbert to the library, where he gives them another lecture in a friendlier tone. Although he encourages friendships between the sexes, they have to be very careful with Hilde. Because she has a strong tendency to suffer, she must be treated like a delicate plant. He enjoins them to leave her alone during the upcoming Pentecost holiday and to resume contact when school starts again.

Throughout his long journal entry, Edgar tries to justify himself by casting aspersions on his teacher. His theory is that Kranz's reckless behavior was motivated by jealousy. After all, the teacher had been acting inappropriately with Hilde during the trip, keeping her close by his side whenever possible. In a later entry he becomes more generous. Perhaps Kranz was just sympathetic with Hilde and wished to protect her. Edgar never confesses to what's really bothering him, but clearly he is smarting under an angry accusation that's unjust and a direct insult to his respectability and self-control. Worse, the accusation is full of disturbing aspects. There's lurking sexuality, which is not directly discussed in his world, and irresponsible behavior with a girl. The liberality of the school and its experiment with coeducation were suddenly revealing a darker underside.

Edgar was right; he never forgot the episode. Sixty years later, after Brigitte's death, he renewed a correspondence with Hilde, who was living in Wiesbaden with her husband. Hilde had spent her life in Germany and was then enjoying a new grandchild. She had been rereading Thomas Mann's *The Magic Mountain* and could imagine herself back in their old schoolroom, listening to Kranz talk about the novel. Edgar must have taken up the reference, because Hilde responded in surprise:

> I wanted to write to you because I was astonished that you still remember Kranz at the Plauersee. It wasn't that way with me, because I could never endure that anyone could be angry with me. . . . You must remember that I grew up among sisters, with no experience of boys, and was probably behaving in a way inappropriate to a coed situation. The evening itself was innocent enough. But I knew that Kranz was somehow right, and as he thundered away, that it was something to pay attention to. And because the thunder came from such a re-

> spected hand—I couldn't, afterwards, be such a naïve coquette. In any case he has remained a hero to me. And I always thought it was the same for you—in any case he would be proud of you now.

Hilde, at least, was perfectly willing to admit to the ways she had contributed to the "catastrophe," though in Kranz's version—as reported by Edgar—she had been the victim rather than one of the alleged perpetrators of scandalous behavior. From a historical distance the episode suggests the confusion of attitudes toward sexuality and female propriety in the 1920s. Many girls of good family were as sheltered as their mothers' generation had been, but some were freely beginning to have affairs before marriage. The Grunewald crowd was kept as innocent as possible. They mostly walked to the dinner dances at the homes of their friends' parents, and Hilde later recalled a party at which only one girl in the room was seen wearing lipstick. Kranz, Edgar, Herbert, and Hilde were all caught in the uncertainties of a transitional moment in relationships between young men and women, in a city renowned for its edgy high life. When school resumed after the summer break that year, Kranz had clearly decided that the matter should be taken up on a higher plane. He organized a symposium for his advanced students on Eros in Aristophanes, making sure to emphasize that true Eros was trained upon the eternal whole.

The schoolmates completed their *Abitur* in February 1926, and Edgar was sent on a grand tour to celebrate his success. The notebook of that year is primarily the journal of his travels to Cologne, Paris, Biarritz, Spain, Geneva, Caen, Brittany, and Brussels. As he set out westward on the D-train in March, he celebrated his release from family life. On trains, or when he was walking alone, he could think better. At home, there was too much going on, and one appeared to be moping when lost in thought. Now, at last, he was free to prepare himself for the life ahead. He was just eighteen, and ready to take the world by storm—after a bit more practice.

At first, the trip was an art and architecture tour in which Edgar applied the principles of art viewing that he had begun to learn at school. His judgments were careful and rather conventional. Although he thought of himself as something better than a tourist, he was acting much like one—most especially when he generalized about national differences between the old enemies, the French and the Germans. Spain didn't figure in this nation comparing contest; the obligatory bullfight duly horrified him, but he fell in love with the paintings of El Greco. Their weird wild spirituality stimulated his romantic tastes and his eloquence, while the painter's political situation under Phillip II intrigued him. "Maybe I'll write a book about it," he mused, "How frightful it must be to be in the vicinity of such a despot! What purpose has this power? Does power only have purpose when it is used for the social good?" Forty-five years later he would publish a book called *Power, Law and Society*, in which he would counter Nietzsche's "will to power" with Bodenheimer's "will to law."

The later part of the 1926 journal becomes a record of his reading and intellectual life; he was intent on becoming a person of note. In a lecture to himself, he wrote: "I have a life that few others enjoy. The range of my experience and impressions is wider than that of most people my age. According to my abilities, I have a duty to do something high in life. If I fail, it will be an admission of weakness. I have determined, more fully than ever before, to give my full attention to whatever comes before me on every single day. Total concentration and self-discipline will help me to grasp the substantial and the valuable. Surely no one can do more than that." He had earnestly absorbed the values of his father and his teachers. Now he was going to apply them, he hoped, from the inside. His handwriting had changed, becoming larger, bolder, and more Germanic, as if to signal an emergence from the oversight of schoolteachers—or the acquisition of a new fountain pen.

Living the ideal was not exactly possible in a world largely determined by the behavior of other people. And, however carefully he tried to keep his notebook free of unpleasant experience, there were moments when dismay and disgust seeped through, suggesting strong emotional reactions to various unnamed kinds of disillusionment. When he was angry with someone or disgusted by what he saw, his writing suddenly became vividly concrete. Near the end of the 1926 notebook, back in Berlin, he felt annoyed by his own life, which was turning out more mundane than he had hoped. He was impatient for something meaningful: "The legal studies have not been satisfying in any way, and it's hard to concentrate on intellectual matters in Berlin, because the demands on one's time are too large." No doubt the need to participate in family life instead of poring over books was part of the trouble. His attention to Schopenhauer would have to be postponed.

Edgar's 1926 journal also reports on a conversation between young men under the influence of two widely read works: Thomas Mann's popular novel *Buddenbrooks* (1901) and Oswald Spengler's pessimistic take on European culture, *The Decline of the West* (1918). Edgar and his friend "discussed degeneration and wondered why so many families degenerate already in the second generation—and indeed, exactly those families of outstanding intelligence. It's probably because powerful commitments to intellectual life diminish physical strength. It may be nature's way of assuring that intelligence doesn't interfere with the future development of a healthy race." It is hard not to smile at this young man's theorizing; amateur social-Darwinist notions were freely bandied about in those years, in support of German nationalistic sentiments. At the same time it is disturbing to recognize how fully Edgar was taken with the race and degeneration theories that were growing ever more virulent around him.

Searching for intellectual heroes, Edgar was willing to find them whenever he was moved by eloquence, or grand abstraction. A Jesuit father lecturing on the differences between East and West—that is, Russia and Germany—impressed him with his *Bildung*, his freedom from one-sidedness, and his "holy earnestness." What he learned: the Russians are a "people of chaos"; deprived of a Christian Renaissance, they were helpless before Bolshevism. Dostoevsky's "chaotic souls" display Russia's spiritual illness, antithetical to German ideals of classicism and order. Such nationalistic generalizations were familiar to the enthusiastic listener: Edgar had made similar contrasts between the French and the Germans when he was visiting France. The French had enjoyed a longer cultural development, he wrote, but were now in decline, its people marked by signs of illness and degeneration. Germans, on the other hand, were in the ascent. Their true cultural awakening went back only as far as Goethe. Germans, then, had an expansive future awaiting them, along with the will and the energy to pursue it. As he came to the end of his meditation, he saved himself from being *einseitig*, conceding that the French could teach the Germans something about clarity and logic, as well as aesthetic beauty in material life.

Edgar studied law in the German fashion, moving among various universities to attend lectures before settling down to a series of state examinations that would qualify him for law practice as a member of the German Civil Service. He spent time in Geneva, Berlin, and Munich, ending up at Heidelberg, where he completed his degree and wrote a doctoral dissertation. The earlier years of law school featured occasional bouts of study mixed with good times: ski trips, mountain excursions, theater, opera, independent reading, and conversations with friends. He spent the summer break of 1927 playing tennis, billiards, and piano in a well-heeled boarding house in Maidenhead, England, where he was sent, like many of his class, to practice his English. The semester at Munich was especially packed with sociability and amusement; the South German university was well known for its easygoing atmosphere, quite different from the sternly Prussian context in which Edgar was brought up. In the journals, enthusiastic descriptions of trips, conversations, and lovely landscapes alternated with meditations on what he was reading. For a while Nietzsche was an obsession, but others follow, in organized notes that would help him master basic concepts. He learns to critique high capitalism and the dehumanizing pace of professionalized modern life, in which "whole people don't exist any more." He, of course, is an exception: "How lucky I am not to suffer under this and to be able to follow my interests."

Did he want to be studying philosophy rather than sitting through lectures on legal procedure? It is possible that his profession was chosen as a compromise to placate his business-oriented father; law was considered a good preparation for a variety of respectable careers. While Edgar was pursuing his degree at Heidelberg, he was also working in the Mannheim law office of his teacher Karl Geiler, counsel for the German coal syndicate and some other large industrial enterprises. His thesis, *The Principle of Equal Treatment of Shareholders in Corporation Law*, suggests an attempt to please Siegmund while advocating for equality. It was published in a collection of legal monographs on commercial law, edited by Professor Geiler.

Edgar's attempts to take his freedom and make a place for himself in the larger world did not go altogether easily. Siegmund remained in control, and had to be elaborately convinced of each new project, and each new funding request. As with earlier father-son pairs among the German Jewish bourgeoisie, the son assumed that the father's wealth should be used to support the higher aims of the next generation.[9] Edgar became adept at letters of persuasion: why it was a good idea to go to Caen and take a French course, why it was important to stay on at Heidelberg once he had finished his dissertation. At the same time the correspondence reveals his closeness to his family and his wish to keep them on his side through charm and affection. He reports on meeting someone everyone at home would like, "so handsome that Bebs and Maus [Helga] would immediately fall in love with him." He admits that Papa was right about some contested matter: "I hope this was the only time I gave you cause for a bad mood." From Geneva, he reports on the people he's met at an international union: there are lots of "inferior Germans," but there are also the sensible ones, including himself and his friends: "Auf Deutsch, nur Juden!" (To put it bluntly, just Jews!).

His sense of superiority could also slide into full-blown arrogance. After a letter from England in which he had performed an extensive character assassination of one acquaintance, Rosi reprimanded him. "Do you think so well of yourself that you can allow yourself such a criticism of a fellow man?" Edgar did not back down. He can't waste his time on people who think they are cultured when they are not. Maybe *she* would like the good-natured quality of this fellow, but he finds it a sign of an indifferent, uncritical, "milk-soul." Papa, he is convinced, would not be pleased to hear himself described as "a good-natured man." He lectures Rosi on the difference between good nature and goodness until I want to shout back, "Don't talk to your mother that way!" That's what *my* mother would have said. I do not know if or how Rosi continued the dialogue.

Edgar's rather ambiguous entanglement with Hilde did not end when the classmates completed the *Abitur* early in 1926. His sister Bebs recalled the relationship as a "big love" in her shy brother's early life, though it is barely traceable in his writing after he left the Grunewald Gymnasium. Hilde studied law as well, sharing Edgar's semesters in Berlin and Munich before she completed a doctorate at the University of Kiel. For Edgar, she was the only bright spot during his Berlin semester. In an unusually personal note, he writes, "I think, that this semester would have been *öd und leer* without Hilde." (His reference to the bleak and empty sea separating the lovers in Wagner's *Tristan and Isolde* suggests the nature of their dialogues.) "I have given Hilde almost all my free time, and I'm very happy about it. Every hour that I spend with her is special, something out of the ordinary. How sad, that such a pure and original mind, such a talented and loving nature, such a splendid character, are trapped in the over-sensitive, weak, easily disrupted body she was dealt. Otherwise she would be an entirely wonderful person."

When it came to the test of the Greek ideal, a sound mind in a sound body, Hilde's temperament did not seem to fit the bill. What happened between them can only be surmised from her fervent love letters, written between 1928 and 1933. Edgar kept them for the rest of his life, as if he did not want to destroy the evidence of her uninhibited adoration. If he admired and enjoyed Hilde with reservations, she seems to have been suffering from an intense case of romantic young love. Some of her letters are about arrangements to meet during her time at Kiel, and express her unending hopefulness that somehow everything will work out between the two of them. She addresses him with a tone of intimate knowledge stemming from their childhood companionship, always pulling him closer and drawing him in. Planning for a 1928 visit, Hilde figures out how they can spend time alone together at a northern resort town without letting their parents know. It involves an elaborate plan for meeting in a train (where they must pretend not to know each other), and a postcard he will write to his parents, which will be sent by Hilde's friend from another town. She has bought a sweet new red dress for the occasion. The project excites her; it's the kind of thing one can tell one's children about someday. Although it would be hard to guess this from the emotional flood of her writing, she repeatedly comes out at the top of her class in exams, and in her doctoral dissertation.

While Edgar made repeated attempts to declare a moratorium on the relationship, Hilde's battle between despair and hope went on until 1931.

Her suffering is brushed with highly romantic literary overtones, as if she were, in her very early twenties, identifying with famously doomed lovers like Tristan and Isolde, or Goethe and his Lotte. She had a taste for drama that probably enchanted the serious-minded Edgar, when it didn't make him nervous. In one of her recollections, Hilde reminded him of something he had said to her during a visit at her parents' house, when she was telling him about the lovely ski excursion some friends were enjoying. "But surely, Hilde, we are not envious?" was Edgar's response. I can easily imagine the kind and slightly mischievous smile that might have come along with his words. For her, it was the "we" that saved it from feeling like a rebuke.

In spite of the romantic fizzle, the friendship held. Hilde and Edgar were welcome in one another's homes, but Siegmund, for one, would have disapproved of any commitment before Edgar had established himself in a secure financial position. Edgar's own reservations about Hilde's suitability as a life companion were substantial, and by 1931 he was already interested in someone else. Did religious difference play any role? Hilde later married and spent her life in Germany, so she was clearly not Jewish. Yet this fact never surfaces in Edgar's writing.

For Edgar's eightieth birthday in March 1988, Hilde sent him some detailed memories of their school days. Her first memory dated back to his first day at the Grunewald Gymnasium. Religion classes were required, and he was asked about his faith. "'I think, I am a Prussian,' was your hesitating answer—the answer of a small, serious boy, who was taking trouble over the classification demanded by adults, and who, in the end, didn't fully grasp all the implications of what he said—and only an equally enlightened Biblically trained teacher could have done better than 'Behold, an Israelite, in whom there is no guile.'" The teacher had quoted the Gospel of John 1:47, in which Jesus recognizes the skeptical Jew Nathanael and converts him instantly into a believer.

If this memory is accurate, it raises questions about Edgar, as well as Hilde's ways of interpreting him. Was he quietly challenging the requirement that he classify himself by religion, or did he not want to call himself a Jew among strangers? Did he fully identify himself as Prussian rather than Jewish? Was Hilde, in retrospect, trying to cover for him when she implied that he didn't entirely see what he was saying? And how, exactly, did she read the rather double-edged "enlightenment" of the teacher's response? These are unanswerable questions, but her memory does suggest that young Edgar was uncomfortable with the personal aspects of being a Jew in Germany. That fact was something he preferred to ignore or put aside.

His first mention of *Judentum* (Judaism) as a subject appears in his journal for June 1927, in a list of intellectual problems he must think out:

1. Nationalism and Jewry
2. Pacifism
3. Northern vs. Southern people
4. The essence of music: melody and rhythm
5. Democracy
6. The essence of opera.

At nineteen, the relationship between Judaism and nationalism appeared to him as a problem of intellectual concern, on par with abstractions like "the essence of opera." It was, after all, a historical subject that had occupied writers, both Jews and non-Jews, as the Jewish populations of Europe were gradually granted citizenship and civil rights during the nineteenth century. The old arguments were heating up newly in Weimar Germany, at the height of Jewish participation in German public life.[10] To what extent could a Jew, identified with the special history of Judaism, fully belong to a European national culture or history? To what extent was that merging of historical identities desirable at all, from either the Jewish or the European point of view? Was assimilation possible or desirable? Rabbi Leo Baeck of Berlin, the revered leader of the German Jewish community, was an assimilationist who nonetheless urged his flock to save their souls by keeping faith with the Hebrew religion.[11] At the same time the Enlightenment ideals adopted by German Jewry as a modern form of belief were facing a new kind of nationalism, one that looked back to a pre-Enlightenment Teutonic past.[12]

Of course, these questions were not generally posed in such a benign way. To take just one prominent case, there was Richard Wagner's essay "Das Judentum in der Musik" ("Judaism in Music"), published anonymously in 1850 and republished under his name in 1869. The essay sets out to explain why Jews cannot contribute to the arts, with particular attention to the "Jewish elements" that spoil the music of Mendelssohn and Meyerbeer. It also gathers together some of the more general emphases of anti-Semitic discourse. Wagner begins: "With all our speaking and writing in favour of the Jews' emancipation, we always felt instinctively repelled by any actual, operative contact with them . . . we have to explain to ourselves the *involuntary repellence* possessed for us by the nature and personality of the Jews, to vindicate that instinctive dislike which we plainly recognize as stronger and more overpowering than our conscious zeal to rid ourselves thereof."[13] Once having established that anti-Semitism is the fault of the Jews, Wagner goes on to highlight those repellent qualities: the Jew's "disagreeably foreign appearance," and, "far more weighty," the way Jews speak their adopted languages only as aliens. Because Jews are "outside the pale" of "an historical community," they are incapable of speaking European languages as natives can. And they are incapable of evolution: because the Jew is stuck "with his Jehovah in splintered, soilless stock," there can be no "self-sprung evolution" (83–84). This line of thinking will be familiar to anyone who has encountered racist attitudes toward colonized peoples: capable only of "mimicked speech" (89), "they" are not like us, nor can they ever become like us, because they are stuck in a historical dead end.

It is not just that Jews cannot speak European languages idiomatically but that "the Jew's production of voice sounds is a creaking, squeaking, buzzing snuffle. . . . The cold indifference of its peculiar 'blubber' never by any chance rises to the ardour of a higher, heartfelt passion" (85). (The contemptuous German verb for Jewish speech intonations or gestures was *mauscheln*.) For Wagner it follows that Jews have no aptitude for song, or music in general. And the cultured Jew who cut himself off from his own roots is left nowhere; "it has conducted only to his isolation, and to making him the most heartless of all human beings" (87). With no roots, this Jew can have no authentic passions, "so does the Jew musician hurl together the diverse forms and styles of every age and every master" (92). In the early twentieth century, this cold, rootless, cosmopolitan Jew would be held responsible for the outrages of modernist experimentation in music and the other arts.

Despite his claim that Jewish listeners cannot grasp the essence of German music, Wagner the composer was an artistic hero to the huge Jewish audiences who faithfully followed his work and contributed funds to support his grandiose ambitions. He seems to have made an exception for them, and they reciprocated by forgetting about his sentiments.[14] It would have been bad form to allow the personal anti-Semitism of a great artist to interfere with one's worship of his transcendent art. To meet intolerance with dignity and forbearance was the mark of a civilized person.

Yet the effort of German Jewish assimilation was in many ways an effort to disprove the ideas of Wagner and other anti-Semitic German writers. Those ideas would emerge during periods of national crisis—military defeats or economic recessions—and lie dormant in periods of optimism and prosperity.[15] To resist prejudice meant accepting its terms; if German Jews were bent on dissociating themselves from anything obviously Jewish, it was a measure of their desire to exist in harmony with their culture. Middle-class children were taught to erase any leftover Yiddish inflections in their speech or gestures; *mauscheln* had to be trained out of them. As late as 1934, running a school for Jewish children who had been expelled from German classrooms, Rosi Bodenheimer's cousin Vera Lachmann was still horrified by it. She wrote to Edgar about one little pupil "who *maus-*

*chelt* fantastically and talks with his hands. But Edgar, if *we* don't change his habits, he'll grow up and pass the poison on. He's now ten—maybe it's still possible!" A passionate student of classical and German literature, Vera would continue to indulge her fantasies until the very last moment, emigrating only in late 1939 after Hitler's invasion of Poland. Edgar's life would take a different course. But as he made his list of topics to ponder in 1927, any directly personal threat that lurked in the pairing of nationalism and Judaism was, as yet, inconceivable.

2

# Emigration

The "fatal year" 1931 would always be a black memory for Siegmund Bodenheimer. On July 13, the Danat-Bank collapsed and shut its doors. He and his partners had made heroic efforts to save it, meeting with Chancellor Heinrich Brüning to negotiate government support, but their efforts had failed. The US stock market crash in October 1929 had precipitated a severe liquidity crisis as US bank loans were called in, and the Germany economy had fallen into a serious depression, with unemployment affecting nearly a third of the workforce. The Danat-Bank, as Siegmund explained in *Mein Leben*, was also undermined by the failure of the Austrian credit system in May 1931, as well as by fraud and collapse in a large Bremen textile firm that had enjoyed the bank's generous credit.

Presenting to government overseers the truth about the Danat-Bank's inability to meet its responsibilities was, Siegmund wrote, one of the heaviest assignments of his life. He could not help but add a bitter remark about his prominent Jewish partner, Jakob Goldschmidt, whose risky, unconventional financial practices had always worried him: "The great Jakob Goldschmidt was so small that he didn't have the nerve to undertake this unpleasant task." Goldschmidt, who had apparently felt free to use the bank's resources for his private investments, would soon disappear from sight. But the public failure of the Danat-Bank had broader consequences, contributing to a general loss of trust in the German banking system. Detlev Peukert describes the aftermath: "In a chain reaction, the international finance system began to break down, nations tried to seal themselves off from world markets, the German financial system became badly crippled and Germany, along with the rest of the world, braced herself for a further, disastrous slump in production." He describes Germany's answer to the crisis as a "headlong rush to abandon the Weimar 'system' altogether."[1] Amid the growing evidence of mismanagement in business and financial institutions, Siegmund began to despair of Germany's future, and his own.

"The months-long uncertainty about the bank's fate and our personal fates, combined with the catastrophic background of the German business and political crisis was a difficult test of the nerves," Siegmund wrote. Finally, in April 1932, what remained of the Danat-Bank fused with the Dresdner Bank. Unlike some of his colleagues, Siegmund was welcomed into the Dresdner Bank as a member of its newly merged executive board. His professional integrity had been recognized, but the appointment led only to a tentative and difficult coda in his banking life. He signed a one year contract and tried to protect the jobs of at least some of his former colleagues during the restructuring process. His anxiety and dismay, along with the "more than human" efforts he was making to negotiate his way through the disaster, threw a large shadow over the family circle. For a fifty-seven-year-old man who took pride in success, an association with the failure of a major bank would have been devastating. Siegmund's prominent position as a co-owner of the Danat-Bank had lasted for only nine years.

By this time the Weimar Republic had ceased to function as a democracy. The conservative Chancellor Brüning and his right-wing successors were governing under an executive dictatorship. The Reichstag (Parliament) had been essentially paralyzed since the election of 107 members of the Nazi Party in elections called by Brüning in 1930. Under article 48 of the Weimar constitution, the chancellor could govern by decree during a state of emergency. This was the legal loophole that brought down the Republic well before Hitler exploited it in his 1933 seizure of power (*Machtergreifung*).[2] In Siegmund's Wagnerian image, Weimar Germany was on its way toward *Götterdämmerung*, hovering in the twilight before the collapse of the ruling gods.

In this increasingly melancholy and unstable atmosphere Edgar carried on with his legal training, in the hopes that someday he would preside as a judge over a German courtroom. His path to that courtroom was clearly laid out. In 1930 he had passed the first state examination, the *Referendarsexamen*, which was followed by a period of apprenticeship in a range of civil and criminal courts. After that required service, he could take a second exam to become an *Assessor*, which would allow him to clerk in higher courts. Finally he could proceed to a career as a fully qualified judge or lawyer. If it all went smoothly, he could expect to attain this professional status before the age of thirty.

Legal training could lead to other kinds of civil service positions as well, though it is likely that Siegmund preferred a course that would place Edgar firmly within the world of commercial and business law. But in 1932, as Siegmund was serving his term on the executive board of the Dresdner Bank, Edgar was migrating toward academics. He was living in Heidelberg, working on his doctoral thesis, and commuting irregularly to nearby Mannheim as an apprentice to the law practice of his academic mentor Karl Geiler. He was thrilled to be working with eminent professors at Heidelberg: the legal philosopher Gustav Radbruch, the Roman law scholar Ernst Levy, and the Christian existentialist philosopher Karl Jaspers. By the end of the year, his thesis complete, he was studying for the oral exam that would culminate in the award of his degree, Juris Doktor, magna cum laude. Engraved in Latin, his diploma was signed—in Latin—by "Ernestus Levy," not yet revealed as Edgar's future father-in-law. Around Christmas, he wrote to his parents, he had said good-bye to Professor Levy, "who was charming and said that my high honors degree was unusual for Heidelberg." He had been working hard to convince the skeptical Siegmund that it made professional sense to remain in Heidelberg, take his oral exams, work for Karl Geiler, and learn more about commercial law.

The account of his academic success bears little relation to the romantic and political turbulence in Edgar's internal life during the early 1930s. A cryptic note on a slip of paper suggests that in May 1931 he became engaged to a woman called Helga. A separate slip records a parting from her in November of that same year. In 1932, letters home from Heidelberg mention a person he calls *die Hase*—the Hare—with whom he often spends his social time. The nickname is something he shared with his sister Bebs; he always requests that his parents pass that news item on to her. During the summer break of 1932 he took a long and quite romantic journey with the *Hase*, including stops at Salzburg, the Italian Dolomites, and Venice. He described the trip to his parents without naming his companion, perhaps because they already knew, perhaps because they did not. In the margin of this letter Edgar in old age has penciled—for whom?—her full name, though in later letters of the 1930s she will appear under another nickname, Hesi. Perhaps Siegmund was not altogether wrong in suspecting that Edgar had an unspoken motive for remaining in the Heidelberg area, rather than acceding to his father's wish that he return directly to Berlin after completing his dissertation.

However he might present himself to his parents, the tone of Edgar's journal in the early 1930s was quite different from the optimism of his earlier musings. This notebook, covered in red, is more battered than the others; it stayed with him from April 1930 to June 1952, primarily as a place to record his political reactions and to develop his political ideas. The handwriting veers from one style to another during the first five years, until it gradually settles down into the clear forward-slanting hand that would later become familiar to me. A Goethe poem, "Beherzigung," sets the tone on the inside front cover. In translation it reads:

Cowardly thoughts,
timid shaking,
womanish hesitation,
fearful lamentation—
they ward off no misery,
they do not make you free.

Gathering all your forces
for the offensive
never to give way,
showing yourself powerful:
this calls the arms
of the Gods to your side!

Edgar is calling himself to arms, warding off emotional weakness, and flexing his internal muscles for the challenges ahead. In his last entry for 1932, written in April, he says only: "Life = getting the better of tension." He sounds very much like his father. Yet, during his twenties, a significant part of Edgar's battle lay in the effort to thwart Siegmund's desire to control the course of his life while remaining on good terms with his family. At the height of this German son's classic bid for independence, National Socialism arrived on the scene.

As the red journal opens, Edgar's earlier focus on the aesthetic aspects of personal *Bildung* has shifted. He is still thinking about individual self-development as the highest form of life, but he is now conscious that this can happen only within a social politics that allays suffering, allowing for self-development to occur. In January 1932, however, he records this antithesis: "Liberalism is atomizing, analytical, autonomous, vs. collectivity (therefore, specifically Jewish)." Whose opinion is this? Is he summarizing Nazi doctrine in a formula that attacks his own (Jewish) liberal individualism? Or does this mark a rightward political conversion in the face of Germany's economic crisis? After two more brief apolitical entries, the journal goes silent. When it resumes, it is April 9, 1933. On April 1, Edgar had been dismissed from the state's legal apprenticeship system because of "non-Aryan" extraction. He was no longer qualified for admission to the bar. His German legal career, barely begun, was now over.

Only two months had passed since Hitler's appointment as Chancellor, on January 30, 1933. The appointment was based on a tragic misjudgment made under pressure by the aging President Hindenburg. Hitler was supposed to bolster the conservative right wing in its bid to overthrow the Republic from within; instead he used the old-guard conservatives for his own purpose. Once in office, he moved with great rapidity. After the Reichstag fire of February 27, 1933, he pressured Hindenburg to pass an emergency decree suspending citizen rights and instigated a purge of Reichstag Communists declared responsible for the fire, along with mass arrests of Communists in general. On March 23, 1933, the newly constituted Reichstag passed the Enabling Act, ceding full legislative and executive power to Hitler. A series of decrees followed to implement the so-called *Gleichschaltung* (synchronization) policy, which consolidated Hitler's totalitarian control over every aspect of the state.[3]

Actions against Jews began early in 1933, starting with the cultural domain where Jews were prominent and moving quickly to other realms. Dismissals of Jewish bank directors sped up in March; meanwhile Hitler's cabinet prepared an April 7 decree that would exclude Jewish lawyers from the bar, along with civil servants in many other branches of government. This decree, the Law for the Restoration of the Professional Civil Service, was especially notable for its definition of "non-Aryan" as "anyone descended from non-Aryan, particularly Jewish, parents or grandparents. It suffices if one parent or grandparent is non-Aryan." The definition established the basis for all the persecutions that were to follow.[4] For apprentice *Referendare* like Edgar, who were not yet members of the bar, dismissals occurred on April 1, the same day that a nationwide boycott of Jewish businesses signaled to the German populace that Jews were now fair game across the land.[5]

Edgar's dismissal was abrupt, but the subsequent paper trail extended over a period of months, and he kept it among his files. A blurry carbon copy dated April 2, 1933, declares that the decree banning Jews from the civil service is also applicable to any *Referendar* of Jewish descent. The notice, like all the ones to follow, is littered with numerical citations of freshly minted Nazi laws. On May 29, Edgar was sent a form and given a week to return it. The form required him to name his parents, his mother's maiden name and both sets of grandparents, along with the maiden names of each grandmother. He was then to sign a statement declaring that neither he nor any of these relatives were non-Aryans or practitioners of the Jewish religion, and that he further understood that any falsehoods on the form would lead to his dismissal. "If you are not in a position to give the assurances designated on the form, you will send me a short statement of the reasons," states the cover letter. His path was clear enough. He sent his reason and kept the blank form. Looking at it now also allows me to imagine the non-Jewish civil servants who were also sent scrambling to prove their heritage within a week. The required signature was an act of coercion, forcing signers to collaborate with the regime under threat of losing their jobs.

For Edgar, the legal farce was not over yet. On June 9 he received another notice, still addressed to Referendar Edgar Bodenheimer. "Since you are non-Aryan, and none of the exceptions apply to you, your dismissal from legal services is imperative." He is given a week to make a statement if he wishes to initiate a search—presumably a legal justification—of his dismissal. That was too much for Edgar. He addressed himself to the President of the Supreme Court. "I allow myself to remark the following," he begins. "The opportunity to search out my dismissal with respect to a law, whose purpose is to alienate non-German elements from the civil service, is of no use to me, since I see no cause in my upbringing or world view to count me among such elements." His position as a lawyer disbarred by a "law" he considered both absurd and illegal was a first step toward the natural law philosophy he would develop in later years.

It was not until August 1933 that Edgar got his "official" dismissal in a notice from the Prussian Minister of Justice. His degrees and testimonials were to be returned to him, and indeed, on September 5 he received a testimonial that listed his credentials and the steps he had successfully passed in his legal training to that point. Assuming that similar documents were sent to everyone in Edgar's position, the Civil Service Restoration Act alone must have generated enough bureaucratic business to contribute significantly to the rising employment rate for "Aryan" citizens of the Third Reich.

Despite his sudden loss of profession and status, Edgar's nationalistic identification with the German state was not so easily expunged. Like many assimilated Jews, he was stunned and dismayed to discover that he—a loyal German—had suddenly been transformed into a "non-German element," a Jew, and a foreigner. In the face of this personal crisis, Edgar's attempts to work out the relation between nationalism and Judaism led him in a strange direction. At some point in 1933 he joined an organization called the *Verband Nationaldeutscher Juden*, the League of Nationalist German Jews. One purpose of this association was to convince the Nazis that at least certain kinds of Jews—the assimilated, truly German ones—would be assets to the nationalistic goals of the new regime. It was not yet clear to most people, with a very few exceptions, that the anti-Semitic policies of the Nazi Party lay at the very heart of Hitler's mission. Amid widespread Jewish attempts to downplay the significance of early Nazi actions, Edgar placed his allegiance with those who promised to maintain his sense of privilege as a member of German society.

The League of Nationalist German Jews was the brainchild of Dr. Max Naumann, who had announced its formation, backed by the signatures of eighty-eight Jewish businessmen and professionals, in March 1921.[6] Naumann was a Berlin lawyer with a militaristic bent, who had been decorated and promoted in the First World War. In opposition to the Central Union of German Citizens of the Jewish Faith (*Centralverein deutscher Staatsbürger jüdischen Glaubens*), an organization born of the need to resist German anti-Semitism, he took an extreme position against any kind of Jewish separateness. In his view the work of German Jews was to eradicate any lingering feelings or external signs of Jewishness, in a wholehearted commitment to the German nation that would assure the withering away of anti-Semitic sentiment. Zionism was Naumann's particular enemy, but he also insisted on complete disassociation from the so-called *Ostjuden*—Jewish immigrants from the east—whose numbers in Germany had doubled between 1910 and 1920. According to Naumann, the "primitive" *Ostjuden*, stuck in a shtetl mentality and practicing outworn religious rituals, represented an unassimilable element. With their tendency to align themselves with undesirable political radicals and Communists, such Jews would sharpen German anti-Semitism and pose a threat to the German realm.

The extremity of Max Naumann's revulsion had a milder echo in the prejudices of many middle-class German Jews, who were well known to feel embarrassed by the Jewish mannerisms and religious rituals of Yiddish-speaking Polish and Russian Jews. Like other groups who have worked their way up the social ladder of a culture fundamentally hostile to their presence, they did not want to be associated with people who reminded them and others of their ancestors' social and religious origins. Social class, rather than Jewish self-hatred, was primarily at issue here: they had staked their claim on German high culture, from which they could avoid or condescend to more recently arrived *Ostjuden* fleeing from pogroms, imported as cheap labor, or following their merchant ambitions westward from Poland or Lithuania. At the same time, liberal German Jews had a history of charitable responsibility for the impoverished Jewish immigrants who had begun pouring over the border in the 1880s. Many of their beneficiaries in those days were transmigrants, sent through Germany on sealed trains toward ports and ships for the Americas, in an eerie preview of Nazi deportation methods. Whether the new immigrants travelled through or settled in German neighborhoods, however, long-established German Jews were forced to experience their modern European identities against an uncomfortable awareness of their "Asian" Jewish counterparts.[7]

Max Naumann yearned to leave *all* traces of Judaism behind, to merge entirely with a German *Volk* heritage, and even to abandon a Jewish for a German God. In 1932, Naumann endorsed Hitler's National Socialist Party, supporting the Nazi campaign against left-wing "internationalist" ideas held by a good many Jewish artists and intellectuals. The League quickly alienated the other Jewish organizations that were attempting to work against anti-Semitism. By 1933 it was isolated, ignored by Hitler's regime, and increasingly vilified in Jewish opinion.

How did twenty-five-year-old Edgar, a Weimar liberal, get mixed up—if only for a few months—with the Fascist-leaning League of National German Jews? His entries in the red journal for 1933 suggest that he was compelled by the hope of finding a solution to the huge identity problem that now confronted him. Somehow, I imagine him thinking, there must be a way to synthesize—or eradicate—this unwelcome new opposition between German and Jew. Many of his Jewish age mates responded by joining either Communist or Zionist organizations, but Edgar's tendency to consider himself an exception to any commonly shared situation, along with a sense of disbelief that he could have been permanently excluded from German professional life, may have played into his decision to join the League. He was an enthusiast, readily swayed by compelling rhetoric, and some of the most compelling rhetoric in the floundering Republic of the early 1930s came from the Right. Oswald Spengler's *The Decline of the West*, calling for a collective German fight against degeneration, a national rebirth of the *Volk*, and a great leader, had generated a wide spectrum of shared language that the Nazis exploited.[8] As we have already seen, it was a language with which Edgar and his generation were quite familiar.

Entries in the red notebook between April and August 1933 reveal Edgar's attempts to define Judaism in relation to an ideal Germany. As so often is the case in the journals, I can't tell whether the ideas are his own or someone else's; nor can I tell to what extent he believed them. On April 9: "About the Jewish Question: maybe the Jews are especially fit to recognize the essence of Germanness; a certain distance is conducive to that. Self-knowledge is harder than the recognition of the other. The actual being shines only in opposition. Maybe Jews are chosen to serve a foreign spirit, to mediate a foreign spirit, bringing them to themselves through criticism and example. This is—above all with the *Volk* of the future—the German destiny, that must be great." Somehow, he hopes, Jews can be the moral mirrors who will restore Germany to its true destiny.

On May 26: "Judaism is intellect (*Geist*). But spirit can break down if it is not paired with 'blood.' Jews in the Weimar Republic overvalued intelligence. This lesson must be learned and proven in this difficult time, which is a new exile." Here Edgar tries to force the German Jewish split into the familiar dichotomy between *Blut* and *Geist* (body and mind/spirit), which was already taking on sinister new meanings as the Nazis defined race by bloodline and exalted the physical training of the body above all else. "The new exile," harkening back to the exiles of Jewish Diaspora history, imagines a kind of internal exile during a transitional period to the apocalyptic new Reich that Hitler dangled before his audiences.

On July 11: "The *forms* that the German Revolution takes (anti-parliamentary, totalitarian, the leader-principle, a strongly bonded society) are good. The content with which this form is filled (race romanticism, the craze for Germania, anti-classicism, pro Lutheran) cannot be refused. The Third Reich is supposed to bring the Third Humanism."

On August 26: "National Socialism melds the ideas of 1789 [i.e., French Revolutionary ideals, which Hitler rejected] to nationalism, and takes from communism the socialist element. Nationalism, formerly a privilege of the ruling class, is now for the whole people. Socialism, the privilege of the proletariat, is now for the whole people. The self-confidence of the *Volk* is not created through *class*, but (and this is the new element) through *race*, and further in the deepening of racial superiority (the Germanic, the German Middle Ages, etc.). This is a new central European ideology evolving between France and Russia." While it's hard to feel any comfort in such sentences, they do suggest that Edgar wanted to see Hitler's revolution as a way toward something better and that he was temperamentally addicted to the notion that antitheses can somehow be reconciled.

By September someone or something had brought him to his senses. On October 3, a few days before his departure for New York, he resigned from the League and wrote a long letter to Dr. Naumann explaining his reasons:

> I have been a member for a few months, and also joined the paramilitary organization. As positive as I am about the goals of the League, so little do I agree with its methods. I think that the spirit that reigns in this endeavor is out of touch with the real situation. The battle of the new Germany is not just with certain Jews who are considered not-German (*undeutsch*), but against the Jews as a race. At first I thought the race theory was a dispensable element in National Socialism, at least one that could be grown out of. But during its development, and through the study of National Socialist literature, I have been convinced of my error. The anti-Semitic revolution—that's what it is, and therefore the Jews cannot support it—didn't just come about because of Jewish behavior during the war. Its roots lie far deeper. It is a revolution of blood against spirit; as such, it doesn't ask what spirit is, only what blood is. In this dismissal no one asks whether the dismissed has German or other feelings. The exception for veterans is unfortunately a concession to sentiment, which will be ignored in the future. In future people will only qualify by race—the Nazis leave no

> doubt about that. Certain concessions to the economy or business mean little or nothing. Surely our league could not go along with it if, as in the middle ages, Jews were to be stamped out.

He had figured it out. As I read the letter, I breathe a sigh of relief. It is difficult to imagine Edgar in a paramilitary organization, but he had learned from it. "The emphasis on assimilation also puts the League against all other Jewish groups. I was struck by the disgracefulness of some of the behavior in the paramilitary. I can't endorse the *deutschen Gruss* (the Hitler salute)." As for other Jews in the Third Reich, raising his arm to the Führer had set off a powerful repulsion.[9] Since he cannot consent to the League's present forms and methods, Edgar concludes, he must submit his resignation. He does not mention that he is about to leave for America.

I have access to this letter because someone copied it into the red journal. The feminine handwriting almost certainly belongs to Edgar's sister Bebs. The resignation, then, may have been something of a family affair. Did his father know about Edgar's membership in the League? Was it Siegmund's realism that had prevailed, or had Edgar correctly read *Mein Kampf* on his own? Was Siegmund's decision to send Edgar to New York connected to his son's blind nationalism, or was it something that he had been planning to do since Edgar was dismissed from the civil service? I can't answer these questions.

What I do know is that in March 1933 Siegmund was already planning to protect his own interests against Nazi pressure on banks to purge their remaining Jewish directors. After the *Machtergreifung*, he wrote, his one-year contract with the Dresdner Bank ended. He agreed to a six-month extension, to expire on September 30. In this way he prevented a discussion about whether, as one of two Jews on the Executive Committee, his contract could be renewed. The family myth has always been that Siegmund voluntarily resigned from his position because of his refusal to negotiate with Nazis. This was partially true: in his shrewd way he had forestalled the humiliation of being fired. But for him the life-changing crisis had come earlier, with the failure of the Danat-Bank. It was the time between its collapse and its merger with the Dresdner Bank that he called "the unhappiest period of my life." About the retirement itself, he wrote simply, "On 30 September 1933 I ended my connection with the Dresdner Bank. With that my business career came to an end; after 43 years of strenuous work I returned to private life. Convinced that it was impossible to have any hope for Jews in such a fallen country as Nazi Germany, I began to prepare for emigration. My son went to the United States in October 1933; my daughter Gerda was already outside, studying at the University of Bern. In March

Figure 7. Siegmund Bodenheimer in 1944

1934 we shook the dust (not to say the filth) of Germany from our feet and travelled with our daughter Helga to Switzerland."

Of course, it had not been quite so simple. At his father's seventieth birthday celebration in New York (November 22, 1944), Edgar made a speech. Addressing a large table of family members who had escaped Hitler's clutches largely through the help of Siegmund Bodenheimer, he reminded them of what might have happened had his father shared in the illusions held by many influential Jews in the early years of the Third Reich. In the worst case, it would have meant "a trip to the hereafter." (By 1944 the sad journey to death in a concentration camp had been taken by three of Siegmund's sisters and their families.) At best, Edgar continued, it would have required a much longer and more difficult rebuilding of their lives in a new country. The speech was a thanksgiving, and an apology. After praising his father's foresight, Edgar turned to his mother, remembering her reaction to the election of 107 Nazis to the Reichstag in 1930. That day at the family dinner table, he said, "Mutti had argued energetically and earnestly for immediate emigration. This, at a time when we didn't just have a roof over our head and a chicken in the pot, but ate roast goose on silver plates. One should have had full respect for her prophecy. Instead, not only our father but especially her nationalistic, loyal-German only son bore down on her and denounced her as a defeatist and a Cassandra." He concluded in English: "Now the record is straight." He regretted the follies of his younger self; *that* record needed to be set straight, above all.

His twenty-five-year-old self had disembarked from the *Europa* in New York City on October 11, 1933. His German passport was still valid, and his father's wealth had helped secure him a visa to enter the United States, at a time when American consuls abroad were advised to withhold visas from applicants likely to become public charges in the American economy.[10] Siegmund's international connections would also have provided American sponsors who signed the affidavits required for entry. According to Edgar's letters home, the first months in New York were full of excitement and enterprise. Armed with a working knowledge of English and plenty of introductions from his father and teachers, he set about making contacts with bankers, lawyers, and anyone else who might know about a position or be able to put in a good word for him. A month later, recommended by "a charming old rabbi" who was the friend of one contact, he landed a job at a downtown law firm, Rosenberg, Goldmark, and Colin. Mr. James Rosenberg, "an unusually nice man," had told him he'd have to start again at the bottom until he had learned more about American law. He was taking night-school courses to work on that. This good news was his birthday present to his father in November 1933; Papa would be glad to hear that the salary would cover his room and board. By December he was joking, "Once they found out I was only half as dimwitted as I seemed at first, they started giving me more interesting work."

He moved rapidly from a boardinghouse to the International House on Riverside Drive, and then to small-apartment life. And his social life flourished; it seems that there were innumerable German Jewish American people who were ready to invite him into their circles and introduce him to the greener areas outside the city. His old friend Hilde turned up briefly on a visit from Germany and treated him to a lovely weekend at a friend's house in Greenwich before moving on to Washington. Edgar reported eagerly about American friendliness and hospitality. And he was careful to let his parents know that he was keeping occasional company with a fellow émigré who had arrived in New York just a month before him. Her name was Brigitte Levy; she was the daughter of Ernst Levy, his Roman law professor in Heidelberg. Edgar had met her briefly before in Europe, at an Austrian ski resort. She was completing a Heidelberg law degree and studying American law at Columbia. Before he left Germany someone had promised to send him her address, but he had run into her quite early on, in the Columbia Law School library.

What more could a parent want to hear? The plan for Edgar's emigration seemed to be going splendidly. At home in Berlin, Siegmund was carefully watching the temperature of the times. He had not yet decided exactly when to leave; it's likely that he was using the first months of his retirement to figure out how best to secure his financial assets in the face of increasingly stringent Nazi regulations. By the end of March 1934 the moment was nearing. In the Jagowstrasse the Bodenheimers were packing; Bebs had come home from the University of Bern to help out. On Friday, March 30, they had an unannounced visitor who slipped into the house with Rosi's cousin Kaethe Sachs. It was Edgar's girlfriend Hesi. She and Edgar had become privately engaged before he left for America—or so she thought. In a letter describing the weekend, she told Edgar, "There was hardly a minute among the preparations for travel. I helped Gerda [Bebs] a little, and she asked what I had heard from you, how things stood between us. I said, 'I think I can now call you sister.' We kissed and were happy. Immediately I asked her not to tell anyone yet, you had not given your permission."

On Sunday Bebs got in touch with Hesi and asked her to come back that afternoon. The final decision to emigrate had been made on Saturday, and the family was about to depart permanently for Switzerland. Under these tense circumstances, Bebs had told her parents about Hesi's visit and they had summoned her for a conference. During the discussion Hesi learned that they knew nothing of any engagement or understanding; Edgar had not mentioned it. Great difficulties were raised. "I kept things back, and perhaps appeared less decided than I really am," Hesi wrote. "Therefore I want to say to you that I am happy and sure in myself. . . . Our parents will now begin difficult negotiations. But the main thing is that we will find our way to each other."

Long before Hesi's letter arrived in New York, Edgar received an angry telegram from his father. On April 5, he replied. "I acknowledge your telegram. I was surprised by the rapidity of your conclusions. . . . I don't see any reason to be 'indignant.' For reasons, much like your own, I will attempt to explain why I would like to get Hesi quickly out of Germany. The question now becomes—who knows?—years of separation. We should now arrange for her to continue her training here, to prepare her for early employment; there's a special need for her kind of work here. Your March letter from Zurich, dear Papa, has strengthened my desire to press for a quick emigration. I can understand how, under the circumstances, you might be horrified and send a spontaneous telegram. But the situation is now so changed that one can't make the same arguments as before. . . . I am convinced, despite the telegram, that we will come together on all issues and leave 'indignation' behind on both sides, never to give it room again."

Brigitte Levy had evidently fallen out of sight in the family crisis. By linking his concern for Hesi's safety with Siegmund's own push to get his family out of Germany, Edgar was attempting to beat his father at his own game. The tactic only fanned the flames of Siegmund's opposition. In the midst of his flight from Germany, to be confronted with the unwelcome surprise of his son's secrecy about an important family matter like marriage? And who was Hesi? According to family rumor, she may have been an actress—most certainly not an appropriate match for his son. The whole situation seems to come from a Victorian novel in which a young man gets secretly engaged to an actress and is threatened with disinheritance by his wealthy, indignant father.

Edgar learned only a week later of Hesi's disastrous visit to Jagowstrasse, and apologized to Siegmund: "I ask for your forgiveness for having put you in this difficult and upsetting situation. Of course we will now work everything out in mutual understanding." Apparently deaf to his father's refusal to consider Hesi an appropriate match, he reemphasized the Nazi danger: "The situation in Germany and generally in Europe has come to a point when in an instant anything could happen. I would not be able to sleep at night, were I not sure that Hesi was doing everything to emigrate soon." Suddenly, war seemed imminent. He also took a stand on his tentative new roots in America, insisting that such marriages were common here. Young couples could live cheaply in small apartments, eating at home and offering each other refuge from the strains of city life. "We live in a new world where things don't depend on commercial success but on courage. . . . I know that Hesi thinks the same way I do, and would manage if we were together. . . . I beg you not to think of Hesi as an enemy to family peace, but to support her in her wish to come here." As usual, he was concerned to restore family harmony as soon as possible while refusing to bend to his father's will. Distance and the ten-day interval between mailed and received letters may have helped to muffle the impact of Siegmund's alarm. And emigration had given Edgar a taste of independence: he was on his own turf now. I can't tell whether he was still interested in marrying Hesi, or whether he wanted to defy his father's control in the name of "saving" her.

The father's reply was uncompromising. Writing from a perch in Montreux, Switzerland, on April 21, he lets Edgar know that the roots of the family's objections lie very deep. They are pleased that he doesn't want to set himself in opposition to his family, but that will surely happen if Edgar forces his intentions. The hurry and the suddenness he has shown are based on a false apprehension of the situation in Europe. An immediate war was highly unlikely. Germany was not prepared, and neither France nor England would wage a war of prevention. He has reason to believe that Hesi's parents were also opposed to forcing the issue. He and Rosi hoped to visit New York in September, when they would carry on the dialogue in person, giving Edgar time to consider this enormous life decision and to balance his sentiments with reason. The letter is moderate and ostensibly friendly, though it implies that no one but Siegmund himself, and certainly not his overhasty son, knew how to assess reality correctly.

Who *was* Hesi? Edgar kept some of her letters, written on blue paper in an attractive, confident hand, illustrated with little nature drawings and sprinkled with phrases in French, English, and Italian. During 1933 she wrote playful, imaginative, and emotionally forthright love letters, reveling in his tanned handsome looks and trying to arrange for places they could meet without being observed by her companions. That year she was living at a school in western Germany, where she was training for a career that is never named. Whether or not the stage was in question, Hesi was certainly acting when she attempted to hide her Jewishness from her fellow students. "They talk a lot about politics; it all comes out of the newspapers, no individual opinions, and they're also anti-Semitic of course; it can't come out that I am from other shores." In recompense for that secret, she had another: "Sometimes I have the thought, at home there's something golden I'll soon put on again." Their engagement, or understanding, seems to have dated from the early months of 1933. Whether or not she knew of Edgar's membership in the League of National German Jews, she sometimes complains that he doesn't tell her enough about what he's thinking and doing.

When Edgar left Germany, he and Hesi had not decided what was to happen next. His new life in New York did not help to clarify matters, and they may both have been ambivalent about their prospects together. At the end of February 1934 she wrote, "You know and say often how important my work is to me. And I think you know that a lot depends on my training. This will last just another year. And we have no idea how things will develop over the next few years. I really need you to say what you think. You write 'Come over!' but it's not such a simple matter; I can't just pack up and be at the dock all at once! And how do you think of what's to follow—I can't even imagine it." Siegmund was not the only one who was upset by Edgar's way of leaving things ambiguous. Amid the growing horror of Nazi Germany and the upheaval of emigration, questions of old and new personal commitments were looking quite different from before.

Hesi was sensible enough to see that they were living in a wholly new set of circumstances. On March 6, 1934, she sent a telegram. "Beloved, understand me and decide without pressure. There's nothing to blame yourself for. I must act in relation to you. You know that the past is now concluded. I thought we would come together. Decide what's best for you. I will abide by our agreement." Under this decided pressure, Edgar chose to go on with their relationship, precipitating the family showdown of late March and April. But by June Siegmund had won. Perhaps he threatened the permanent rift that Edgar could not bear to contemplate; perhaps Edgar reconsidered the bond in the light of his new American life. The engagement was broken. On Friday, June 30, Hesi wrote a final line to Edgar: "My Beloved—and nothing any more."

What happened to Hesi? Did Edgar ever know? The tragic answer, death at the hands of the Nazis, leaps all too readily to mind. But Hesi was well aware of her danger, and she was enterprising. Someone with a name like hers, of the right age, arrived in New York from Bremen in August 1937. It's not an uncommon Jewish name, so I can't be sure. But I would like to think she was the girlfriend my father left behind.

The father-son struggles of 1934 were not yet played out, but as the year proceeded, all the Bodenheimers were consolidating their postemigration positions. Siegmund and Rosi placed thirteen-year-old Helga in a Lausanne *pensionnat* and attempted to recoup what they could of the family fortune. With a banker's concision, Siegmund put it this way: "The emigration was naturally bound up with heavy financial losses. There was a 25% emigration tax on one's entire fortune, and the rest was subjected to a barrier: it had to be extracted in *Sperrmarken*, only to be sold in the markets of Switzerland and Holland. Non-liquid assets like houses, material goods and life insurance could, if at all, only be saved by great expenditure of time and ever-increasing shrinkage of profits. If we had to live a new, much more limited style of life, we had the contentment of knowing that—as we only learned later—the role of Jews in Nazi Germany had been played to its end."

The 25-percent Reich Flight Tax and the *Sperrmark*, or blocked mark, put in place to reduce capital flow out of Germany during the financial crisis of 1931, came to play special roles in the Nazi campaign to appropriate Jewish property. Until 1935 the *Sperrmark* could be exchanged for foreign currency only at 50 percent of its value; after that year the percentage decreased quickly until it reached 4 percent in 1939. If anyone knew how to make the most of this bad situation, it would have been Siegmund. He travelled frequently to Zurich and Amsterdam to negotiate sales of his *Sperrmarks*, and, despite his financial losses, he remained a rich man for the rest of his life.

Putting herself in some danger, Rosi returned to Berlin at least twice to dissolve the huge Jagowstrasse household, and managed to get a good deal of the furniture, art, china, crystal, and silver out of the country. The chauffeur's residence on the property was consigned to her young cousin Vera

Figure 8. Rosi Maass Bodenheimer in 1948

Lachmann. For six years, until the Nazis shut it down, Vera used the building as a school for Jewish children who had been excluded from the German education system under the April 1933 Law Against the Overcrowding of German Schools. The entire Jagowstrasse villa was later destroyed during the Allied bombing of Berlin. Even the address was erased after the war when the street got a new name, Richard Strauss Strasse.

Siegmund and Rosi travelled constantly from their Swiss base, thinking about where to settle or paying last visits to the capitals and natural beauties of Europe. They did not, as threatened, visit Edgar in New York in 1934. Instead he returned to Europe that July and spent some time with them in the Swiss resort town of Villars, where he introduced them to his new girlfriend, Brigitte Levy, who was also visiting her parents in a nearby village. The Bodenheimer parents spent the month of October in Palestine, where Rosi's brother Alfred Maass had emigrated with his family. In a letter to Edgar, Siegmund conveyed his impressions. It was disappointing that so little of Jewish antiquity was visible in the Promised Land, but the energy of the present was impressive. His description of a classless society in which former lawyers had happily become chauffeurs was entertaining enough but clearly not to his taste. Nor did the principal cities tempt him. Although Edgar, already disenchanted with America's financial scandals and poverty, had urged him to consider Palestine as a place to settle, Siegmund responded only with an ironic remark about Edgar's sudden embrace of Zionism.

Edgar himself was having some trouble getting used to the melting pot, American style. He worried about the anti-Semitism in his new country, though, like so many German Jewish émigrés, he had tremendous faith in Roosevelt's leadership. If Roosevelt's program fails, he wrote, things here will be critical for the Jews. He was already caught up in American politics, celebrating Democratic victories after the midterm elections of 1934.[11] Edgar's prejudices were also apparent. He joked extensively about the mixture of types, races, and mixed-race people in New York, but he was not very happy about taking the subway to work, sandwiched, as he put it, between a Negro woman and a gangster reeking of brandy. He couldn't figure out what Americans found funny in Hollywood movies. "Will one end one's life as a naturalized Hottentot? Who knows?" Humor aside, those luxurious Berlin ways of life were not so easy to give up.[12]

He was doing well at work and in his night classes in American law at New York University. Just after the turn of the year Mr. Rosenberg told Edgar that he'd recommended him for partner in the firm. "I have the impression I am a 'bright fellow' and will be given a chance to build a future." He would be placed in a division where he could use his knowledge of foreign law and languages, the unit that handled the liquidation of Ivar Kreuger's International Match Company, "whose fraudulent activities," Edgar later wrote, " were a cause célèbre at the time. My work in this office led me into a study of various aspects of international law." (Kreuger, the Swedish "Match King," engaged in financial swindles on a grand scale.) Rosenberg also suggested that Edgar Americanize his German-sounding name, but Edgar refused. "I see no reason to conceal my Jewish-German roots and father-name for reasons of 'Americanization,'" he told Siegmund. Emigration had solidified his sense of who he was, and that person aspired to no American dream.

Despite Edgar's successes, Siegmund did not trust him, especially when it came to family matters. On October 24, 1934, Edgar wrote to his parents, who were somewhere on their travels between Tel Aviv and Lausanne, announcing his decision to marry Brigitte Levy. It would not, he thought, come as a surprise to them after what they had learned about her at Villars that summer. They knew that he considered her in every way the right woman for him. Everyone who knew her spoke of her in the highest possible terms, and he was amazed to think she had agreed to become his wife. You will ask, he wrote, why I have bound myself so early. I can only answer, "because this attachment simply seems obvious, because she makes me feel happy and free. When two people know with unshakeable certainty that they belong together for life, then the attachment is simply there." The doubts and equivocations that complicated his dealings with Hilde and Hesi are absent in this description of Brigitte. If she made him feel free, it was probably because she was not the one who was trying to pull him closer and lay claim to him. He was now in full pursuit of a young woman who was decidedly rational, sensible, and free of inclinations to emotional drama.

Edgar's announcement reached his father just four months after the end of the Hesi affair. When Siegmund returned to Lausanne and picked up Edgar's letter, he was beside himself with anger.

> In your most important life decision you have had neither the sense of duty nor the decency—not to speak of the heart's affection—to make sure of your parents' approval. You have broken your word, because you promised me not to present me with this question as a completed fact—and you did so just two months after our conversation about the matter. . . . That I am deeply hurt by this, everyone will understand. The matter has thrown a shadow over my 60th birthday, and I will require time to recover from this disappointment, which I had not thought possible. The experiences of 1934 have been a bitter lesson for a father who had had a different picture of his only son.

Siegmund couldn't help seeing Edgar's quick engagement as yet another instance of his son's irresponsible folly, but this letter lacks his usual measured control. This time he had no reservations about the appropriateness of Edgar's choice. Instead he was simply enraged by his son's refusal to make his father a central figure as he forged ahead with his marriage plans. In his view Edgar continued to make light of him by responding to his father's anger with his usual pleas that harmony be restored and bad feelings swept aside. Siegmund would have none of this; he let Edgar know that what he had done was unforgivable. "Maybe your approach is the result of a weak character, or a determination to declare your own will. There's not much difference between them as far as I'm concerned. The disappointment is the same, even if your behavior has other wellsprings." He had also been very embarrassed to receive a note of congratulation from one of his sisters, when he had barely heard the news himself. Brigitte's parents had printed engagement notices in late October, at about the time Siegmund, returning from his travels, received the announcement from his son.

Why did Siegmund allow himself to attack Edgar so directly? His insistence that being a weak character is the same as declaring your own will gives him away: he couldn't tolerate the idea that Edgar had a will apart from his own. Siegmund may once have cherished the thought that his son would continue the family dynasty he had begun in his rapid ascent to financial and social success. From his perch in Switzerland he had barely had time to register the fact that everything he had so proudly built was essentially lost, dissolved into nothing by the Nazis. Nearing sixty, he was temporarily homeless, though his family could stay at the best hotel in any city or resort they happened to be visiting. His shrewd assessment of the political situation had saved many members of his family—and now his son was flagrantly ignoring the obvious importance of a father who had supported his life in every possible way. Unlike this exemplary father, Edgar had not waited until he was earning enough to support a family before leaping into yet another engagement. Siegmund had lost command of a small empire he had built, and now he was losing command over his son.

For his part, Edgar at twenty-six was making his own way. He must have been tired of submitting every decision of his life to judgment at his father's court, where he had to ratchet up his powers of persuasion against an always skeptical magistrate. He *had* been inconsiderate to Siegmund, most likely because he was unstoppably committed to getting married as soon as possible, establishing a household apart from his parents, and securing the approval and affection of his new in-laws-to-be. It would be hard to say whether he had deliberately withheld things from Siegmund or had simply been carried along by the force of his feelings for Brigitte and the opportunity to settle the whole vexed matter of marriage for once and all.

As 1934 reached its end, father and son found a kind of accommodation. Bebs, always the family member with the greatest emotional understanding, managed to overcome her hatred of letter writing long enough to send a plea to her beloved brother. She made it clear that she was writing in the spirit of their special brother-sister alliance, not as a parental emissary. Richly sprinkled with endearments, her letter implored Edgar to help their father get over his hurt feelings. On December 20, Edgar did his best:

> On my side it was neither a sickness nor a rebellion—it was not that I rejected my parents' participation in the most important decision of my life. It was really about the question of whether a connection in the *present* case was right or not. And I'm of the opinion, that a son one sends to America should be given a certain freedom of decision. There are so many other considerations besides the economic one. If those were the only grounds, no marriage would happen. One has to take into account that a connection with a worthy girl in our situation means a lot for the *soul*, especially when one lives in a country one doesn't love.

In addition to her other virtues, Brigitte was a part of home, in particular the intellectual and academic Heidelberg milieu that Edgar especially cherished. That, at least, he would be allowed to carry with him as he tried to imagine a future in the country he didn't love. He had emigrated against his own inclinations, but the change had given him some independent authority that might have been harder won had he been able to stay in Germany.

This letter and a subsequent one included some real apologies, and Siegmund warmed up, only hoping that in future Edgar would bring more psychological understanding to his treatment of his parents. Soon after the New Year, he wrote to Brigitte, welcoming her officially into the Bodenheimer family. It was an odd, comic production, designed to glide above the recent embarrassment. "Newly baked fathers-in-law are in a bad way," he began, pleading inexperience and pretending to have consulted his bookseller for a guidebook that would help him out. He promised to spend a half-hour a day dutifully studying "how to be an ideal father-in-law" and hoped that the task would be made easier once he and Brigitte met again in the coming March. With greetings to both of them, he signed it with the plural "you," *eure Vater*. The family crisis was over, but it was not the last time that Siegmund would object to his adult children's financial and personal decisions.

In March 1935 Siegmund and Rosi began an extensive tour of the United States, appearing for Edgar and Brigitte's modest New York wedding on June 6, 1935. Bebs, who had been living a gloriously Bohemian life as a medical student in Bern, refused her parents' invitation to join them. She intended to spend the time in Berlin with her boyfriend, Teddy Blau. After her parents returned, Bebs and Teddy travelled to their big hotel in Lausanne and got formally engaged, "which was something you had to do at the time, to please your parents." As Bebs recounted to her son, Siegmund and Teddy took "an endless walk around the garden and, you know, I guess Dad got the third degree. And at the end of the conversation Opa said it's OK, you can get engaged."[13] No doubt Siegmund would have preferred to take a similar walk with Brigitte Levy.

Bebs and Teddy married in March 1936 and left shortly afterward for the United States. It was September before Rosi and Siegmund completed their European business and landed in New York with sixteen-year-old Helga, to begin life in what Siegmund called "a new, better Fatherland." A year before they arrived in Manhattan and set up their elegant apartment at 315 Central Park West, Edgar and Brigitte had already moved west, well beyond the parental orbit. They were both working toward American law degrees at the University of Washington in Seattle.

# 3
# Brigitte Levy

The German childhood of my mother, Brigitte Levy, comes in a small cardboard box, off-white with a design of scattered blue cornflowers on its cover. The box is crammed with old letters in their envelopes, some bundled together with small pieces of colored string or ribbon. As I struggle to untie and retie these tiny bits of string, my hands remember my mother doing up food parcels to send to German friends long past the end of the war. My job was to put a small finger on the first stage of the knot so her hands would be free to tug it tight.

Cracking the code of these remnants appears difficult. The box itself is stuffed, as though twenty-year-old Brigitte had given herself just this much room to preserve letters from German relatives and friends when she emigrated in September 1933. Or perhaps the girlhood box was brought over by her parents when they left Germany three years later. But that is the least of its mysteries. Both sides of her Berlin-based extended family—grandmother Hedwig Wolff and grandfather Robert Levy, along with various *Tantes* and *Onkels* and cousins—were dedicated to the habit of cramming as many words as possible onto small postcards or pieces of paper. Both the Wolffs and the Levys were well off, so a lack of paper is not in question, though old family habits of careful saving may be at work. Written in mixtures of Gothic and Roman script, most of these letters are barely legible. I content myself with figuring out who the correspondents were and where they lived (mostly in the comfortable neighborhoods of Berlin-Charlottenburg) while getting a rough idea of the occasions marked by the letters. Birthdays and the passing of academic exams invite congratulations, advice, and family news. Letters from high school friends left behind after a move are bundled together by correspondent. They sport lovely handwriting and wider spaces, but I can't make out all of the words. Brigitte is sometimes called "Bärchen" (little bear), and one of her friends signs herself "Rikki-Tikki-Tavi" from Kipling's *Jungle Book*, so I know there's a history of affection among the schoolgirls.

Helpfully, there's a little group in English from a household in the town of Dorking in Surrey, where fifteen-year-old Brigitte boarded for a while in 1927. They come from Josephine Craven, her landlady, an aging teacher at a Dorking school that Brigitte attended for some months, who signs herself "your English aunt." She urges Brigitte to return in 1930, hoping for her company and household help. And there are letters from Pickles, Miss Craven's English orphan "niece," a schoolgirl perhaps a year or two younger than Brigitte. Pickles, who does not seem to have another name, helps Miss Craven with household work and is specializing in domestic arts at Christ's Hospital, Hertford. Her letters sound as if they are drawn directly from *Schoolgirls' Annual*. She is mad about sports and full of "jolly goods." In one note, she teases Brigitte, whom she calls "My dear old Buggins," about writing postcards in that tiny illegible script. Beyond the fact that Brigitte, like Edgar, was sent abroad to practice her English, I learn just a little more about Brigitte herself. Her two improbable companions loved her enough to correspond with her for two years after her sojourn with them. I learn as well that she disliked her new school in Heidelberg, where her parents had moved in 1928. She was tired of losing school friends and moving to new places.

While Edgar's childhood was grounded firmly and luxuriously in Berlin, my mother's early life was full of transitions. She was born Brigitte Marianne Levy on September 27, 1912. Her first two years were the ones her father would later recall as the happiest time in his life. In 1909 he had married the lovely Zerline Wolff, always called Marie, and begun his legal career as a lower-court judge in Oranienburg, a town just north of Berlin. Now, at thirty, he had been invited to teach law at the University of Berlin and was working toward his *Habilitation*, the written thesis that would qualify him for the lowest academic rank as a *Privatdozent*. Ernst Levy's uncommon abilities had been recognized early. Among the fragments left behind, there is a small envelope addressed to Herrn Amstrichter Dr. Ernst Levy in Oranienburg, containing the business card of Dr. Emil Seckel, the Roman law scholar at Berlin who had been his primary teacher. Thanking his former student for New Year's good wishes in 1910, Seckel hopes on the back of the card that Levy's practical work allows him time to foster his "splendid talent in the service of Roman law." It was a kind of praise that Ernst Levy would not have publicized himself.

Unlike my Bodenheimer grandfather, Ernst Levy had grown up in a well-established Berlin family. His father, Robert Levy, was a successful businessman. His mother, Betty Landsberger Levy, could trace her ancestry back through the Sephardic line of Spanish Jews to an ancestor who served as physician to the royal Spanish court in the early 1500s. Her more immediate forebears had been rabbis, teachers, and physicians. Ernst's uncle Joseph Landsberger was well known in Berlin for his work in bacteriology and public health.[1] In such a context *Bildung*, high achievement, and the personal modesty that properly went with it were simply assumed.

As a youth Ernst attended the Friedrich-Gymnasium where Edgar was later to pass his early school days. Finding academics easy, he aspired to be a concert pianist and reached the master-class level of study at the Stern Conservatory, which trained a number of important German musicians. His powers of concentration and discipline were intense, and so was his capacity for self-criticism. Perhaps he abandoned a career in music because he felt that he lacked the talent to meet the demands of his own perfectionism. The last remnant of his early musical talent now stands in my living room: a Bechstein baby grand, built in the early 1890s, which traversed the Atlantic and the continental United States several times before it came to rest in our house. I never heard my grandfather play it. Bored during a childhood visit to my grandparents, I struggled to learn a Mozart sonata and fell in love with the piano's sound. But my grandfather never said a word about his own musical experience. Was he secretly horrified by my impatient readiness to let mistakes fly by? Or was he simply a man in his late seventies whose mind was elsewhere? There was something uncanny about Ernst Levy; his intense gaze was almost otherworldly in its focus.

During Brigitte's infancy her family was living in a peaceful apartment in Grunewald. While *Vater* wrote steadily in his study, Marie was absorbed in creating a loving home for her husband and children. She was accustomed to the household needs of scholarly men. Her brother Fritz Wolff was an expert in Sanskrit and Persian culture whose extensive research was financed by their businessman father, Emanuel Wolff. Her older sister Flora had married Gustav Mayer, a historian of socialist theory and the German labor movement. As a young mother, Marie doted on her outgoing, talkative, willful two-year-old son, Wolfgang, who filled her with pride and laughter. Brigitte, a shyer, more solemn baby, worried her a bit at first. Soon after her second birthday, however, the mother felt reassured: "My little problem child has developed into a regular, little, sweet girl. She is so good and loving. I just can't be angry with her. She is so tender and gentle, like a regular little female, originating from me. That is the way it should be. . . . Her speech is very cute, always with a fine thin voice. But then she is embarrassed that she has said anything at all."[2] In the journal she kept about

Figure 9. Ernst Levy (third from right) with his unit in World War I

her children, Marie's attention to their doings and sayings is saturated in love and appreciation. She comes through as a mother full of responsive feeling life, while Ernst remains a respected but somewhat judgmental presence in the background, playing his fatherly role as necessary but somewhat surprised that children take so long to grow up.

At the end of 1914 the young family idyll came to an end. Ernst was conscripted into the army and went to war. He spent a year as a sergeant training recruits and was then sent to the Russian and later to the French front. Under a "civic truce" of 1914 Jews were officially welcomed into the German army and joined in great numbers, but anti-Semitism was common in the ranks. As the war began to turn sour for the Germans, scapegoating predictably followed: wealthy Jews were accused of war profiteering, enlisted Jews of avoiding front-line duty. A *Judenzahl* (Jewish census), initiated by the Prussian War Ministry in October 1916, attempted to count the number of Jews who served in various military positions. When news of the count became public, Jewish leaders and organizations mobilized in protest, demanding that the results be published to reveal just how wrong the anti-Semitic assumptions were. A Jewish population of just over half a million sent about a hundred thousand soldiers to war, thousands were decorated, and at least twelve thousand died for Germany. But the results were not published, and suspicions about Jewish participation did not die out in the postwar years. For patriotic German Jews eager to show their commitment to the fatherland, the discriminatory census, singling them out to fail a test of patriotism, clarified the extreme shakiness of their status as fully accepted German citizens.[3]

Only two of Ernst Levy's wartime letters to Marie have survived. The official army letter, a faded green *Feldpostbrief* folded over once, allowed little room, but Ernst's tiny script packs the small pages. Dated July 2, 1916, the first was written from the French *Feuerstellung* (front) just after the Battle of the Somme, a prolonged slaughterhouse for both sides, had begun with devastating results for the Allies. It's impossible to tell whether Ernst was stationed anywhere nearby, though he opens the letter noting calmly that the French had made themselves quite noticeable during the evening, so that real sleep was impossible. The compensation was that he was still awake at 11:00 to receive and read her *liebevollen 308*—her loving 308th letter, numbered so they could keep track of correspondence sent and received or lost in transit. For Ernst, the crisis was not the battle war historians would write about. He was serving under a senior officer, "S," with whom matters had come to a critical point. He was applying for a transfer, because he could not sustain the depressed mood and the stifled sense of personal freedom and dignity that this officer imposed on him. A difference of religion is named as just one aspect of the tension between them. Ernst is trying to figure out how best to forward his application: directly to Frankfurt, or through the officer, who wants to get rid of him in the worst way but can't be relied on to take the necessary steps. I do not know how this conflict ended, but it seems clear that my grandfather was suffering, as a Jew, at the hands of a loutish superior.

The second letter, his #375, was written a year later on August 13, 1917. "My saving grace, beloved child, now you must hold your nerves together and be brave. It is not unthinkable that the French are planning a big attack here, and that you will read in the newspaper what I unfortunately, unfortunately, cannot prevent." Air and artillery bombardments had been heating up as they always did before an attack. He had been in command that morning, and had no choice but to send his men back to the trenches. A benevolent heaven opened up its sluices and the rain gave them a glorious two hours of sleep at midday. They were working like gardeners, digging trenches further back and using the cut mounds of grass as additional safety barriers. He feels well, body and soul, he assures her. She, his *Goldkind* (his golden child, in their love-talk), must be hopeful, even if she doesn't receive mail immediately. They have careful leaders and a favorable position. Once this mountain has been climbed, they can look forward to his leave and a happy future will light up before them. Not for the first time, Ernst was looking death in the face, but the letter is characteristically thoughtful about his wife's emotional well-being.

The hopes it expressed were fulfilled, at least for a time. Shortly before the end of the war Ernst was released from military service. Like so many other veterans of that terrible conflict, he never spoke of his war experiences after his return. Despite the horrors, stresses, and personal humiliations, his nationalism seems to have remained intact. After Hitler's seizure of power in 1933 he believed for some time that his military service in World War I would exempt him from Nazi restrictions on Jewish life.

The father who returned when Brigitte was six was ready to throw himself all the more deeply into the solace of intellectual work. His rigidly disciplined way of life became the ordering rule of the household. Mealtimes, rest time, and walks had their sacred places in the schedule of each day. The children were expected to honor them; disturbing their father at work in his study would have been unthinkable. On the home front, the family had not had an easy time during the war years. Marie could not have kept her worries from the two small children in her charge. Wolfgang and Brigitte loved and played with each other, but the war was on their minds, too, and Marie recorded some of their childish responses. Brigitte sees a soldier with one leg. She says, "He probably left his other leg at home." (Ever practical, helpful Brigitte solves a troubling problem.) Wolfgang calls from the backyard, "Mother, I took 500 Russian prisoners. Shall I look for more, also English prisoners?" Marie tells him that prisoners of war have to work. Wolfgang: "Do they have to work like Vater at his desk?" (A fate fit for prisoners, from Wolfgang's point of view.) Marie comes into the room to find Brigitte in tears: "Mutter, Wolfdant kills me all the time with his stick." (She had trouble pronouncing both her brother's name and her own.) Brigitte says, "My doll is not called Anna anymore, because Anna is French. She is now called 'Mops.'" Wolfgang asks, "What happens to our enemies after the war? What are they to us then?"

The temporarily fatherless family had some support. Marie's widowed mother, Hedwig Wolff, lived near them in Berlin, as did Ernst's younger sister Anna, who had married the pianist/composer James Simon and had two sons about the ages of Wolfgang and Brigitte. The Levy grandparents sometimes invited Marie and the children to Brunshaupten, a small town on the Baltic sea, for summer holidays. Marie recorded a little interchange after they had visited with the grandparents and Brigitte had, as required, been especially nice to them. "On the way back I said to her, 'Little girl, I love you very much.' She was beaming but did not say a word. At the dinner table we had barley with dried fruit. One lonely plum was floating in her

Figure 10. Wolfgang, Marie, and Brigitte Levy in 1915

barley. She fished it from the barley, gave it to me and said 'You should eat it because you are always so good to me.'" Marie fostered an atmosphere of mutual love and goodness to others that survived the grim wartime supper.

Marie's messages to her daughter were not just traditional women's fare. The third of four children, she had yearned to go to medical school, but her father would not allow it. Although she would have been just seventeen when Emanuel Wolff died in 1901, she was probably expected to stay close to her widowed mother, Hedwig, until her marriage to Ernst Levy in 1909. Marie did persuade someone to let her leave home for a while to study horticulture, and her green thumb helped to sustain her in later life. But her frustration at being deprived of real work in the world was always evident to her children. Wolfgang lived out his mother's dream and became a physician. Brigitte knew she was expected to learn something, marriage or not. And, if Wolfgang's outgoing personality made him his mother's son, Brigitte was her father's daughter. She later recalled that her brother was never interested in his father's work, and that Ernst turned to her when he talked about law. Her mother's desire, her father's attention, and her own strongly rational intelligence would later combine to make legal studies her natural course.

Brigitte's childhood in postwar Germany presented other struggles. In

Figure 11. A Levy family portrait, 1924

1919 Ernst took a position at the University of Frankfurt, and the family moved away from their Berlin relatives. Three years later he was called to the University at Freiburg im Breisgau, so they moved again. The inflation of 1922–23 was at its peak. Brigitte remembered those years as a horrible time. "My father—everybody who had a set salary—was very poor. Every week my father would get money, and by the next day it would be worthless. He would get money on Monday, and by Tuesday it would be worth *nothing*. My mother bought seven loaves of bread and a few other things to eat."[4] Like other city people, Marie would go into the country and appeal to unsympathetic farmers for an occasional egg or two. The blows to middle-class pocketbooks were amplified by blows to middle-class dignity. The fact that everyone—with the exception of families like the Bodenheimers whose finances did not depend on weekly salaries—suffered from the economic crisis couldn't protect a shy child from personal embarrassment. My mother used to tell the story of going to school wearing a dress made from her mother's old coat. "The teacher said, 'Take your coat off.' And I went home crying because I couldn't take my coat off, it wasn't really a coat." Explanations to a teacher in a new school may have been more than ten-year-old Brigitte could muster.

Once the inflation was under control, Brigitte's six years at school in Freiburg brought good friends and a new sense of stability. Freiburg, in southwestern Germany, was more liberal and relaxed than Prussian Berlin. Beautifully situated on the edge of the Black Forest, it allowed Brigitte and Wolfgang easy access to skiing and hiking trails. The letters from three close girlfriends preserved in Brigitte's box of correspondence come from this period. A Lutheran religion teacher, Erika Heyd, also became a lifelong friend. Shortly after my mother's death in 1981, an elderly Erika Heyd wrote to me and recalled their meeting:

> I met her in the school at Freiburg. It was my first position, and I was a beginner and at first had only defeats. But one day two girls, between 15 and 16, came to me and one of them asked me whether Brigitte could also come to my religion class. I said of course, if her parents allow it. Brigitte, who had been silent, said 'I may.' She was such a shy Jewish child, with wonderful eyes and splendid braids. I saw her and loved her. And she sat there in the first bench and listened. Once we came across the tax collector Levi in the Evangelist [The Gospel of Matthew]. And the children cried 'See, Brigitte, you occur in the Bible!' I said something like this: 'Yes, she belongs to the chosen people.' That was about 1927, and that was obvious to everybody.

I'm not certain what was obvious to everybody: that Brigitte was one of the chosen, that she was Jewish, or that the students were getting a lesson in tolerance. The religious open-mindedness that Brigitte shared with her parents, her desire to learn about the New Testament, and her wish to be part of a class that her girlfriends attended—all this does emerge from Erika Heyd's anecdote. Brigitte's cousin Ulrich Simon, who attended the Grunewald Gymnasium and became an Anglican priest after emigrating to London in 1933, describes in his memoir the sense among certain liberal Jewish families that there need be no insurmountable boundary between Jews and Christians, since the historical Jesus was a good man who preached a compatible social ethics.[5] Throughout her life my mother kept a reproduction of the beautiful head of the Virgin Mary by the Sienese painter Simone Martini, from his "Annunciation" of 1333. In my eyes, it was a familiar image of home.

At sixteen Brigitte had to pull up stakes again and move for her last two years of *Gymnasium*; her father had accepted an invitation to fill the chair of Roman law at Heidelberg. The friendship with Erika Heyd continued; in fact Brigitte remained loyal to this rather lonely Lutheran woman for the rest of her life. She and a friend visited Fräulein Heyd at her new school in nearby Mannheim. "The two of them came, ate all the cake there was, and

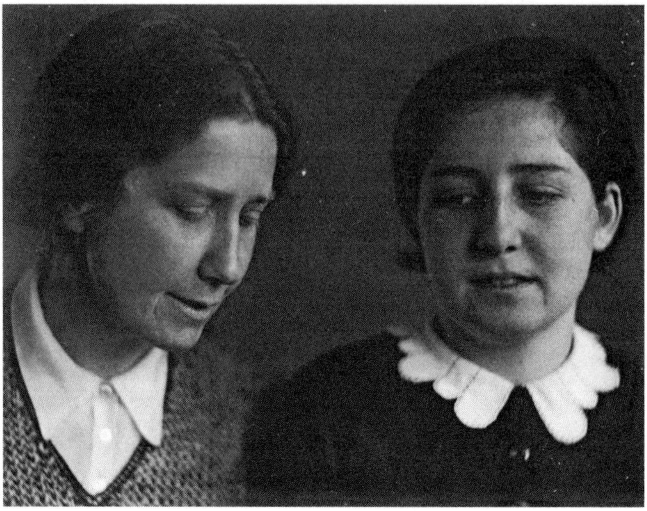

Figure 12. Marie with eighteen-year-old Brigitte, 1931

laughed and laughed. And this was not silly but rather touching, because they were simply happy, as happy as one later can no longer be." As Erika Heyd explained to me, the girls were at the *Backfisch* stage—the German word for girls in the awkward age between childhood and young adulthood.

It would not be long before Brigitte's childhood braids vanished, replaced, to her great relief, with a 1920s bob. Her mother did not succumb to the fashion. Marie's long light-reddish hair, never cut, was always worn in a bun at the nape of her neck, though the floating wisps around her face defied severity. Brigitte inherited her grandmother Wolff's wider face and her father's substantial nose. She was always dubious about her attractiveness and disliked being photographed even after she had matured. Only rarely could a camera catch her in a relaxed pose that captured her forthright charm and open, intelligent gaze.

Ernst Levy's Heidelberg years, 1928–1935, confirmed his status as the foremost German scholar of Roman law. When the University of Bonn tried to hire him in 1931, the Rector at Heidelberg protested in the name of his law faculty: Herr Professor Levy was now the top Romanist in Germany, equally superb as a scholar and a teacher, and a move to Bonn would be an irretrievable loss for Heidelberg.[6] The family joined the liberal academic elite clustered in that ancient city and moved into an apartment at Ziegelhäuserlandstrasse 17, a villa of lovely proportions overlooking the Neckar River. Professors were highly esteemed in German society, and Brigitte was used to the way her mother was formally addressed as Frau

Professor Levy, despite Marie's native lack of pretension and her natural way of attaching others to her. But their way of life remained relatively modest, at least compared with the rather conspicuous high-bourgeois style favored by the Bodenheimers.

Wherever they lived, the Levy apartments were sparely elegant. Small Persian rugs were scattered about, simply shaped tables covered with tapestry cloths held lamps and books, Marie's plants lived in an old inlaid cradle. Furniture was chosen for its clean, solid lines, not for its pretensions to taste. Siegmund Bodenheimer had acquired three pleasant Impressionist landscapes he bid for at auction during his heyday in Berlin—as well as a hideous German canvas featuring a massive black bull in a lowering dark-green landscape. The Levys passed on a quite different art legacy: a contemporary lithograph by Oskar Kokoschka that caught the mood of postwar Germany and resonated with personal meaning. It is a sad, slightly distorted sketch of a woman called Camilla Swoboda, one of a series Kokoschka did of her in 1920 as she listened to music played on the piano by her husband, the Viennese art historian Karl Swoboda.[7] The effect of inward attention and sadness is so intimate that the portrait was always hung in my grandparents' bedroom.

Ziegelhäuserlandstrasse 17 was an ancestral home of the political economist and sociologist Max Weber, whose intellectual spirit remained alive in the minds and work of his Heidelberg colleagues and followers after his death in 1920.[8] His widow, Marianne Weber, had moved back into the villa, devoting herself to editions of Max Weber's works and a biography of her husband. By 1928, when the Levys moved into their apartment, Marianne had reestablished the intellectual salon she had run in the Weber apartment before World War I. She maintained a cordial relationship with her new neighbors. As a result, Brigitte became acquainted with two powerful older women, Marianne Weber and her close friend Else von Richthofen Jaffé, who were quite different from the devout schoolteacher Erika Heyd.

Marianne Weber was a feminist sociologist, a prolific writer and speaker who had served as chair of the German National League of Women's Associations. A feminist trailblazer, she was among the first generation of women to receive university degrees in Germany, which had become possible only in 1897. Yet her positions were conservative by contemporary standards. She insisted that women should be trained to work and argued for economic equality in marriage and independence from women's reliance on the support of men. At the same time she was adamant that the ethical relation of marriage, including a women's service to her husband and children, formed the basis of her selfhood. As the arena of struggle between patriarchy and women's rights as autonomous individuals, marriage was the proving ground of the soul, where the ethical self fought to overcome the merely animal instincts of the human being. Marianne Weber fought simultaneously on two fronts: against patriarchy and against feminist ideas that threatened the ideal of marriage and sexual fidelity. The titles of her books suggest her focus on family law and ethics; they include *Career and Marriage* (1906), *Marriage, Motherhood and the Law* (1907), *The Question of Divorce* (1909), *Authority and Autonomy in Marriage* (1912), and the later, more popular *Women and Love* (1935), which explored ways that childless women could achieve fulfillment by mothering other people.

Brigitte was certainly informed about the major tenets, if not the details, of Marianne Weber's work. As she made the transition from high school girl to law student, she would sometimes be invited to the afternoon salon next door, where she would drink tea and listen to the lively discussions among liberal Heidelberg intellectuals. Both her own career in American family law and her life choices were to echo the kind of liberal conservatism that Marianne Weber represented. It was a complex position, because it required a woman to pursue her career, to maintain equality with her husband, and—at the same time—to subordinate herself to his requirements. All of this, along with the raising of healthy, ethically sound children, was to be accomplished without complaint or loss of self-control. Other models for a woman's career in law or public life would have been limited when Brigitte began her studies in 1930. Women had been eligible to take the German state examinations and enter the legal profession only since 1922. Members of the pioneer generation who became lawyers and judges during the late 1920s were often oriented toward feminist concerns, such as equality in marriage law and the treatment of juveniles. Overlapping with Weber's sociological emphases, these were the fields in which Brigitte was later to make her mark in American family law.

Marianne Weber's own marriage was conducted according to her beliefs.[9] She was Max Weber's cousin; their marriage was sexless and childless. After his teaching at Heidelberg had been interrupted by a massive nervous breakdown in the late 1890s, she tended and travelled with him for years. From then on the battle between his depression and his ability to work remained at the center of their lives together. She pursued her own work, while wholly supporting the man in whose genius she had put her faith. Her best friend, Else von Richthofen, had earned a doctorate in economics under Max Weber and served for a time as the first state-appointed woman factory inspector in Karlsruhe. Else remained a close friend of the Weber couple and a denizen of the Heidelberg circle. In 1902 she married Edgar Jaffé, another Weber student, and had children with him before the marriage dissolved. For a time Else and her sister Frieda were caught up in the erotic liberation movement preached by the psychoanalyst Otto Gross, who had affairs with both sisters. Frieda von Richthofen lived out her commitment to the erotic life when she abandoned her English marriage and children to elope with the novelist D. H. Lawrence. Her sister, more intellectual and controlled, drew back from the fray. But in the later years of his life she became Max Weber's lover, all the while maintaining her friendship with Marianne. By the time the Levys moved to Heidelberg, Else was the companion of Max Weber's brother Alfred.[10] Marianne Weber's battle against the doctrines of free love and sexual liberation had been fought on very intimate ground—possibly more intimate than she had fully allowed herself to know.

It is not likely that a young girl like Brigitte would have been told directly of these histories, but she must have been aware of them. She knew both "Frau Jaffé" and her half-Jewish son Friedel, who took his law degree at Heidelberg a few years before Brigitte began her own studies. Passing her *Abitur* at seventeen, she entered university in 1930, spending her first year at home in Heidelberg and returning there after semesters away at Munich and Berlin. I do not know whether the sexual liberation movement affected her student life, though I would guess that she remained a somewhat innocent and protected girl. When she emigrated at twenty, she was still deeply bound to her parents and had spent only brief periods away from them.

Her brother had loosened his family ties at eighteen, leaving Germany in 1928 to begin medical school in Vienna. The following year Wolfgang fell in love with a fearlessly energetic fifteen-year-old American student, Ruth Jacobs, who was studying in Austria for the summer. Ruth returned the next summer and the relationship held. In her old age, my aunt Ruth Jacobs Levy recalled meeting my mother sometime during this period. "She was charming," Ruth said. "She approached me holding out her hand, on which she had placed some tiny toy animals to greet me and put me at ease." Brigitte loved tiny animals and made them part of her affectionate life. In her fifties and sixties she couldn't bear to throw out the little ceramic beasts that came in Red Rose Tea boxes, and displayed her favorites on the kitchen windowsills in Davis. In Ruth's case she was sweetly trying to soften the edges of the younger girl's encounter with Wolfgang's family, who may have appeared formidable at first sight to an American teenager.

Once she became a young lady of eighteen, Brigitte began to enjoy social engagements among adults. Her box of letters contains a set of invitation cards addressed to "Fräulein Brigitte Levy," which she considered important enough to keep among her personal correspondence. Whatever her reasons may have been—the pride of being grown up, or amusement at the forms themselves—the cards open a small window on the rituals of social life among the German professoriate. Many were partially engraved with the hosts' names and the formulae of invitation, with spaces for the handwritten details of a particular occasion. The third person was the rule: Frau und Herr Professor X would be happy to see Guest Y at their home at the filled-in date and time. The gatherings would be of certain kinds: tea at five in the afternoon, *ein einfaches Abendbrot* (a simple supper) with or without dancing, or an evening get-together at 9:30 *im kleinen Kreis* (in a small circle). There are variations, according to the humor of the hosts: one couple invited Brigitte to a *sehr juristischen Thee* (very juridical tea). Marianne Weber's invitation was almost entirely engraved and promised "tea with collective conversation," the formula for her salon discussions. Brigitte kept over forty of these cards from her university years. When she left home to study in Munich and Berlin her father's colleagues were sure to invite her, so she got a lot of practice in making the kind of conversation appropriate for a female law student who was also the daughter of a well-known legal scholar.

The Levys were close to other liberal Heidelberg figures who would remain important to the family even in the postwar years. In a collection of Levy family photos I found formal portraits of several members of the law faculty, including Gustav Radbruch, a liberal Weimar politician and legal philosopher, Walter Jellinek, a Jewish scholar of constitutional law, and Max Gutswiller, a colleague in Roman law. Beyond the law faculty, the existentialist philosopher Karl Jaspers and his Jewish wife, Gertrud Mayer Jaspers, were the most prominent of their friends. In fact, they were part of the family. Marie's brother-in-law Gustav Mayer was the older brother of Getrud Mayer, and Karl Jaspers, who befriended both Gustav and his brother Ernst Mayer, was almost an honorary sibling in the Mayer family. As wives of Heidelberg eminences, Marie Levy and "Trude" Mayer were quite close. Both counted Marianne Weber and Else von Richthofen Jaffé among their friends.

Karl Jaspers' intellectual life could hardly have been more different from Ernst Levy's. While Ernst burrowed deeply into the minute details of Roman legal history, Jaspers' scope included medicine, psychiatry, philosophy, art, literature, ethics, and politics.[11] His tall, handsome Nordic presence enhanced his charisma as a public intellectual. (After I met him on a visit with my grandmother in 1959, I would not forget his frail but towering blue-eyed presence, wrapped in a blanket. Jaspers suffered from a lung ailment throughout his life, and was fiercely protected by his small wife.) In the Enlightenment tradition, he championed the cultivation of individual freedom through reason and creativity, which could allow the individual to understand and transcend the constraints of historical circumstances. It was a view that would certainly have appealed to Edgar when he studied with Jaspers at Heidelberg. As for Brigitte, Jaspers recalled to Edgar after the war that in his seminar Brigitte would sometimes ask, “Das muss so sein?” (Does it have to be that way?). The disarming quality in her intellectual skepticism sounds very much like my mother.

When she retired from teaching at the UC Davis Law School, Brigitte allowed herself to be interviewed by a law student called (as it happened) Stella Levy.[12] As her university life proceeded, she told Stella, the Nazi period was beginning in earnest, with brown-shirted storm troopers marching in the streets. Brigitte recalled her own young obliviousness to the threat. “I wasn’t reading the newspapers very much at that time. . . . And then I wanted to go back to Berlin [to study], and my father said, maybe you’d better not go anyplace else, things are getting too—grim. So I went to Frankfurt because that was close to home—closer. Then I began to—then you *had* to become aware—the big flags that people put out, the swastikas and so on.” Although she hesitated to say this to an American student, her class position had prevented her from taking seriously the political shenanigans of lower-middle-class thugs like those Nazis parading in the streets.

Brigitte had not yet taken the first of the German state examinations, which would qualify her as a *Referendar* and initiate her three years of apprenticeship as a law clerk. Unlike Edgar, who was four years older, she had not tangled with Nazi politics or bureaucracy. But when she returned from a ski trip in March 1933, Marie confronted her with the political realities. “My mother said, well, you’ve got to leave, you’d better go to the United States. She was always ahead of everything, anyhow. I was still not convinced. So we began to plan it, and pretty soon it became clear that I wouldn’t be *admitted* to that state examination. So that I couldn’t go on with my studies anyhow.” After obtaining a visa and the sponsorship of distant relatives in New York who took her on as an au pair girl, Brigitte crossed the Atlantic on the *St. Louis*, arrived in New York harbor on September 13, 1933, and found herself in suburban Mount Vernon, where she was expected to babysit and teach German to the children. She had no experience, or interest, in childcare. Two weeks after she arrived she turned twenty-one.

When Stella Levy interviewed Brigitte for the *King Hall Advocate*, it was 1979. The women’s movement was on Stella’s mind, and she was especially interested in how a woman of Brigitte’s generation had come to have a notable career in law. She was expecting stories about fighting gender discrimination and some Nazi period horror, but Brigitte did not oblige. She and her brother had had comparable educations, she insisted. Yes, there were separate schools for boys and girls but the teaching was very similar, and she got a dispensation from art class to study Greek for a while.

"That's probably why I have so much trouble understanding the problems that so many women have about discrimination. I didn't know any discrimination, didn't feel any in my younger years." As for being Jewish: "At that time I studied at the university, and it was very free and easy, no discrimination against women, or Jews—at least none to know of, under the circumstances. . . . The first years of studying were very free and easy, really no awareness of anything, except I knew my father was getting increasingly pessimistic." Historians would dispute her impressions on both counts, but Brigitte's life among Heidelberg liberals may have created a protective envelope that she did not care to unseal.[13]

Even a retrospective self-presentation for an audience of American students could not tempt Brigitte to dramatize her position as an exile. "I was one of the people who left very early, in September 1933," she told Stella, "so I really never experienced that much of what was going on there." Emigration, too, was presented as a matter of course. Although her childhood moves had not been easy for her, she told Stella, "I've moved around all my life, so it was nothing new to come to the United States and move again." She was being true to her nature and training: one did not complain about one's status as a woman or a Jew, nor did one draw on the vocabulary of victimization. It was not that she didn't understand American feminists, as she politely put it during the interview, but that she didn't really approve of their aggressive attitudes and methods.

At the same time Brigitte represented her own forms of feminist action with great energy and detail. She loved to recount episodes when she overcame outward obstacles and inward doubts because she was intellectually prepared. The most triumphant of these stories was the one about how she was accepted at Columbia Law School soon after her arrival in the United States. It began with her Mount Vernon situation: "Babysitting—and I hadn't had *anything* to do with kids, at that time. And I said, I want to go to law school. And they said, oh no, maybe after a while you can become a social worker. I was *stuck*—and I didn't even know how to use the subway." As she spoke, Brigitte was diverted into one of the memories omitted from the write-up in the student paper, though it is an essential part of her immigration narrative:

> That's a very funny story. I remember I went to the place where you could change the money, at the subway—at that time it cost a nickel, and I thought I wanted to get a ticket. So I gave him some money and said I wanted a ticket—that's the way I went on the subway in Berlin. And he gave me all that change, and he didn't give me a ticket! So I said what do I do next, and he said take a nickel. I didn't know that

> that coin—the 5 cent coin—was a nickel, and I wasn't being treated too well, he thought I was an *idiot*! And then I had the nickel but I didn't know what to do with it—put it in that slot. But I got on the subway and got to Columbia Law School.

It's a classic case of unforgettable foreign-feeling; only know-how can help to overcome the pain of feeling seen to be stupid. Once she figured out which coins to put in the slot, the gates of Columbia opened for her, too, though it took a bit longer:

> So, the director of admissions at Columbia University was a very stiff kind of person, and he said, there's not a chance in the world that you can go to law school. I said, I've already had so much, six semesters of German law, I wanted to continue here, I wanted to start over. Well [he said] you have to take an exam, and I'm sure you can't pass that—in a week. So I said, all right, I'll take the exam. The exam was a big book—like an LSAT, I suppose. I had never seen such a type of exam in my life. It was a four-hour exam, and I had to figure out all these mathematical differences—decimals and groups—and it was all written a little differently. By the time I was supposed to be finished, I had done about *half*. I handed it in, and that was that.

The next step was Brigitte's appeal to two faculty members she knew because they had previously been visitors at Heidelberg. She was allowed to audit as a special student but required to pass several undergraduate courses in history and government in order to be accepted as a regular student. She found these courses dreadful. There had to be a better way.

> There was some agency in Albany that had to approve that I had all the prerequisites for law school in New York. So this was my main first accomplishment in this country. I sat down one night—I think it took the whole night—and wrote a very long letter to—I think his name was Mr. Field. And I took this out of my study book—we had books that showed which courses I had had in Germany—everything that had *any connection* with American government or American history. It so happened that there was one professor from Harvard who taught at Heidelberg the year before I left, comparative constitutional law, or something like that. And a few others. So, I listed all these courses, I pointed out what I had done. After I had done this of course I didn't expect anything but at least I had done what I could. And really, I *did* get a letter back, you do not need to take these courses, you

> can get into law school. I think that was the greatest accomplishment of my young life. It was the first time I had really done something more or less on my own, because otherwise I had been under the wing of my parents.

Having achieved this victory, Brigitte said, she became "a very bad law student." She meant that the American system required constant testing, while she was used to the "academic freedom" of German universities, where you didn't have to go to class or prepare daily in case you were called on. Her fellow students warned her, but "it didn't make any impression on me at all, I just went about my business, and when I was called on in class I said 'unprepared.' Until the first exams, and then I practically had a nervous breakdown, because I was reading the casebook from the beginning just before." She passed, with B's and C's, and did better the next year. Modest as she was, my mother was capable of drama when it came to immediate, concrete challenges. Much later, at family dinners in Salt Lake City, she could fill our ears with tales of recalcitrant legislators she was battling in her quests for legal reform.

For both Brigitte and Edgar, the opportunity, presumably financed by their parents, to start over in American law school guaranteed that their ejection from Germany would not erase the expertise they had begun to gather in their early years. Retraining was essential because the German and American legal systems operated on different principles. The German system, based on Roman law, rests on a collection of codified laws. Proceeding from abstraction and general principles, cases are decided by judges through an inquisitorial process. The American system derives from British common law and relies more on precedent, on the principle that similar facts should not be treated differently on different occasions. The judge's role in criminal cases is less critical, because of the Anglo-American commitment to trial by jury. The thick legal casebooks that Brigitte struggled to master for her first Columbia exams were new to her, as was the method of arguing by way of particular precedent-setting cases. Going to law school twice was a burden for Brigitte and Edgar, but it meant that emigration did not force them to live entirely different lives from those they had imagined. For many of their fellow émigrés, promising middle-class careers in Germany were simply wiped away with the move to a new country.

In 1934 it still looked as if a return to Germany might someday be possible, and Brigitte had left on the verge of earning her doctoral degree. She went home to spend the summer of that year with her parents in Heidelberg, working at top speed to meet the degree requirements. Like Edgar, she earned the Juris Doktor, magna cum laude, with a dissertation called

"Toward Equality in Joint Liability for Debt." Her examiners were her father's colleagues; perhaps they were not terribly hard on her under the circumstances. Preparing for the degree was not her only worry, though: What was to become of her parents? Emigration was almost unthinkable for Ernst Levy, whose work in Roman law depended on a long tradition of German scholarship in a subject of virtually no interest to American legal academics. During the summer of 1933 the number of Jews on the Heidelberg faculty had already been cut down substantially after the early April decree that Jewish professionals and academics be fired or forced to retire. Nazi student groups were beginning to boycott the classes of Jewish professors and to denounce them in "theses" posted on university buildings and public billboards.[14] As a frontline soldier and veteran of World War I, fifty-two-year-old Ernst Levy was, temporarily, exempt from dismissal. He clung to his position, hoping that matters would somehow reverse themselves while probably knowing that they would not. Like other women in her situation, including Rosi Bodenheimer, Marie had read *Mein Kampf* and recognized the extent of their danger, but she had to repress her desire to leave in order to remain loyal to her husband's needs. The stress in the household was palpable.

Brigitte's thorough immersion in her parents' lives and anxieties comes through in a letter she wrote to them on March 16, 1934, from New York, during her second semester at Columbia. Like the war letters between Ernst and Marie, it is numbered (55) and acknowledges receipt of their letters 46 and 47, noting the irregularity of the ships that carry transatlantic mail. She and her parents had been separated for seven months, but their dialogue remained constant, detailed, and intense. The letter is typed single-spaced on two sides of a page, all mixed together in one long paragraph with an occasional dash to indicate a shift of topic, and many abbreviated words. The family habit of crammed correspondence had not changed. Getting things down was more important than style, and Brigitte was, as usual, pressed with work. She addresses Ernst and Marie by their pet names "Lenchen" and "Miezchen," suggesting more intimacy and equality than was usual between generations in the Bodenheimer family.

The letter begins with a response to tragedy. Someone close to Marie had died in ghastly but unnamed circumstances that sound like suicide under Nazi pressure. "I just hope that now you will leave," Brigitte insists. Both she and her brother, Wolfgang, had been trying unsuccessfully to persuade their father to resign and emigrate. Launching into gossip about a hapless academic acquaintance in New York, she assures Ernst that he would not experience America in that way. He would like teaching in a law school here, "so let's wait and see." She expresses her gladness at Wolfgang's good news: he and Ruth had been married a month earlier, and Wolfgang, completing medical school in Vienna, had arranged a residency in radiology at the Montefiore Hospital in New York. "Those two have really accomplished something, and have earned a lovely restorative trip."

As for herself, she deserves no drumrolls for hard work, though she is working harder than in the previous semester. Her classmates work far harder, to the point of madness, she thinks, but she will soon have to buckle down to it, too. Miezchen has had painful dental work: Why must the dentist hurt her so much? And Lenchen, who's always slaving away like a madman, needs a vacation, too. She urges him to do some reading in a book about America she has sent, and then complains about the press of social life in New York: people are more accustomed to being constantly with others here. It is *Menschenüberlastung*: human systems overload, a New York disease. Meanwhile, she is entranced with a little girl, the daughter of family friends, in whom she sees something of herself, though the child is cuter and less shy. Despite her obsession with working (and not working) Brigitte is full of ready affection; in her letter everything goes on at once.

Then she turns to Edgar ("Bodenh"). She had already mentioned him to her parents after they recognized each other in the Columbia Law School Library. Edgar doesn't seem to suit Miezchen, she writes (Marie must have met him briefly when he was Ernst's student at Heidelberg). But she likes him and thinks that her mother misjudged him at first glance despite her excellent instinct for people. He's not insincere, but the opposite: rather reserved at first, which she likes better than people *die gleich alles auf der Zunge haben* (who immediately have everything at the tip of their tongues). She sees him seldom, because he respects her need to work. She did see him two days earlier for his birthday, and they ate in a lovely French restaurant with an elegant menu. Oysters to start. He laughed himself silly because she had never eaten them and had to ask him how to do it. But over here these things are a lot cheaper. Without pause, she chides her father for terrorizing her about how quickly her Heidelberg exams are coming up, which doesn't help her to study. And then, to parting: let yourself be caressed by me, Miezchen, Lenchen will do it. The intimate, uncensored range of tones she can take with her parents astonishes me.

After the Heidelberg degree was completed in 1934, Brigitte and Marie took a vacation together in the Swiss mountain village of Adelboden. By this time Edgar was wholeheartedly in love. Their separation during that summer has made it possible to glimpse their courtship through the letters that passed between them. Unlike the letters my father kept in his files, this set was sent to his sister Bebs for safekeeping after Brigitte's death. At some point after Edgar's death in 1991, Bebs passed the letters on to me. "Enjoy them!" she wrote on a pink Post-it note. It is easy to do so: my father's enthusiasm is infectious, and my mother, proceeding far more cautiously, was gradually catching it.

The first three notes in the set were written at the turn of the year 1933–34 in New York City. The first is addressed by Edgar to an unknown Herr Sachs, thanking him for sending Brigitte Levy's address in New York. As might happen in a small town, he writes, he had already run into *das Mädchen* (the girl) during his first days in New York, at the Columbia Law School Library, and has seen her frequently since. At this point Bebs took out a red pencil and wrote in the margin "Aha!" Late in her life she was entertained to discover that her brother was already seeing Brigitte when the Bodenheimers became embroiled in the last act of his relationship with Hesi. On January 6, Edgar writes a rather formal note to "Fräulein Brigitte" inviting her to a play. Brigitte's response captures her amused impatience with the old forms. "Dear Edgar (since we are in this land of first names, it is more sensible to save oneself the trouble of the last name—and for you to drop the Fräulein)." Nevertheless they are still on terms of acquaintanceship: she calls him "Sie" rather than the familiar "Du," and signs "Brigitte Levy." She has already received an invitation to the play, with friends visiting from Philadelphia, but she hopes that he will find another play for them—even better if they could go after her exams are over. She is utterly straightforward: she isn't going to turn him down, but she is going to mention the realities of her life (omitting all those unread casebooks) as she postpones their date.

By June, when Brigitte is back in Heidelberg, things have progressed rapidly, and Edgar is pressing his case against some resistance on her part. After telling her his latest news, he writes,

> I know that I have made mistakes, if it is a mistake to tell someone that one feels love for her. You didn't believe it at first, and sometimes you still have doubts. I do not think I have given you cause for such doubts, Brigitte. I don't want to 'take you as you are,' I want to love you without reservation, knowing that love is not so much something you drift into as a choice that requires a full investment. We all have the failings of our virtues, and what's decisive is just that a couple grows together and gives one another strength for life. Alone one can't always quite find it.

He was moving too fast for her. Concerned for her parents and anxious about her exams, Brigitte was not quite ready to trust a man she had known for only a few months. She was attuned to family affection but rather inexperienced in romance, while Edgar was over-eager to forget Hesi, end his loneliness in New York, and establish a stable comradeship with a young woman whose intelligence, loyalty, and gameness for life he recognized and appreciated. He responded to her doubts by tuning up the persuasive powers he had practiced with his father and offering her an ethically charged vision of love and marriage. Four years older, he assumed the role of the wiser one who could quell her doubts about her own worthiness and desirability, while representing her as essential to his happiness. "Worrying so much about yourself is rather unfruitful. For me you are *everything*, that is becoming clearer to me every day. In my thoughts you are always with me, and I simply cannot imagine how my life could go forward without this hope." Her diffidence had turned him into a very single-minded lover.

In mid-July Edgar went on vacation to Italy, on the way to visit his parents in Villars. He wished Brigitte were with him. They had been stuck in the Manhattan *Steinmeer* (sea of stone) all winter and had never been in nature together. He wanted to be able to talk everything over with her—indeed, his criterion for a good marriage, as he always told his children, was one in which the partners could always have good conversations. For the moment, he wrote about his Italian adventures with his usual enthusiasm for travel and its pleasures, and she wished in return that she could share them with him. But everything was crazy at home. They talked plans constantly but her father refused to make any commitment and seemed frozen in place. She and her mother would go to Adelboden and then sail to New York together at the end of August; could Edgar perhaps visit them in Adelboden? Her father was sailing for America early in August, but he would only consider it a vacation trip; he would probably stay with relatives and refuse to do anything about finding a position in America.

As Brigitte's exams loomed and passed, expressions of love and affection began to flow more easily back and forth in the correspondence. Cousin Vera Lachmann comes to visit the Bodenheimer family in Villars, and Edgar entertains Brigitte with his description of their deep discussions "in the realm of pure, abstract empyrean spirit." They have done some proper mountain climbing, and he is slowly beginning to feel himself whole again; in New York one is only half-human. In early August, he goes to visit Brigitte and Marie in Adelboden and brings Brigitte back with him to meet his family and do some mountain touring together. The two visits, in the glorious setting of the Swiss Alps, are decisive. Marie is won over by Edgar, the Bodenheimers and Brigitte like one another, and, once separated again, our two principals write to each other with joy, excitement, and confidence in their future together. Edgar has written a declaration of love that pleases Marie and does at least half the job of winning over Brigitte's father, still away on his visit to America. Although the contretemps with Siegmund about their formal engagement is yet to come, the young couple is launched.

Before Edgar leaves Villars, Brigitte urges him to convey her greetings and thanks to his family. She has taken their measure and wants to be sure that they are aware of what's going on. She jumps into her social and practical duties as a proto-wife, giving advice about New York apartments and assuring him that they will make the best of the stony city together after their return. She is also getting better at love talk. Although she tells Edgar she's not one for sentimentality, she has her own versions, sometimes mediated through little animals. She almost loses a little dog on the train with her mother; when finally found, he is rather battered and woefully tailless. "This will not interest you at all, yet you have to hear it. You will be hearing a lot of things that don't interest you." She is still a bit dubious about her power to please Edgar; sending along greetings from her mother, she adds the proviso "who is much nicer than I am." She had reason to be nervous. Marie was a model of wifely and motherly love, but Brigitte also had a serious drive toward professional activity. She was entering uncharted territory in a new country with no assurance that anything would work out. Edgar supported her career and enjoyed sharing their common legal know-how, but would he turn out to be a demanding German husband in the long run?

Reading these letters of upper-middle-class love and courtship, set in the Alpine resorts where such German families were accustomed to spend their summer holidays, it is sometimes difficult to remember what was going on next door in Germany. An eerie sort of normality seems to prevail. For many people, both Jews and non-Jews, that feeling of normality, punctuated by the sudden eruption of a fresh Nazi action or decree, was the prevailing mood of the early 1930s. No one could tell what would happen next. In the meantime, people went about their lives as best they could. Travel between America and Europe was perfectly possible for those who held German passports and could afford the journey. Brigitte and Edgar returned to Switzerland again in August 1935, after their early June wedding at the Hotel Alden in New York. It had been a small, subdued affair. Siegmund and Rosi Bodenheimer were there at the end of their preemigration American tour, while the bride's side of things fell to Edward and Rose Jacobs, the parents of Brigitte's sister-in-law Ruth. Later that summer the newlyweds visited the Levy parents in the Swiss town of Zug. Brigitte and Edgar were preparing to move to Seattle, while Ernst and Marie were to return once more to their apartment in Heidelberg.

Figure 13. Edgar and Brigitte's wedding at the Hotel Alden. From left: Rose Jacobs, Siegmund, Brigitte, Edgar, and Rosi

As yet they had come to no decision, but the teaching career of Heidelberg's eminent Roman law scholar had effectively been shut down earlier that summer. On May 11, 1935, Ernst received a letter from Berlin announcing that he had been placed on leave from his teaching duties as of July 1, though he was given a research assignment at the university library. No official timetable was likely to remain stable, however. In May and June the Nazis instigated a new wave of student boycotts aimed at "non-Aryan" professors. At the end of May Ernst Levy had entered his lecture room to find no one there. On June 4 (two days before his daughter's marriage in New York) he wrote a note to his dean:

> Highly honored *Herr Dekan*,
>
> On 21 May 1935 I had to abandon my lectures, because no listeners showed up. After this strike in which, as I hear, the whole student body participates, the attempt to take them up again would probably be unsuccessful. Under such circumstances I am constrained to consider my lecturing duties as ended.
>
> With best wishes.
>
> Your devoted, E Levy[15]

Dignity and pain come through these formal sentences in equal measure. Liberal Heidelberg was as ready as any other German university to look the other way as Jewish colleagues were made to disappear. For the time being Ernst retreated to his research post, which was subsequently cancelled. On July 8, he wrote to his colleague Wolfgang Kunkel from a two-month retreat in the Swiss Engadin, telling of his attempts to reimmerse himself in his several academic projects. "Walking takes its turn with working: a makeshift attempt to glue together what is inwardly broken."[16] His great grief is beautifully contained in the form of that quiet sentence.

On September 15, 1935, Hitler proclaimed the Nuremberg Laws at the end of the annual Nazi party conference in that city. They included the Citizenship Law, which stripped Jews of their civil rights, making them "subjects" rather than "citizens" of the Reich. In the wake of this law, exemptions for veterans of World War I that had briefly protected Ernst Levy were no longer enforced. In October he was placed on permanent leave; in December he was fired.[17] The couple's prolonged tension after enduring nearly three years of Nazi misrule cast its shadow on Edgar and Brigitte's wedding visit in August and would seriously affect Marie's health after emigration.

The Levys brought a wedding gift from Marianne Weber to Switzerland, and Brigitte wrote to thank her on August 19, before her return to the United States.[18] She was very conscious of the Weberian ethics of marriage as she described her newlywed state and the couple's future plans. "At the moment, in the first time of sheer happiness, we have not yet encountered the assignments and duties of marriage, and we can't show that we have tackled them. But we are strongly convinced that it will go well, and this belief isn't entirely irrational or blind. There are strong and good foundations." It won't be until they reach Seattle that she'll confront the experiment of running a household while completing her law studies, and she is curious about how it will work out. "My husband won't be very pleased if a meal doesn't appear. But he will just have to help." She is, of course, worried about her parents. Although she and Edgar have been able to infect them with a bit of their own joy, such moments are just glimpses of light in a general situation that weighs heavily on them. Brief postscripts from Ernst and Marie, written after they have taken the young couple to the train station, suggest the sadness of the parting. As yet they had no emigration plan.

Despite the obvious danger to his professional and personal life, Ernst was so closely bound to German academic culture that emigration threatened to undo his being. The hard-won decision finally emerged in January 1936: they would go to the United States even though he had no prospect of a position and mistrusted his facility in English. As he wrote to

Wolfgang Kunkel, "The risk at my age [55], with the loss of an enormous part of my assets, is great, and in this respect the whole undertaking may come to seem reckless. If we take it on anyway, it is not simply because of our children's urgent pleas." He meant, I think, that he had finally yielded to his wife's long-standing desire to leave. They had a final photograph taken at their breakfast table the morning they left Heidelberg, crossed the Swiss border on March 3, 1936, and sailed from Amsterdam to New York, where they stayed with Wolfgang and Ruth. After a month they set out for Seattle, where it was quieter and cheaper, to live with Brigitte and Edgar. To Ernst's dismay, part of his valuable and extensive library had to be left behind in New York with colleagues at Columbia, and when they reached the small house in Seattle, more book boxes had to be stored in the basement. Still, he could rejoice that his own desk stood there "in person, in a little attic room with a view into greenery."[19]

After the war, Brigitte was quick to reestablish connections with the non-Jewish friends and mentors of her youth. Both Marianne Weber and Erika Heyd received early greetings and food packages, and Brigitte would continue to look after them in this way long after others had given up. Marianne Weber's letter of July 23, 1946, makes it clear how much this meant to her. "I am extraordinarily thankful and happy, and feel more secure for some time to come. You can hardly imagine *how* comforting and gladdening such help is—materially but also *seelisch*—for the soul." It was especially comforting not to be blamed by a Jewish émigré for the sins of Nazi Germany. She was impressed that Brigitte, now expecting her third child, has managed to sustain both motherhood and a career. Among the younger women in postwar Germany, she writes, that would be extremely difficult. Many are intellectually deadened, turned into proletarian workers who have to forage for food in the countryside in order to survive. Three years later, Marianne Weber acknowledges another package, telling Brigitte that she's the only one left who still sends them. One can get almost everything now, she writes—though little rice and very little meat—but the prices are fantastic. At seventy-nine, she is tired and ready to die, though the work of her Heidelberg circle goes on. (She would live another five years and die in 1954.) She wonders, a bit wistfully, at thirty-six-year-old Brigitte, still in the thick of life with children growing around her, praising her as a "marvelously able and talented person" and hoping that heaven will bless her.

In the letter she wrote to me after my mother's death, Erika Heyd grieved Brigitte in more emotional and spiritual terms. In 1933, she writes, she visited the Levy parents during the boycott of Jewish businesses on the first of April. "I went to your grandparents in their lovely, cultivated apartment and they were so composed and dignified that I have never forgotten it. I was allowed to accompany Brigitte to the train when she emigrated. We made no promises, but we knew we would never lose each other." After the war was over, Brigitte's was the first greeting, the first food package, the first coffee and chocolate to share after long deprivation. In 1953, during our family's stay in Germany that summer, the former teacher and student were reunited. "We saw each other and there was no separation, no foreignness. She came back to the homeland from which she had been evicted—without bitterness, without hate." Wolfgang Kunkel used the same words to describe Ernst Levy's postwar attitude: "Bitterness and hatred were completely foreign to his nature."[20] Like Marianne Weber, both of these German citizens expressed gratitude that their Jewish friends had not abandoned or rejected them. But Erika Heyd went further. "From [Brigitte] I learned what I should have learned long before from the Old Testament, that justice is not a legal concept but a high virtue that understands others, an understanding that is full of goodness. Your grandmother said sometimes, Brigitte is wise, and I must say that for me she was love itself." Erika Heyd had cherished a special feeling for Brigitte since her school days. But my mother could have that effect on others who knew her, worked with her, and received her generosity.

# 4
# Seattle

When Edgar and Brigitte married in June 1935, Brigitte had completed her second year at Columbia Law School and could look forward to graduating the following spring. Edgar, still working on Wall Street and accumulating American law credits from his evening courses at NYU, knew that his parents and sisters would most likely move from Switzerland to New York within the coming year. Why, then, did the newlyweds suddenly pick up and move to the furthest corner of the West Coast, to a city where they had no connections?

The simplest answer is that Edgar had come to detest New York City. Being crushed into subway cars at rush hour was intolerable; the vertical urban landscape felt like a rat maze. Two years of New York had only increased his homesickness for Germany and his disgust for the brutalities of American commercial life. Being Edgar, he turned his feelings into theory—Marxist theory, this time. On New Year's Day 1935 he returned to his red journal, the keeper of his private intellectual development, for the first time in his American life. He began with this pronouncement: "New York is the ultimate expression of the capitalist spirit. It is mirrored in its construction, its aspect, its atmosphere, all the characteristics of its form (or better, lack of form). The anarchy of the capitalist system is expressed in the stylistic mix-up of buildings, the planlessness of the city." His analysis—and his unhappiness—spread beyond the urban scene and into American law: "The capitalist character of American law is expressed in the law of torts that grants a 'business visitor' a higher ground of protection from negligence than the mere 'social guest.' Someone who wants to bargain with me can expect more respect that someone who visits me out of pure personal affection." In April 1935, preparing for marriage, he summarized his state of feeling, finding America "the most extreme embodiment of everything I dislike—whether it comes to business, politics, law, philosophy or personal relationships." He did not think this reaction would fade.[1]

Moving to Russia was a possibility, but he saw practical difficulties: the language was hard to learn, and the Russians needed technical and business people, "not theoretical Western jurists." Brigitte's leftist cousin Jörn Simon had gone there, he mused, and had had to abandon his degree in economics to become an engineer, though "he had neither interest nor talent for this profession." (Jörn Simon would disappear in Russia two years later, a victim of Stalin's purges.) Edgar yearned, instead, for a homegrown Communist Germany in which he might participate, if only the time for such an ideal might arrive.

Edgar's turn to Soviet love came later than Jörn Simon's, though both of them participated in the widespread European belief that espousing Communism was the best way to oppose Fascism. Fragments of writing between 1934 and 1937 suggest that Edgar was reading in socialist theory and attempting to formulate a personal philosophy of history, through which he could predict the future course of twentieth-century upheavals. His categories were large: Nazism was the last, desperate stand of capitalism, which would be overtaken by Communism. Yet Fascism retained a few good points, which might be absorbed into an ideal socialist order. Among them were the recognition that people were unequal despite the promises of democracy and the belief in "great men" capable of transcending the pressures of their historical moment to lead the world toward a new and better phase. Despite Edgar's new ideological leanings, remnants of his earlier thinking were still apparent. His lifelong tendency to set up two opposing principles, and then to fill up the space between them with qualifications and distinctions, was beginning to emerge.

Not unlike the nineteenth-century British politician Benjamin Disraeli, Edgar sometimes imagined a world organized around a harmonious relationship between "the people" and an aristocratic class of enlightened rulers. And, like the Jewish-born Disraeli, Edgar now reserved a special place for the Jews. As he saw it, the Old Testament Jews had laid the groundwork for the development of civilization and its ethics. Marginalized by Christianity, the Jews would now reanimate their founding principles of social reform by joining the Communist revolution—and, presumably, by shedding the taint of greedy capitalism with which they were all too often associated. For the moment, he ignored the fact that the Nazis were equally content to condemn Jews for being capitalists and for being Communists.

The trouble with Edgar's theory was that it merely inverted the Nazi association of evil Jews with evil Communists. As David Nirenberg has argued, both kinds of thinking use historical Judaism as a special playing card in a game of world-historical theory that, more often than not, worked to the advantage of anti-Semitic sentiment.[2] Edgar was to remain devoted to the idea of the Old Testament as the founding document of civilized life, but he retained his discomfort about being Jewish. In one journal entry, he mused that all the important Jews of modernity—Spinoza, Marx, Disraeli, and Heine—distanced themselves from Judaism in their ascent to some higher plane. He did not bother to specify the particular circumstances that shaped each of those four lives—excommunication in Spinoza's case, Christian baptisms in the others. He was struggling to integrate his own conflicts into an overarching worldview that might hold them steady.

From a post-twentieth-century perspective, Edgar's solitary ruminations may seem ungrateful to the country that rescued him, and as naively idealistic about Communism as he had previously been about German nationalism. But he was participating in a spirit shared by many intellectuals, both European and American, who clung to Communism during the 1930s and 1940s as the central hope for a definitive answer to Fascism. His journals also tended to echo the attitudes of other educated German Jewish émigrés who found Americans ignorant of history, overly pragmatic in their reasoning, crude in their willingness to talk about money, and far too permissive in the way they brought up children.[3] As political scientist Henry Pachter mused in a retrospective memoir, "Americans did not react to the same appeals that could move us. Americans do not easily respond to abstract ideas. They don't admire a man for what he proposes but for the way he carries it out."[4]

Established European intellectuals, notably the Marxist sociologists Max Horkheimer and Theodor Adorno, who organized the Institute of Social Research in Frankfurt and moved it to America during the Third Reich, did not hesitate to apply European methods of analysis to the failings of American mass culture. Unrestrained by the pressure of publication, Edgar's private writings show the influence of Marxist sociology, but they also suggest the pain of his loss, his yearning to go home, and his angry resistance to a new life he had not chosen. His new orientation was also a way to resist his capitalist father, on whom he continued to depend, especially after he quit his Wall Street job and moved west to complete an American law degree. The escape from New York City to Seattle was one way to ensure that the geographical distance from Siegmund and Rosi Bodenheimer would be maintained after they arrived in America.

Moving west was not an unusual thing for young émigrés to do, especially if they had left Germany early and spoke English well. Refugee organizations encouraged newcomers to leave New York City and disperse throughout the country, if only to better their prospects of employment.[5] In a retrospective summary of his career, Edgar explained the move to Seattle as a purely professional calculation: "My wife and I, at the recommendation of Professor Karl Llewellyn, moved to Seattle, where we both took the law course at the University of Washington." Karl Llewellyn was at the time one of Brigitte's professors at Columbia, a spokesman for the school of legal realism in jurisprudence. Born in Seattle, he had spent time in Germany and took an interest in the young émigré couple. Knowing of the small but well-established community of German and German Jewish immigrants in Seattle, Llewellyn argued for a native city whose charms he knew. But when Brigitte recalled the decision during her retirement interview she wasn't so sure that his advice had been the deciding factor. Edgar's hatred of the New York subway, his love of mountains, and photographs of Mount Rainier may have determined the choice. "Anyway, we went, and that mountain my husband promised me didn't appear from behind the clouds for about a month, and I didn't believe him, that it was there."

Characteristically, Brigitte underplayed the sacrifice of her Columbia law degree during her retirement interview, though she did refer to it. "The people at Columbia were *horrified*. They said, 'how can you throw away a Columbia degree and go out there and get a degree from some other law school?' I said, 'I don't care.' And they said, 'well, you're pioneering,' because going out west for people in New York was very unusual." Caught up in a new marriage and a spirit of adventure, perhaps she didn't care. One American degree was as good as another, and at the University of Washington, she claimed, "The instruction was very good; I must say we were prepared very well." Still, the move to Seattle marked the beginning of a pattern in which she would go where Edgar needed to go, at the cost of her own professional and personal commitments. He was the theoretician and she the practical one, but the urgencies of his will were paramount.

Mountains were a real need for Edgar, and Brigitte shared his enthusiasm, if not to its fullest extent. Soon after their arrival in Seattle, as yet carless, they found ways to take buses or catch rides to skiing areas, staying in tiny woodland cabins and walking along roads balancing skis and luggage as best they could. Practical discomforts were not the point. Being in the mountains meant freedom, escape from social requirements, and the grandeur of the nonhuman world, which lifted the heart above the idiocies of human mess making. It meant physical and mental well-being—the exercise, the ascent, the panoramic views, the packed sandwiches, and the happy tiredness of the well-used body. Edgar communicated the need to his children, and we all became true believers and avid practitioners. Boots or skis on the trail meant joy in the heart; there was no denying the power of it.

In September 1935, however, Edgar and Brigitte were busy arranging their new law school courses and setting up their first real household. Brigitte's letters, along with small pocket diaries she kept in 1937 and 1938, provide the details of everyday life in their new city. Writing to her parents in Heidelberg, she exulted in *unserem kleinen süssen Häuschen*, the tiny sweet little house, "so nice and so cheap." It did have some failings: heat had yet to be installed and would bring the rent up to $22.50 a month. They would have to buy a stove and an icebox, and use their neighbors' telephones for a while. But the neighborhood delighted her. Ravenna Place was almost rural, with charming little wooden villas, fruit trees and bushes, and the green stretch of Roosevelt Park just two minutes away. Her excitement was real, but it was also a form of persuasion. The Levys needed to get out of Germany before it was too late, and she was offering the new house as their American destination. Some of her parents' furniture would be welcome—those massive European wardrobes especially, since there were too few closets—and Miezchen's horticultural skill was needed in the overgrown garden. Brigitte listed every item of furniture they bought, making sure her parents knew that the new blue couch could be made into a bed for two once Lenchen and Miezchen arrived. She praised the open friendliness of everyone they met and dealt with; she had never experienced anything like it.

Reading these letters almost eighty years later gave me visceral shocks of recognition. That blue couch was the very one that resided in my father's study in Salt Lake City during my childhood. If I felt bad during a meal, I would be sent to lie down there until I was better. When Edgar conducted his "Sunday school" classes, first with my two brothers and later with me, he would tell us stories from the Old Testament as we sat on those fading blue cushions. The study would smell of the German cologne 4711, which suffuses my memories of the ancient tales Edgar summarized for a child's understanding. My parents' bedroom set in American maple also came from that Seattle shopping trip and lasted through their lives together. As a teenager I lounged on the dresser while I talked to my friends on the phone, idly playing with the little pile of change that lived there. Those unremarkable pieces of furniture were the unquestioned givens of my childhood, and the knowledge that they had actually been chosen and acquired on a particular day in Seattle, 1935, was quite a revelation.

Brigitte and Edgar had about seven months to build a life in Seattle before Brigitte's parents joined them. They endured their American law courses, putting up with what seemed to them a senselessly complicated system of credit hours. In a letter of February 2, 1936, Brigitte wrote to Else von Richthofen Jaffé and her son that the area was beautiful and the campus glorious, but "the intellect comes up a little short. We do our assignments and honestly we are bored." She would be finished by June 1936, but Edgar had a few more credits to fulfill, and then the job search loomed, "which will be less happy. The dislike of foreigners isn't small here, and of course anti-Semitism is added to it." Like her fellow refugees, she complained that Americans lacked individuality and were "the same everywhere," and noted that reactionary Fascism was on the rise in the university system as well as in politics generally. Although she had grown up with a father whose devotion to work was legendary, she was still amazed that Americans "work so much, and one doesn't know for what."

At the same time, the young couple began to make friends with Americans. They became especially close to Lawrence Seltzer and his wife, Claire Wheeler Seltzer, who shared Edgar's interest in socialist theory. Just a few years older than Edgar and Brigitte, Lawrence was working as an attorney; Claire comes through as a woman passionate for every cause in which she could identify with the underdog. Brigitte also struck up a friendship with a German American woman called Helen Wunderlich. Cooking was their main topic: with Helen's help, Brigitte was learning to cook the German recipes she would keep in her repertoire. An older German Jewish physician, Hanna Kosterlitz, became part of the close family circle after she landed in Seattle. These names turn up frequently in the spontaneous comings and goings of the household recorded in Brigitte's daily diaries for 1937 and 1938. She and Edgar were closely entwined in their daily life: they walked to campus together, studied together, and often shared picnic lunches in Roosevelt Park. But they were not isolated in their Seattle community.

Brigitte and Edgar stayed in the small house at 5307 Ravenna Place throughout their five-year sojourn in Seattle, filling it to capacity when Brigitte's parents arrived in the spring of 1936. After the Levys moved into a place of their own and my mother completed the courses she needed for her law degree, the family expanded with the births of Peter in 1937 and Tom in 1939. Life was a bit crowded and quite frugal, but Ravenna Place was always remembered with fondness. For three generations, it was the ground on which an American life began to take root.

When Ernst and Marie arrived in April 1936, bringing two huge wooden crates of furniture, the little house was stretched almost to the breaking point. The most obvious crisis they brought with them was the question of Ernst's professional future in a country that had little use for Roman law. That problem was rapidly addressed. Some summer school courses in ancient history needed staffing, and Ernst—doubtless through Brigitte's intervention—was invited to take them. As Brigitte retold the story, he was reluctant at first: "And he kept saying, look here, my field is Roman law and now you say ancient history. And I said, it will be all right because you know more about ancient history than many many other people! So he consented." Faced with ten hours of instruction a week, he was imme-

Figure 14. Ernst Levy in 1944

diately overwhelmed with the task of preparing new material and translating the script into English. "Every day he wrote his manuscript for his class," Brigitte recalled. "And every evening he came down and he read it to us and we corrected some of his mistakes. In the first weeks, it was mostly read, and then after a while he became more fluent, and became a very good teacher."

Although Ernst had no assurance that he would be kept on, he received an official university appointment early in 1937, as well as the award of a Guggenheim Fellowship for 1937–38. That busy summer of 1936 turned out to be the beginning of a sixteen-year career at the University of Washington, where he would teach history, political science, and law, including seminars in Roman and Comparative law, and become a popular, admired professor.[6] During that period Ernst Levy would also publish his major scholarly work, including the first volume of *West Roman Vulgar Law* (1951). Although it was originally published in English, the work solidified his commanding position among German legal historians who studied the variations (or popular "vulgarizations") of classical Roman law practiced in outlying regions of the late empire.[7]

Marie's crisis, as it happened, was much harder to address. She was devastated by the years of tension in Germany and the difficulty of adjusting to America, especially since her English was weak. Seriously depressed, with her husband suddenly immersed in his new teaching life, she could not tolerate her double exile from Germany and the more familiar European community of New York. During the next three years she spent some

Figure 15. Marie Wolff Levy in 1942

of her time in New York with her son and daughter-in-law, or as a patient in a sanatorium, suffering through each new development in Hitler's war against the Jews. Brief mentions in Brigitte's diaries suggest that her parents' marriage was strained during this period. But Brigitte shrank from describing family stress even in private diaries. At such points, when her mother was upset or Edgar was angry, she would switch to writing in German shorthand.

Marie's distress through the Seattle years was compounded by the fates of old friends and family members who lost their lives to the Nazis or moved beyond her reach. Her older sister Flora was safely in England with her husband, Gustav Mayer, but her younger sister Elwina and her husband, Georg Neustadt, committed suicide in the face of deportation threats. Her brother Fritz Wolff died in Auschwitz in 1943, as did her niece Ruth Neustadt Kaufmann in 1944, along with her husband and two young sons. Ernst's sister Anna Simon left Berlin for Switzerland in 1933, but for some reason her husband, the pianist and composer James Simon, moved only as far as Amsterdam. In 1944 he was deported and killed in Auschwitz. I have mentioned the death of their son Jörn Martin Simon in the Stalinist purges of 1937. Their second son, Ulrich Ernst Simon, who attended the Grunewald Gymnasium shortly after Edgar did, emigrated to England in 1933, converted to Christianity, and was ordained as an Anglican priest in 1939.

It was Brigitte, of course, who bore the main burdens of her parents' situation on the West Coast, while Wolfgang and Ruth tended to Marie during her intervals in New York. After she finished her law school courses in June 1936, Brigitte became the family caretaker. She had two rather demanding men on her hands, both requiring intellectual and practical support. If her father needed a new suit, she would take him to the clothing store and translate. When he or Edgar was invited to give a talk, she would vet the script and assure the speaker of its success afterward. If her mother required winter clothes, or if her father went east to reunite with his wife and his library, she would make sure the right things were packed. When her mother returned to the West Coast, she would listen to her complaints and sympathize. When her parents moved to an apartment of their own, Brigitte directed the move. She could not get paid work: although she had her law degree in 1936, she was, at that time, banned from taking the Washington State Bar exam because she was not a US citizen. For the next four years she was, as she put it in her retirement interview, in one of those "interim periods" when she could do nothing except have children. By the time of her twenty-fourth birthday in September 1936, she was pregnant.

Edgar had a few more courses to complete, but he faced the same delaying prospect when it came to employment as an attorney. An academic appointment would be desirable instead, but on what basis? Had he been in Germany, a book that could serve as a *Habilitation* thesis could pave the way, if it found favor with established professors who could help get him a university appointment. Perhaps that route would work in America, too? He decided to write a book on jurisprudence, hoping it would serve as his ticket into the American legal academy, and apparently unaware that hands-on law practice was the usual prerequisite for an American teaching job. Writing a book meant continuing to rely on his father's financial support, which was unfortunate but necessary if Edgar was to fulfill his potential as a scholar and thinker. In January 1937, ready to begin writing, he secured a desk—a cave, as he called it—in a dark corner of the law school library. Brigitte found some intellectual stimulation as his research assistant, reading and extracting relevant passages from the twelve volumes of Sir William Holdsworth's *History of English Law.*

Edgar was also trying out his public American voice as an expert in European matters. Early in 1937, both he and his father-in-law were invited to give talks to various Seattle groups who wanted to learn about developments in Germany or aspects of European law. Ernst Levy joked to his German colleague Wolfgang Kunkel that he had lectured at an evening black tie affair that had gotten splendid reviews in the local paper—about what the society ladies were wearing. Edgar kept the scripts of his talks, allowing me to admire the clarity in his analysis of current affairs, his command of English, and the accommodation of his private views for a largely uninformed American audience. His talk for a University of Washington sociology class, "The Sociological Basis of German National Socialism," presented an analysis of German class and economic structures that had supported the rise of the Nazis. He explained Hitler's anti-Semitism as a strategy to garner support from both capitalists and socialists by scapegoating only the Jewish practitioners of either ideology. In a lecture to the Herzl Conservative Congregation on "The Rise of anti-Semitism in Germany," Edgar reviewed and critiqued some of the arguments about why German anti-Semitism had taken so firm a hold. He had learned that Jews could not get around prejudice through assimilation, no matter how hard they tried. He did, however, express his own continuing prejudice against German Jewish writers and journalists who "indulged in a super-intellectualist, lifeless, unconstructive kind of writing which was disliked by many Jews as well as by non-Jews." Jewish irony, satire, or extreme subtlety was anathema to Edgar. He had internalized the notion that Jewish irony marked an irreconcilable difference between Jews and Germans.[8] But he was capable of being lighter-hearted on other subjects: some informal remarks on "My Most Striking Impressions of America" named drugstore ice cream sodas as one of America's most delightful surprises.

By 1938, Edgar was also giving talks on topics like "Recent Trends in Legal Philosophy" and "The Concept of Law in the Autocracies and in the Democracies of Today." Drawing from the research for his book, he was beginning his push for academic recognition. In both 1937 and 1938 he visited the deans of several western colleges and universities, looking for a position in law or sociology. His situation was quite anomalous, and nothing came of it. But he was making contacts, both with American academics and with émigré intellectuals who visited Seattle for one reason or another. In the spring of 1937 Karl Korsch, a German revolutionary Marxist associated with the Frankfurt School, was lecturing at the University of Washington. Edgar and Brigitte, along with their friends Claire and Lawrence Seltzer, were caught up in the controversies he brought. Korsch rejected Leninism and Stalinism, arguing for a self-generated proletarian revolutionary socialism that could come about only through widespread progressive education. Still hoping that Soviet Communism would succeed, Edgar argued with him, while Claire championed Trotsky. For a time the four friends constituted themselves an informal seminar to read and discuss the writing of Trotsky and Marx. A discussion that didn't go well could leave Edgar angry for some time; Brigitte would have to calm him down.

In July 1938 the director of the Institute for Social Research, Max Horkheimer, also visited Seattle, apparently interested in moving the Institute from its temporary home in New York to some spot on the West Coast (eventually they moved to Los Angeles before returning to Frankfurt after the war). Edgar served as Horkheimer's guide and driver. "I liked him quite a lot," Edgar wrote to Ernst, who had met Horkheimer in Germany. "I asked whether he might be able to use me at the Institute. He said I should publish something in a journal, and we would go from there." This unlikely prospect never came to anything, but the story illustrates Edgar's hope of finding a position by making a good impression on well-established scholars.

On March 31, 1939, he and Brigitte had the opportunity to drive the great German novelist Thomas Mann and his Jewish wife, Katia, around Seattle. Passing through on a lecture tour, Mann was an international hero of public resistance to the Nazi regime during that time, and Edgar made the most of their two hours. "He is straightforward and informal," he wrote of Mann. "Conversation was lively and developed naturally." Edgar grilled the novelist about all of his own concerns—freedom and equality, Fascism, Marxism and democracy—faithfully noting how Mann's opinions differed from his own. At the end of his life, reading Mann's published diaries, Edgar would find "the little Bodenheimers" mentioned in a footnote to that day in Seattle.

Although he may have cherished the fantasy of becoming a Marxist sociologist, Edgar's political views were actually in flux. To begin with, his father had forbidden him to speak of his Communist sympathies to anyone. The Bodenheimer parents visited the young couple in Seattle for the Christmas holidays in December 1936. Edgar wrote extensively in the red journal about his attempt to explain their political beliefs, and his father's response. "He required from us, that we keep our beliefs entirely to ourselves, and not tell a single soul about them; that I had entirely to bury my Marxist principles in my scholarly work; that I allow no danger to interfere with my American career. The alternative was, break with the family." Still holding the purse strings, Siegmund resorted to his well-worn threat, knowing that it would work. He also opined, Edgar wrote, "that my nerves were not strong enough to take on the dangers of my political beliefs in practice. He also seemed to assume that all this was probably temporary, since in Germany I was so nationalistic." Edgar was deeply offended by "the level of acknowledged opportunism that lay in every word [Siegmund] said" and by the notion the his father could not place "high ideals over respect for the family." As usual, however, a level of harmony was reestablished the next day. Siegmund was right about the purely theoretical nature of his son's Marxism, and about its potential dangers to his career in America. I wonder whether Edgar recalled, during the McCarthy period of Communist-baiting in the 1950s, that his father's insistence had done him a favor.

In the red journal, Edgar began recording his doubts about the Soviet experiment. In January 1937: "The decisive thing will be whether Communism brings forth creative people. If just a contented herd emerges, and everyone is the same, perhaps all the energy is wasted." The next month brought news of Stalin's show trials. By New Year's Day 1938 Edgar had come around: "The year 1937 brought about a shift from radicalism to skepticism about developments in Russia. If the ideas and viewpoints that remain from the revolution—namely a planned economy and a clear social system—have to be bought through endless blood and the loss of freedom of thought and human worth . . . one has to wonder whether all other countries would have to travel the same path." He was not giving up on the perfect society, though; perhaps "one socialized just enough but not too much" could be brought about by the leadership of a great man.

Later that month the red journal turned to other topics, as Edgar wondered about the impact of Einstein's relativity theory on the possibility of absolute knowledge in philosophy. As his thinking developed, he would attempt to find a correlative in physics for suprahistorical laws that could serve as the foundation for a theory of natural law. He was bothered by quantum mechanics, which introduced chance and instability into the calculations of physics, and was later relieved to learn that Einstein, a fellow émigré, remained skeptical about developments in theoretical physics that his own work had generated.[9] None of Edgar's American reviewers would be convinced by his forays into science, but the desire to rope in an amateur acquaintance with physics and other fields attests to the scope of Edgar's quest.

Like the older Einstein, Edgar wanted to be able to imagine a universe that rested on some yet undiscovered theory of stability and order. At some point Edgar also read Einstein's 1934 essay, "The World as I See It," and copied a number of quotations into a notebook he kept for excerpts. The first passage he transcribed suggests that Einstein was also helping him to think about Judaism. The quoted passage begins like this: "The pursuit of knowledge for its own sake, an almost fanatical love of justice, and the desire for personal independence—these are the features of the Jewish tradition which make me thank my stars that I belong to it." As the 1930s took their tragic course, Edgar would have found some sympathetic reassurance in these words.

On April 24, 1938, Edgar wrote a paragraph that formulated his mission as a writer and teacher:

> It is *not* the mission of legal philosophy to express, purely in relative terms, the various possibilities of opinion about the law. That leads

> to error and places students in the arms of demagogues who promise absolutes in the form of radical totalitarian philosophy. *The true legal philosophy must emerge from the conditions of our present being*, must engage students in the stormy stresses and fights of our time, and must explain to them their background causes and goals. It must make it possible for them to see both sides in the struggle between individualism and collectivity, to recognize the tendencies of development, and to meet one's choice on the ground of fact. The teacher cannot entirely hold back from his own opinion. But he should present differing views in a fair and objective manner.

When I came across this statement, written shortly after Edgar's thirtieth birthday, it seemed to express the essence of my father's thinking. Taking a stand against totalitarianism was essential, and the relativism of positivist legal thinking would not suffice in the face of Fascist threats. The legal realist current in European and American thinking emphasized that justice was dependent on its immediate political context, and that the decisions of judges could be read as expressions of their personal psychological situations. That was dangerously cynical, in Edgar's view. The statement also suggests his continuing faith in the possibilities of rational objectivity and his old hatred of the *einseitig*, or one-sided, together with his fierce partisanship on behalf of those Enlightenment principles he had absorbed as a student in Weimar Germany. His embrace of natural law precepts, that certain basic ethical rights and duties were inherent in human nature and that law could not be separated from justice, was an unfashionable position in prewar America. Because of this cluster of beliefs, Edgar would always be an honorable outlier in the landscape of American legal philosophy.

If Edgar's library cave was devoted to abstract thought, the couple's affectionate family life was deepening. The letters they wrote when they were separated are full of affectionate endearments and pet names. He was "Pauzer" "Pürzli" or "Schnautzer" and "Schnautzertier" or, all in one, "Schnautzerpauzertier." She was "Spitz," "Süssmäusel," or "Tierli." Edgar reported to his parents-in-law that when Brigitte was wheeled out of the delivery room after Peter was born, she yelled out "Schnautzer!" the moment Edgar came into view. To adult family members, the couple would always be "Ett (later Ed) and Bitz," though Brigitte had long been "Britze" to her parents. For the rest, they had to put up with a lot of mispronunciation from American friends and colleagues. "Edgerr" replaced the German "Edgah" easily enough, but "Brigitte," a three-syllable, hard-consonant word in German, was another matter. Throughout her American life she had to put up with "Bridget," "Brijeet," "Brigedde," "Brix," and other variants, even from people who had known her for some time.

Before the war started it was not entirely clear whether the children would grow up American or German. The new parents chose names that would work in either language, Peter and Thomas, though the boys were also saddled with embarrassingly Germanic middle names, Herman and Siegmund. With each other, Edgar and Brigitte referred to the babies, even before birth, as diminutive versions of themselves. During her first pregnancy Brigitte believed she was carrying a girl they called "Klein-Bitz" ("little Bitz"). It was easier for her to imagine having a girl until Peter actually arrived on June 29, 1937, impressing everyone with his bright eyes and his obvious intelligence. Peter immediately became "Klein-Pauz," and Tom would later feature in parental correspondence as "Klein-Pauz II." Edgar was happy to have a son, and Siegmund was delighted to welcome a new generation of the family dynasty when he came west to inspect the new baby, finding Peter to be "a real little Bodenheimer!" The year 1937 brought first-born American sons to both families: Bebs and Teddy Blau had Fred in early May; Wolfgang and Ruth Levy had Reuben in late July. Peter was well supplied with first cousins, though they lived a continent away.

Brigitte's first months as a nervous and inexperienced new mother were stressful. Her own mother was in New York, so she and Edgar learned to hold, diaper, and bathe the baby from a nurse, Mrs. Pope, who found their first attempts comical. Nursing was difficult, Brigitte got a high fever, crises occurred regularly, and Peter didn't gain weight for the first month. Finally they were advised to supplement with formula, and things began to improve. By the time Helen Wunderlich gave birth to her son in August, Brigitte had calmed down and was ready to help Helen through her first weeks of motherhood. In September, Edgar and Brigitte got a two-week vacation break, leaving Peter in the care of Mrs. Pope and Marie, who was back in Seattle. That month Peter was ready for his first solid food—and toilet training was already on his mother's mind, as the medical wisdom of the 1930s prescribed. Brigitte was impressed by her son's smiling good nature and by his attentive observation of his surroundings, though she quickly learned that he would react strongly against a sudden exposure to something new.

I learned all this, and more, from a special journal in which Brigitte recorded the first five years of Peter's development. Her mother had kept such a journal; probably it was Marie who gave her daughter the notebook covered in dark green leather, with its stamped gold border. Brigitte didn't actually begin writing until Peter was three months old, but she left enough space at the front so that she could fill in the story of her pregnancy, the birth, and the first difficult months. She didn't get around to writing in those empty pages until June 3, 1939, just ten days before Tom's birth. Perhaps she was preparing herself for the second birth by recalling what had happened with the first, but she also knew she would be too busy for more than occasional jottings once she had two children to tend. The rest of the journal describes the details of each new change in Peter's life: childcare was Brigitte's work for the time being, and she took it very seriously. Although she did not write about her children as emotionally as Marie had done, her love comes through in her close attention to what made Peter happy or angry, in her admiration for each new step he took, and in her accommodation of his character traits.

However she may have felt during frustrating moments, her written observations are quite objective. When President Roosevelt instituted Daylight Saving Time for the summer of 1940, she could see that Peter was fascinated, but she didn't want to explain it to him "because he wants everything—time—to be absolute." After the boys began to talk, Brigitte would note down charming and interesting things they said, accurately reproducing their baby pronunciations. I was amazed and delighted to read that my brother the astrophysicist was interested in "the moon, the worlds beyond the sky," when he was two and a half. At five, he was asking his mother, "When can I see the Northern Lights? When can I go to Norway? Is Norway in this world? Are there other worlds? In the sky? And underneath the world? What is underneath us?" Meanwhile, Brigitte was noting that Tommy—my physician brother—was putting bandages on his stuffed animals. Although the children spoke only English, Brigitte's journal did not switch from German to English until the United States joined the war in 1942.

Brigitte's attention to motherhood was strong, but it had its limits. She hired a young woman to help out for part of the day, and took refuge in research for Edgar's book during many of her afternoons. In 1939 she and Edgar became US citizens and began studying together for the Washington State Bar exam, which they took over three days in September 1940. Shortly afterward Edgar departed for a job search on the East Coast, while Brigitte looked around Seattle for employment. As she recalled in her retirement interview, "I found I had no chance whatsoever. All the offices said 'Can you type?' And fortunately I could *not* type—I still cannot type except with two fingers. So, there was just no chance. They were not going to hire a woman."

By October 1940 she was feeling a bit desperate. She wrote to Edgar, "We are eventually going to have to get some positive occupation for the Spitz [i.e., herself], otherwise it will be unhappy. It is probably entirely right, that most women are best suited to be housewives, but it doesn't *have* to be that way, if one is not really fulfilled with that occupation. At some point one wants to do what one does best, women too." She was afraid she was being "egocentric" in these thoughts and told Edgar that she intended to push them away until his situation was settled. Edgar tried to reassure her from New York, where he had spoken to Professor Llewellyn at Columbia about the question of children and professional life. "He would like it if you were professionally active. Don't break your head over it, it will work out. If war comes (likely) there will be more jobs for women."

By 1940 the European war was already well underway, and by June most of Western Europe had suffered invasion and fallen under Hitler's sway. Everyone's hopes had been darkening since March 1938, when Hitler's imperial ambitions manifested themselves in the *Anschluss*, the absorption of Austria into the German Reich. On the night of November 9–10 that year, Hitler ordered a nationwide pogrom against German Jews: synagogues and Jewish businesses were attacked and burned, while many Jews were shot, or arrested and sent to concentration camps. *Kristallnacht*, or the Night of Broken Glass, was a clear turning point for the worse in German policy toward the Jews, and a wake-up call for those who had made no previous moves toward emigration.

Neither the Anschluss nor Kristallnacht is mentioned in my parents' surviving letters or diaries, perhaps because they were too disturbing to write about. What could be mentioned, and despaired of, was the September 1938 Munich agreement, when English and French ministers succumbed to Hitler, allowing him to annex the Czech Sudetenland. Edgar was horrified by the policy of appeasement. "The yielding of the English and French in the matter of Czechoslovakia will have unbelievable repercussions in the politics of Europe. The English conservative party has decisively weakened the world order," he wrote on October 1. A few days later, he attempted to understand the move by wondering if Neville Chamberlain's strategy had been "a repeat of the Napoleonic adventure: that Hitler will move on Moscow and weaken himself so that England can then be ready, without the danger of a concentrated attack that would risk the English island." Since his youth he had been familiar with this kind of historical thinking about European strategic politics.

His father's response to the deepening horror in Germany was far less detached. As head of the extended family, Siegmund Bodenheimer was now besieged with requests for emigration help, from members of the family who were still stuck in Germany. At the end of December 1938 he wrote a stern letter chastising Edgar for sending money to his cousin Vera Lachmann without consulting him. "The questions must be handled through a consistent principle, and, given the overlarge claims from the family, we must lay down a line that is applied to all family members that come into consideration. The fact that the plea is immediate and urgent is not relevant. Everyone who has remained in Germany has their own reasons for urgency." His annoyance with Edgar spilled over into an attack on his son's course of action and his seclusion in "an isolated corner" of the country. "I am, to be honest, more and more doubtful about whether the program you have set for your future is the right one, and that you shouldn't think of other possibilities, for instance a job as director of something similar in industry, or a job in civil service, which always hires lawyers, once you have become an American citizen." The banker in Siegmund was extending his usual control, but he had reasons to feel anxious. All three of his children were still in unstable financial situations, and he feared that "the family standard" was about to sink "as a result of the horrible events in Germany." The younger people capable of work had to fight against this result, he entreated Edgar. "You will understand with what cares I, on the verge of old age, watch the development of the family."

As a possible fallback position, Edgar picked up a second degree in law librarianship from the University of Washington. By December 1939 his book had been accepted by McGraw Hill. In New York that month with Brigitte and Peter, he worked out the final details with his publisher and reported that *Jurisprudence* was already slated for use in at least one law school course. In May 1940 the book was published and sent to many of the important legal philosophers in the country. In short order, it was adopted for courses in at least four political science departments, allaying some of Siegmund's worst fears. That September Edgar departed alone for a longer stay on the East Coast, hoping to take some of those scholars by storm, at least to garner letters of recommendation, if not to land a position at some worthy law school. On April 14, 1940, he had written in the red journal, "If there's anywhere now in the world for humanist thought, it's in America." The war, and the acceptance of his book, had brought Edgar closer to accepting his new country.

*Jurisprudence* lived up to its all-embracing title: it was a sweeping overview of the history of legal philosophy from the classical period to the present, with a major emphasis on natural law doctrines. It was also a political cry from the heart, a plea for the rational capacity of the human race and its embodiment in a just system of law that might regulate and restrain the will to power. Twenty-two years later, it would be entirely rewritten and republished by Harvard University Press as *Jurisprudence: The Philosophy and Method of the Law*. This work, first prepared in a dark corner by an idealistic young émigré in his twenties, was destined to become the most successful and widely used publication of Edgar's career. Because it makes its survey of legal philosophy readily accessible to students of law and politics, it is still bringing in royalties seventy-five years after its initial publication.

The 1940 letters between Edgar and Brigitte during his East Coast job search offer a rich view of their lives and characters during those critical weeks of transition. Edgar's first stop was Harvard, where he spent some of the most exciting days of his life meeting and socializing with "the Harvard Prominents." The long, detailed letters he wrote to Brigitte almost daily were placed a separate section of his correspondence file, as if the memory of those days had never lost its glow. They are wonderful letters, witty and eloquent about each encounter with personages who had previously been only names to reckon with. On his first day he was sent to see the dean of Harvard Law School, James Landis. "He looks terribly worn out (that's how it is with the American *Wunderkinder*)," Edgar wrote. "By nature he is very energetic and exceptionally conceited. I was also energetic and conceited (I didn't know I could do it so well) and so we got along famously." Landis's advice echoed that of others: don't pursue further academic degrees, but get a position as a practicing lawyer before you think about applying to teach in law schools. Nonetheless Edgar was euphoric about the success of the meeting, and his excitement grew as he met the great legal philosopher Roscoe Pound, now seventy, who welcomed him warmly "out of pure human friendliness. Something so sweet and cute I have seldom seen. A mixture of an Opa and a *Seeschnauzer*. Peter would love him with his walrus moustache and his *Poposcheitel*" (a German expression comparing hair parted in the center with the buttocks crack). "That's Roscoe Pound," he wrote in English. "Isn't he exactly like what we thought he would be?" And, returning to German, "I have seldom been so surprised. A lovely old man, and very unimpressive." Wanting Brigitte to share in every impression, he recorded most of that brief conversation, and many others, for her benefit. The relief of finding that he could hold his own with people, that the big names were human beings, and that some of them already knew his name and his book comes through strongly in the exuberant little character portraits he sketched.

Roscoe Pound invited Edgar to a party at his house in Watertown, where he met the Czech legal philosopher Hans Kelsen, known for a "pure theory of law" that insisted on a complete separation of law from ethics or justice. On the other end of the legal theory spectrum, there was the American natural law theorist Lon L. Fuller. Despite the wide differences in their points of view, both men would command Edgar's respect in the years to come. He also visited the sociologist Talcott Parsons and the Russian American founder of the Harvard Sociology Department, Pitirim Sorokin, still imagining that he might find a job in a sociology department. No one offered him anything except vague advice, but Edgar was so absorbed in the process of making connections that this fact seemed secondary. By September 30, he was in New York with his family, celebrating his sister Helga's twentieth birthday. He planned to go on to Washington, DC, to follow up on job possibilities in both government and teaching.

Reading those long, entertaining and inconclusive letters back in Seattle, Brigitte became alarmed. Was the job search turning into an ego trip with no practical outcome? After consulting with her father, she began sending advice: get letters of recommendation from the people you have met; write people ahead of time to prepare them for your coming; visit universities where there's someone interested in courses on jurisprudence. "Pauzli," she wrote, "I think you now have to crack a harder nut in Washington. . . . I don't think it will be all right if you come back home with empty hands. I think it would be too hard here even with a little attorney job, and you wouldn't be able to stand it. . . . You must try everything, otherwise it will be terrible here, once the first impressions of the trip are past." Tired and harassed by her home duties, she was getting seriously anxious. "Excuse me, Pauzli," she half apologized. "You are sometimes a little dumb."

Edgar quickly reassured her that he would do everything possible in Washington. "Don't worry," he wrote. "Be patient. I will do my duty; it will all come out." He was still being charmed by recognition. Meeting someone at the New School of Social Research in New York, he was greeted with "What, you are Bodenheimer on Jurisprudence?" In Washington, the pattern of enthusiastic meetings continued at first. With a letter of introduction from Karl Llewellyn, he walked in awe through the empty marble halls of the United States Supreme Court and met briefly with Justice Felix Frankfurter. Later he met Justice Douglas and attended a Supreme Court session, describing the impression made by each Justice. He fell in love with the poet Archibald MacLeish at the Library of Congress, where he went for advice about law librarianships. He was quite overwhelmed by a talk with the Jesuit dean of Georgetown University Law School, Francis Lucey S.J., who had already read his book and praised it to the skies. Only God was missing from Edgar's brilliant interpretive analysis, Lucey told him. It was not the last time Edgar's natural law theories would find special sympathies among Catholic thinkers, and he was deeply moved by the way Father Lucey spoke "so directly from the depth of his world view." In him Edgar saw "the greatness of the Catholic Church and its spiritual tradition shine forth in the time of its decline."

The next day Edgar's mood changed as the search for government positions got serious. He was hearing a lot of pessimistic opinions about all the hotshot candidates from Columbia angling for jobs. And there were other contingencies. The Roosevelt-Willkie campaign was entering its final stages. Election Day was just a few weeks away, and Roosevelt was favored for reelection to an unprecedented third term, but no one could be certain. If Willkie were elected, government hiring would be shut down until the following year, and someone like Edgar would not be considered by any federal agency. Another pesky detail was that Edgar was not yet a member of the Washington State Bar, a requirement for federal employment.

The Bar exam results were finally announced on October 19. Both Edgar and Brigitte passed, and Brigitte forwarded Edgar's admission letter to him in Washington, noting in English, "So now we are lawyers, or almost. . . . But the poor twins! Only Evelyn passed!" She could sympathize well enough with what that would be like. To become "complete" lawyers, they had to be personally sworn in, which would require Edgar to be in Seattle. He wasn't sure how that could happen while he remained on the spot in Washington for daily developments. While he waited anxiously for something to happen, he formalized his recent citizenship by signing up for military service, in compliance with Roosevelt's new peacetime draft law requiring all men between the ages of twenty-one and thirty-five to register.

A job in the Labor Department was gradually coming into view, but everything about it was uncertain, and Edgar was advised that it could disappear in a matter of moments. As the tension mounted, he turned sour about the atmosphere among federal employees and yearned for a position in the west, where people were less driven and cynical. "It is all unhealthy" in the east, he wrote to Brigitte; everyone in Washington would move west if they could. He would rather be a law librarian in Utah than a professor at Georgetown, and he didn't want to bring up the boys in a city without mountains. Living quietly in the family circle was all he really wanted; he missed his wife and children. The days seemed to drag on as he waited for various bits of red tape to wend their way across official desks. Finally, at the end of an especially hopeless-feeling day, he was offered the Labor Department job on October 30. The presidential election results were deemed irrelevant; he was to report for work on November 21. Before that, he had to return to Seattle, take the oath for the Bar, and travel back to Washington, DC, with his family. The job search, which had taken less than six weeks, felt like an epic journey. Stopping at his parents' apartment in New York before his cross-country train trip, Edgar promptly came down with the flu. His mother put him to bed and nursed him with her orange-juice cure.

Brigitte had let Edgar know she would be perfectly willing to move; now she had two weeks to get ready. "Can we leave Seattle on the 16th?" Edgar asked on November 1. He was planning the details of their train journey and thinking about places to live, but before he mailed the letter he remembered to add a postscript: "You could certainly get a legal job here." During his absence Brigitte's dual role as mother and lawyer had received a moment of fame in the Seattle press. Brigitte sent a clipping to Edgar: "What do you say to *pictures in the paper*?" She had been busy with newspaper reporters and photographers most of the previous afternoon, and everyone she knew had called to congratulate her that morning. The *Seattle Times* headline read "German Refugee Couple Passes State Bar Exam." There were two photographs: one showed a strained-looking Brigitte holding her two sons on her lap in front of a bookcase, the other a head shot of Edgar alone. After reviewing their backgrounds, the article concluded, "Bodenheimer at present is visiting his parents in New York City and conferring with educators in an effort to get a teaching position in the East. Mrs. Bodenheimer hasn't decided to what use she is going to put her law education." At this point, the uses of her prolonged legal education were rather limited: cheerleading for Edgar, packing boxes, and organizing her one- and three-year-old children for a big move.

The success of this "German refugee couple" may have caught the attention of Seattle news reporters because the city received an influx of far more unfortunate refugees during that fall of 1940. The last remaining window of escape from Nazi Germany and Poland was a route on the trans-Siberian Railroad across Russia to Vladivostock and then through Japan to the United States. Brigitte joined a group that organized transportation and shelter for newly arrived Jewish refugees who had been allowed to disembark at Seattle. She may have been boarding one of them at Ravenna Place when she wrote, "The new one is still terribly depressed and I don't know whether I can succeed in bringing her up. If normal, she would likely be very good, but the people who come here are all shattered. And the journey through Russia and Japan must have been unthinkably awful. Dirt and harassment, and *gaucherie* from the emigrant committees (themselves emigrants!). But the people themselves are especially unearthly." In addition to this worthy but depressing work, she was tending an ailing Hanna Kosterlitz as well as her parents and children. She did not have enough childcare help. She was perpetually exhausted, and apologized to Edgar for the "inferiority" of her letters when his were of such high quality.

If Brigitte worried that the move to Washington, DC, would leave her parents alone in Seattle, she would have been relieved when her brother moved to Seattle around the time of her own family's departure. Wolfgang Levy had completed a residency in radiology in New York, while his wife, Ruth, earned a Ph.D. in psychology. With their son, Reuben, they drove across the country headed for the Levy family center in Seattle, stopping for job interviews at the state hospital in Blackfoot, Idaho. Although they were both offered positions there, they decided to move on, joining his parents on the coast. They would remain in Seattle until 1956, raising Reuben and his younger siblings, Edna and Ralph, who made close connections with their Levy grandparents.

Eventually, Marie put down roots in Seattle by designing a modern house that blended a flat-roofed one-story Western exterior with an exquisitely arranged European interior. It was distinctive enough to be featured in the Pacific Northwest Living section of the *Seattle Times*, with a full array of photographs.[10] They show the unobtrusive rectangle of stained brown wood embraced by native trees and shrubs, the informal stair-free entrances, and the large living room, its long walls paved in floor-to-ceiling bookcases, with plenty of room for each rescued European furnishing to live in its own space. With Ernst's precious library happily arranged on its shelves, and her beloved plantings indoors and out, Marie had fashioned her American compromise.

# 5
# Back East, Out West

The year 1940 was one of historical turning points, though they barely filtered into Edgar's letters and journals. Intent on establishing his professional future, he registered the presidential election and the first peacetime draft law primarily as they bore on his job search. Hitler's rapid advances in Western Europe were followed and deplored in the family but unrecorded in most of the writing that survives. Siegmund Bodenheimer's annual German verses for Rosi's birthdays were the exception. His rhyming quatrains were unstoppable, but during the war years they carried his dark moods about European politics. In three months during the spring of 1940 Hitler invaded and occupied Denmark, Norway, Holland, Belgium, Luxembourg, and France. In the late summer he turned to the Battle of Britain, his intensive bombing campaign of British cities. The powerful isolationist and anti-Semitic sentiments within the American public, rallied by aviator hero Charles Lindbergh's speeches for the America First movement, gradually began to shift in response to Hitler's relentless London Blitz. The country had been nudged toward action against Hitler by President Roosevelt's careful, step-by-step moves toward supporting the Allies with warships and building up the US arms industry. Seattle's Boeing plant, as Edgar and Brigitte would have known, was visibly thriving.

Roosevelt's acceptance of the Democratic nomination for a third term was all about the question of who would determine America's role in the war. Both he and his Republican rival Wendell Willkie knew that the United States had to support Britain, the last standing democracy in Europe, but given the strength of isolationist sentiment in Congress and the country at large, they couched their knowledge in terms of strengthening America's defensive capability. Even before he won the presidency for the third time, Roosevelt signed the Selective Training and Service Act on September 19 and presided over the national draft lottery held at the end of October.[1]

Edgar reported for his new job in the Labor Department Solicitor's Office shortly after Roosevelt's reelection. It was, to say the least, an interesting time to be in the national capital. His first assignment was to draft a pamphlet explaining the terms of Roosevelt's labor reforms. Officially known as the Fair Labor Standards Act of 1938, this legislation was a keystone of the New Deal. It set a minimum wage, established a forty-hour workweek with provisions for overtime, and regulated child labor. Three months into his pamphlet, however, Edgar described the increasing impossibility of the task in one of his monthly letters to the Levys in Seattle. "The Wage and Hour Division becomes more and more exemption-minded in the interest of national defense; the employers travel here, race around with their briefcases in hand and plead with the Administrator to change this or that rule, which often happens. Everything is in flux, and the manual will be out of date the moment it appears." But if the war economy would complicate the actual effects of the Fair Labor Standards Act for some time, Edgar stood firmly behind the legislation in principle; he was impressed by Justice Harlan Stone's 1941 opinion on the constitutionality of the act. By the fall of 1941 the troublesome pamphlet had been left behind, and Edgar reported working on interesting legal issues ranging from child labor in Puerto Rico to piloting planes over Africa en route to the Middle East. He was anticipating war: "The slogan of the day is 'bombs,' not 'due process of law.' If, at least, the bombs lead to a reconstitution of due process, I have no objection."

As Edgar had predicted, Brigitte did not get a job until the spring of 1942, after Pearl Harbor pushed America directly into war and government personnel left Washington, DC, to serve in the military and other war work. For the first year and a half in Washington she settled her sons into a two-story red brick house at 3008 McKinley Street NW, in a leafy neighborhood just a few blocks west of Rock Creek Park. She discovered a recently founded progressive school in Bethesda, the Green Acres School, where Peter could start nursery school; Tom would join him the following year. And then, finding additional childcare where and when she could, Brigitte started the frustrating process of looking for work. "But I really had nothing to offer—no experience, I had just taken the bar exam," she said in her retirement interview. "And I remember some of the interviews; I really had nothing to say. I hadn't done anything anywhere, except doing the research for my husband and going to law school twice. . . . So it took until 1942, and I still remember the interview with the man who was the general counsel for the Federal Housing Authority. I said hardly anything. He asked me questions, and I said mostly yes and no. Then he asked me at the end, do you have anything further to say, and I had *nothing* further to say. I was hired, and I could never understand why!"

Brigitte's modesty about her talents was both characteristic and real: she found her authority only when she felt she knew a great deal about a particular topic. Quite late in her life, when she was widely known for her expertise in family law, she told me that she had always had trouble seeing herself as a *Respektsperson*—a person who commands respect. Her use of the German term may offer a clue; in the male hierarchy of the German professoriate, she could not have imagined becoming a person of standing. Perhaps as a result, she was a quick study. In the early months of her research for the briefs and opinions section of the Housing Authority, she used her spare time to master the previous work of the section. She was quickly set to work on slum clearance legislation, wartime housing standards for each state, and speech writing for members of Congress.

Brigitte's lifelong interest in writing and promoting legislation was nurtured at the Federal Housing Authority, and her memories of that period glow with excitement: "That was during the New Deal, and people were really *really* interested in what they were doing." After two years she became legislative assistant to the Housing Authority General Counsel Robert Frank, whom she admired immensely. "For the first time I had my own office, close to the General Counsel's office, and he sometimes came in to try to figure things out. He always came up with new ideas; he was a very excellent person. I really learned a lot, got a great education from him. So that was—exciting." The rhythm of work in the department was erratic; sudden bursts of activity to meet deadlines were followed by days when nothing happened. Some nights Brigitte would have to work long hours, or bring work home and stay up late into the night frantically finishing a document. Edgar, whose work habits were methodical to a fault, always disliked those last-minute rushes. Throughout her working life Brigitte had to put up with his impatience at the very moments she was most under pressure from deadlines.

Compared with the difficulty of combining work and motherhood, that probably seemed a minor emotional inconvenience. When Brigitte began working in May 1942, she was still scrambling for acceptable childcare. In June Peter and Tom were sent with a maid (as home workers were then called) to spend a month at a Lake Placid summer retreat with their Bodenheimer grandparents and their Blau cousins Fred and baby Ron. Edgar and Brigitte joined them there for their vacation time in July. Then they turned to the Levy grandparents for help. Marie was persuaded to move to Washington, DC, for nearly a year to live with the young family, with Ernst joining her when he had teaching leave in the spring of 1943. Later, there would be two long-term African American maids, Sadie and Sunshine. But Brigitte was rarely at rest with these arrangements. The children were constantly sick, or kept at home because other children's illnesses created school quarantines. Tom got spectacularly ill with high fevers whenever he got one of his frequent colds. Brigitte would stay up with him through the night, keeping a steam vaporizer going. Her pocket diaries from 1944 and 1945 are littered with entries about Tom's illnesses, her lack of sleep, and days when she, or even Edgar, would have to stay home from work. "When you're young you can handle that, you get up and go to your work even if you haven't slept all night," Brigitte told her interviewer thirty-five years later. It was wartime, and many women were working; she did not claim to be unusual. She thought that her children had "managed pretty well. They became quite dependent on each other." However they managed, the boys got used to spending considerable lengths of time away from home when they were quite young, staying with grandparents, or at cousin Vera Lachmann's summer boys' camp in North Carolina once it opened in 1944.

If wartime America had opened a door for Brigitte's legal talents, it also pushed Edgar's career forward, and occasioned an important shift in family letter writing. Once Roosevelt had declared war on Germany, German Jews who had fled Hitler and were not yet US citizens were subjected to the deep irony of being labeled "enemy aliens" who had to register with the government. Edgar, Brigitte, and her parents were naturalized citizens by that time, though the Bodenheimer parents still had a year to wait. They all began to write to each other in English, to avoid the slightest hint of identification with their mother tongue. Edgar's transition to English was seamless; his writing retained its expertise and its shades of humor. Brigitte also sounded just as she had done in German. Ernst Levy's written English was fluent, with the occasional Germanic glitch, but Siegmund Bodenheimer's was carefully formal, copied out in an old-fashioned spidery business hand that had made a belated transition from German Gothic to Roman script. Once the war was over, the correspondence might be written in either language, with the two grandmothers, Rosi and Marie, generally adding bits in German. But the war, while it lasted, did its part to shake loose long-standing family habits.

The long monthly letters Edgar addressed to Ernst and Marie suggest that they were in many ways closer to him than his own parents. Ernst had become the father Edgar wanted—one who shared his intellectual concerns and his dilemmas about working out a legal career in a new country. They exchanged advice about publishing in American law journals and asked professional favors of each other. Edgar could be more forthright in letters to Ernst than he had ever been with his judgmental father, and he occasionally tested out an idea with Ernst that he had no intention of sharing with Siegmund. For her part Marie, imagining she might find a vocation as a seamstress, made her son-in-law a business suit that was duly admired by his Labor Department colleagues.

Edgar was now geographically close to New York City, so he often visited with his own family during periods when his work took him north. He spent time with sister Helga and her new husband, the Hungarian pianist and accompanist Arpád Sándor, taking them rowing in Central Park and sharing restaurants and theater. In November 1943 he wrote to Brigitte during a long New York work assignment to congratulate her on a raise: "I am very proud of you!" He was going out that night with his parents to see *Life with Father*. "My own life with father is not 100% satisfactory, because his many complexes get worse. Mutti [Rosi] suffers quite a bit under it. Nothing anybody can do about it; it is really a mental case. He himself suffers probably most." It would be interesting to know what Edgar thought his father's "complexes" were. The idea may well have come from his psychologically oriented sister Bebs, now established with her family in East Orange, New Jersey.

Much of my information about the course of Edgar's government work comes from letters to his parents-in-law. In April 1942 he was promoted to attorney and assigned responsibility for managing difficult cases and supervising "the boys" in the office. Working on tricky child-labor issues put him in touch with the "kind-hearted old ladies on the seventh floor. . . . Sometimes their tender-heartedness goes a little too far for my taste, but on the whole they are quite sensible." But his frustrations were building: it was difficult to get anything done in the improvised chaos of a large bureaucracy during wartime. In November 1942 he was offered a job as Senior Attorney at the Office of the Alien Property Custodian, a post that made use of his foreign law and languages. The office, recently established by Roosevelt's Executive Order as an independent wartime agency, was supposed to hold and account for all US property, real and intellectual, belonging to enemy nations. What he had learned from his time at the Labor Department, Edgar told Ernst, was "the workings of democracy and the significance of pressure groups." Now he would escape the politics of a large department to work on the reconstruction and analysis of international patent cartels, especially those made by "the Stahlverein [steel association] and other large German trusts." He was thrilled to accept the new position.

A year later, his letters home to Brigitte told another story. He had been assigned to investigate a business in New York, and on October 18, 1943, he wrote in panic to his "Dearest of all Pürzlis." "The first day is over and I am perfectly desperate." There were three floors of files at the factory, none in German, and he was expected to go through them all. No preparatory work had been done. He was horrified at the way the case was being handled.

"You must give me advice, Bitzli. This is terrible." She advised him to talk with his boss and try to get out of the assignment, but a month later, his boss unresponsive, he was still in New York. He went to see the "doggie film" *Lassie Come Home* with his parents and Helga. "It is a little sentimental, and Helga cried half the time and Mutt a little, but I thought (and Pap too) that it was a very, very nice dog." At the end of the letter he added sweetly, "I would like to do the same thing Lassie did."

Edgar did stay with the Office of the Alien Property Custodian. The war-related work provided him with draft deferments, and he had no wish to enter the army as a private, though he did want to contribute to the fight against Hitler and had earlier attempted to apply for an Officer Training School in Seattle. By the end of 1943 he was working on a new case in Chicago, and the office was soon reorganized to his liking when some talented former Labor Department colleagues joined the agency. The General Counsel's office, looking for an expert in European law, repeatedly put out feelers in Edgar's direction, but he retained his position as principal attorney in the Division of Patent Administration.

Edgar's letters to Ernst Levy also tell me about his occasional academic forays. In 1941 he gave one of his historical talks, "The Legal Background of Total Mobilization in Germany," to the American Bar Association, showing how mobilization was "total" in the sense that Nazi laws targeted every possible business, social, and personal arrangement. He also joined the Riccobono Seminar of Roman Law in America, a forum for American and international Roman law scholars held at Catholic University. Most likely Ernst gave him the introduction, and Edgar presented two seminars based on his earlier work. In October 1941 he gave a paper called "Roman Law and the Dispute about Ancient Economy," a subject he must have studied in Heidelberg with his father-in-law. It was a broad survey of sources, but it ended in an Edgar-like way, characterizing classical Roman law as "written reason." In February 1944 he presented "The Position of Administrative Law in the Classical Legal System of Rome," coming closer to his own experience of government work in his careful definition of administrative law as the regulation of relations between the machinery of government and individuals. By this time he was easier with his audience and had achieved a more casual, American style of address. Ernst Levy, a much bigger name, also presented to the seminar in 1944 and was praised afterward as "the best kind of German university professor."

After his 1941 Riccobono talk Edgar listed the attendees for Ernst: they included about forty young priests from the school of canon law and some fellow Europeans. Among them was Stephan Kuttner, a German legal historian of about Edgar's age who left Germany for the Vatican library in

1933, where he wrote and published two books on medieval canon law. In 1940 he came to Catholic University as a visiting professor of the history of canon law and remained in the United States to establish an Institute of Medieval Canon Law, which was relocated to Munich in the 1990s and named for its founder. During the discussion of Edgar's paper Kuttner "threw in some source criticism." At a later meeting he insisted on the use of original sources, while Edgar argued that secondary sources had to be good for something—like his own kind of broadly focused writing. Despite this scholarly disagreement Stephan Kuttner and his vital wife, Eva, remained close friends of my family during and beyond the Washington years. Later they would fascinate me as the Catholic couple with nine children, whose names I tried to remember in their birth order.

Edgar's affinity for Catholic thinkers had begun early and was only strengthened by the reception of a Spanish translation of *Jurisprudence*, published in 1942 by the Fondo de Cultura Económica in Mexico City. In February that year, he wrote to Ernst about his new connection with "the leading legal philosopher in the Spanish-speaking world," Professor Luis Recasens Siches. Edgar wrote to Recasens in Spanish—he and Brigitte had been studying the language together—and received a friendly reply promising reviews in Mexican periodicals. "I am curious what the fate of my book in Latin American will be," Edgar wrote. "It is not entirely impossible that it will have more success there than in this country, where the general line of thought is in quite another direction." He was pleased to be the only US author in the field of legal philosophy whose work had been translated. "Perhaps the reason is that I am not really a U.S. lawyer, for the pragmatist approach which is prevalent here is very foreign to the Latin Americans."

And it was true: Edgar "was not really a U.S. lawyer," but a man who remained forever caught between cultures, systems, and philosophies. If there is anything to be said in theory for the detached position of the exile, my father's private journals tell a more nuanced story that includes resistance and disappointment. Edgar and Brigitte had successfully assimilated in their new country, establishing sturdier professional roots during their first ten years than many of their fellow émigrés had managed. Brigitte was dealing valiantly and practically with everything that came her way. But in the private musings of Edgar's red journal, still composed in German, conflict and dismay were the ruling forces.

The question of Jewish identity was unresolvable, as it would remain for many German and Austrian Jews who had never thought much about their Judaism until they were persecuted and exiled by the Nazi regime. Edgar was always aware of who was Jewish and who was not among his colleagues, but when he wrote of "Jewish lawyers" he did not include himself. He was horrified by the isolationism of his Jewish colleagues at the Department of Labor, and by their apparent indifference to what Hitler represented. "One said to me that he'd choose a Nazi concentration camp over military service in the war. Another said he'd choose German victory over America entering the war," he wrote on February 2, 1941. He tried to solve this puzzle by attributing such views to his colleagues' "left pacifism and anti-capitalism" or their adherence to the current Communist party line, which, as he rightly noted, could change very quickly. His apprehensions about his Jewish colleagues echo his interpretation of what had happened in Nazi Germany. "I don't doubt that the Jews will later be held accountable for this," he mused. "These Jews, and exactly their intelligence, will not be held guilt-free." It was and would remain his deepest fear: that Jewish cynicism and Jewish intellectualism were in some way responsible for anti-Semitism. He was pessimistic about the fate of American Jews whether or not Hitler won the war, and noted with alarm that the American military had acknowledged the French Fascists in the Vichy government.

In daily life, Edgar and Brigitte's way of presenting Judaism to their sons took the form of weekly "Sunday school," when Edgar would tell them stories from the Old Testament. In that activity, Edgar found one place to rest his Jewish head. The sessions also provided him with material for some especially charming family scenes in letters to the Levys. In January 1944, when Peter was six and Tom four, Edgar dramatized two scenes that reveal his delight in his sons' quite different characters.

> When Moses came down from Mt. Sinai and saw the Jews dancing around the golden calf, he asked those faithful to God to come over to his side and join him at the entrance of the camp. Thereupon the members of the tribe of Levi came over to his side, while the majority of Jews continued to dance around the calf. Brigitte (at lunch after the Sunday school lesson): "I think I am from the tribe of Levi, because my maiden name was Levy." Tommy (immediately): "I am from the tribe of Bodenheimer, so I danced around the golden calf!" (!!).
>
> Theological-anthropological conversation between Peter and his mother. Peter: "Mammy, were the first people born of God?" Brigitte (tells how Adam was created by God and then Eve out of Adam's rib). Peter: "And then they had children?" Brigitte: "Yes." Peter: "And then their children had children?" Brigitte: "Yes." Peter: "Mammy, then Adam's children married their brothers and sisters, did they?"

Through the Bible stories, Brigitte and Edgar made sure their children knew that they shared in the history of Judaism, even as they maintained the German Jewish traditions of celebrating Christmas Eve in the German way and coloring hard-boiled eggs for Easter egg hunts. The celebration of Passover would become the family's one formal Jewish ritual. As he read from the Haggadah at a table laden with the familiar Passover symbols, Edgar's voice took on the special solemn quality he reserved for great occasions. He carefully cut the Haggadah text to emphasize the crisis of the Jews as they suffered under the Egyptians and were led out of Egypt into the land of Israel. The drama was effective, but I am not sure we quite understood, as we listened to our father, just how personal the ancient story of persecution and exile was for him.

Edgar's private Jewish question intersected with other recurrent themes in his wartime red notebook: his rejection of permissive American culture, his distrust of democratic process, and his troubled socialism. He kept among his papers an unpublished letter he had sent to the *New York Times* on June 3, 1940, which argued that the youth of America were not ready for war because of the soft and self-indulgent lives they led. "The free countries of the world will perish unless they undertake a basic redefinition of the word 'freedom,'" he wrote. Democracy should be a system of restraint on power, a "disciplined freedom" requiring autonomy and responsibility. The Prussian belief in discipline and self-restraint was powerful in Edgar and came up repeatedly as a personal issue in the privacy of his journals. Asceticism, for instance, had much to recommend it—although he had to admit that "over-sublimation" was also undesirable.

On July 4, 1942, while America celebrated a wartime Independence Day, Edgar tried to explain the historical survival of the Jews as a consequence of enforced asceticism. Whenever the Jews got too comfortable and pleasure loving, he speculates, anti-Semitism rose up and forced them to fight against narrow circumstances. This would explain the vitality of eastern European Jews, who might otherwise have fallen into degeneracy. "Maybe the Jews are the chosen people because they have been chosen to suffer and regenerate," he wrote.

He was still trying to find a redemptive place for Judaism in world history, but where did his own life stand in relation to such theorizing? He had been expelled from a comfortable and pleasure-loving German existence, accepting the more constrained circumstances of American family life with some difficulty. Had he been revitalized in the process? That was not something he was willing or able to consider, at least on the page.

There was one avatar of American culture that Edgar was moved to take on concretely: Walt Disney. I hardly knew whether to laugh or cry when

I encountered his extended diatribes on the evils of American cartoons, though they did remind me that cartoons had not figured in my childhood. The first entry, for February 8, 1942, begins with a general complaint that American films were too brutal or sentimental. That was a predictable point of view, but Edgar's sudden focus on Mickey Mouse, Donald Duck, Pinocchio, and Dumbo was a surprise. "These go for the high point of cinema art, and my colleagues think I am crazy to avoid them," Edgar wrote. But in his eyes these animated characters represented "an orgy of lust for chaos." He was shocked by a cartoon showing a pyramid of elephants that collapses, bringing the whole circus tent down with it (did it evoke the collapse of Weimar Germany?). He found the idea of a baby elephant Dumbo trying to fly "complete idiocy." Where was his sense of humor? Where was his childhood reading of German fairy tales? More than a year later (August 21, 1943) he returned to the subject with renewed vehemence. Someone had persuaded him to admire the technical virtuosity of the films, but that just stoked Edgar's fires. Disney cartoons stimulate aggression and disorder; therefore they are like Fascist dictatorship. He specified, in an entry that goes on for eight pages: characters fall from high places and are miraculously saved at the last minute. Witches can instantly rob characters of sleep. And so on. He adamantly refused to roll with the conventions of this American genre, which appeared to him as a symbol of cultural degeneration and dangerous mass manipulation.

The fearful political emotion in Edgar's view of Disney may be a better indication of the Nazi trauma he sustained than were his ongoing attempts to theorize about the future of political systems. But it did not come out of nowhere. During those same years, the Frankfurt School sociologists Max Horkheimer and Theodor Adorno were attacking mass culture and the entertainment business. Their essay "The Culture Industry: Enlightenment as Mass Deception" appeared in 1944. Mindless chaos imposed from above led, in their view, to the "stunting of the mass-media consumer's powers of imagination and spontaneity" and destroyed what used to be known as culture. Cartoons were among their targets: "Cartoons were once exponents of fantasy as opposed to rationalism. They ensured that justice was done to the creatures and objects they electrified, by giving the maimed specimens a second life. All they do today is to confirm the victory of technological reason over truth." The spectator's enjoyment of cartoon violence "turns into violence against the spectator." Edgar's examples were his own, but the Frankfurt School was there to back him up.[2]

Edgar found American democracy inherently dangerous because it was determined by pressure groups rather than rational decision making. The fact that this democracy had sustained itself for nearly two hundred years, while the first German experiment in democracy began and ended during his youth, could not allay his anxiety about the imminent possibility of American Fascism. His experience in the Labor Department had initiated him into the realities of procedure in the federal bureaucracy, as did Brigitte's work at the Federal Housing Authority. While she absorbed how it was done, learning to draft and defend actual pieces of legislation, Edgar tended to despair about the irrationality of the process and the disorder it could produce. Although he continued to put theoretical faith in an idealized Soviet socialism, he was in fact yearning for an authoritarian state run by wise men presiding over a social order that encouraged the weaker aspects of human nature to improve.

Socialism, as he saw it, was better than capitalist democracy because it enjoined individuals to give up living for the self and to contribute to the good of society as a whole. In effect, Edgar's socialism was primarily a vague ethical ideal in which cooperation overcame competition. After hearing his sons bicker over who had better birthday gifts, he consigned their competitive drive to childishness and immaturity. Disney—he returned to the subject again—fostered the worst aspects of childhood, tendencies that must be fought and overcome as children grow into adults. Although Edgar did not make the connection explicit in his journal, the problem of raising children in a permissive American context was closely linked with his theoretical ideas of government. Meanwhile, Brigitte's diary happily noted the occasions when the boys began to walk by themselves to nearby friends' houses. Her measure of progress for her children was the gradual achievement of independence.

As for many other left-leaning Americans during this period, the lack of circulating information about Stalin's campaigns to destroy the Ukrainian peasantry and his ruthless mass murders made it possible for Edgar to continue fantasizing that Russia was the forerunner of a future synthesis that would produce a just society.[3] Ernst Levy was cannier, fearing Soviet despotism, but Edgar consistently gave Russia the benefit of the doubt, at various times imagining Russian superiority to America in film, news reporting, and music (Shostakovich was his case in point). As the war drove on, Edgar began to predict what would happen in Europe after Hitler was defeated. Interestingly, America was discounted in his imagination. As he saw it, the basic post-Hitler conflict would play out between Britain and Russia, with Britain (oddly) cast in the Fascist-leaning role. Nations, in Edgar's journal musings, were not really nations; they were the names of contending ideas.

I can arrive at no clear sense of what the family did or did not know about Hitler's final solution and the extermination camps, though it is probable that by 1942 they were aware, like most others in Washington, of Hitler's plans. They would have had weekly information through the anti-Nazi German Jewish newspaper *Aufbau*, which they read regularly, and would have seen the terrible concentration camp photos published in the April 1945 issue of *Life* magazine.[4] Their reactions to such horrors were clearly not to be written down or shared with their young children.

For all the discomfort in Edgar's red journal, the Bodenheimer family behaved much like every other American family as the war neared its end. They placed bets on when D-day would actually arrive. "Even Brigitte loses bets these days," Edgar wrote to her parents on June 4, 1944, two days before the Allied landing in Normandy. They kept the boys up to date on how many miles separated the advancing Russian army from Berlin. As Edgar reported in one of the family scenes he wrote to amuse the Levys, Tommy heard his parents talk and ran to inform his brother: "Peta, if one enemy gets the country of the other enemy, then the war in that country is over." In April 1945 they mourned Roosevelt's death along with their fellow Americans, watching the funeral train make its way from Union Station to the White House. "His small political errors seem so trivial beside the great good he did," Brigitte wrote to her parents. "Amazing that everyone, including ourselves, feels that they have lost a personal friend." Peter was worried about Truman, suddenly thrust into a new position: "Does he have to practice being President? Who is going to show him?" Ignored by Roosevelt during his brief service as vice president, Harry Truman was undoubtedly thinking much the same thing.

As the year 1946 opened, Brigitte knew that Edgar would begin to search for the academic position he had put off for the duration of the war. That fall brought two results: Edgar was back in the west, trying out the job he had been offered at the University of Utah School of Law, and I was born in Washington, DC. Edgar left no record of the months leading to these events. Perhaps they were too busy to be recorded; perhaps it was a difficult time that he did not particularly want to remember. Whether or not they had intended to expand their family, Brigitte and Edgar were caught up in the baby boom that swept through the postwar world in a celebration of new life. Brigitte could foresee another period of transition and underemployment for herself—in her words, another "interim period" when it would make sense to have a child. In August, when she was seven months pregnant, it looked as if that period might play itself out in Salt Lake City, the Mormon Zion.

Edgar had been away in Europe for three months at the end of 1945, on a mission for the Nuremberg trials that I describe in the next chapter. Now he was away again, to test the Utah waters before a final commitment to the position. He and Brigitte wrote to each other constantly, leaving me a detailed sense of those complicated months from September 1946 to February 1947. Reading the letters gives me an odd sense of looking in on my own birth. It also allows me to experience another of Edgar's campaigns of persuasion, as he overcame his skepticism about Mormon conservatism and fell in love with the pleasant Salt Lake valley, embraced by mountains and ski slopes that could be reached in a short drive.

Salt Lake City was a peculiar place for a family like ours to land, but the University of Utah School of Law had been on my parents' radar since their days in Seattle. There was a good reason for that; his name was William H. Leary.[5] Dean Leary, a devout Catholic raised on a farm in Massachusetts, had led the Utah Law School since 1916 and was largely responsible for building up its faculty, its library, and its student body after World War I. During a sabbatical in 1939–40, he returned to his alma mater, the University of Chicago, to study natural law under Professor Mortimer Adler, an American philosopher who worked in the tradition of Aristotle and St. Thomas Aquinas. After he returned to Utah, Leary gave a lecture titled "Natural Law and the Totalitarian States," a topic ready-made to attract Edgar's attention to Leary, and Leary's to Edgar. Although Leary adhered to the natural law theory of St. Thomas Aquinas, in which divine law was the ultimate arbiter of human justice, his ethical instincts overlapped nicely with Edgar's. When World War II ended and the School of Law expanded to accommodate the flood of returning GIs, the dean had many new hires to make. It is not surprising that, at sixty-five, he would be interested in hiring a young man who could carry on his own interest in natural law.

Dean Leary's welcome letter of August 9, 1946, displays a generous interest in his new colleague. Edgar had stated his willingness to accept a position split between teaching and acting as law librarian. The administrative arrangements were almost settled, and Leary outlined a broad course in the history of civil law from ancient to modern times that he wanted Edgar to teach, along with a required course in judicial administration. He had already consulted a number of colleagues around the country about a suitable text for the civil law course but had come up with nothing quite right; perhaps Edgar might want to frame his lectures as the raw material for such a book? Leary also told Edgar a bit about the other new men from Ohio State, the University of Wisconsin, and the University of Chicago, as if to reassure him about the national stature of the law school. His concern for Edgar's intellectual interests suggests that he saw the law librarianship as secondary.

It's no wonder that Edgar was moved to accept the invitation, although he went to Salt Lake City still unclear about whether he would stay in Utah beyond the end of that academic year, when Dean Leary was supposed to retire (in the event, the dean stayed on until 1950). He was considering a return to Seattle, which would please his parents-in-law, but the dean there would probably be more interested in him as a law librarian, and there had been no actual job offer. The December meeting of the American Bar Association in Chicago was not far away: Should he attend and inquire about other openings? When he left for Salt Lake City in time for his first faculty meeting on September 23, these questions were still in Edgar's mind. A long-term stay in Mormon country did not seem desirable either to him or to Brigitte.

"We are all a little poor because you left," Brigitte wrote when the family had returned from dropping Edgar off at the airport. She was sure he would make a success of the new position and hoped "the girls won't all fall in love with you." After his reading of the *Washington Post* that morning, nine-year-old Peter had informed her about the dates of the Jewish holidays that month. Yom Kippur fell on a Saturday, which, Brigitte said, "would eliminate that problem." They must have discussed how Edgar should present his Jewishness in the new workplace. Should he cancel classes if they fell on the holiest day of the Jewish calendar? What would it say to others if he did, or if he did not? What would it mean to be Jewish amid Mormon culture?

Edgar's first reports about that culture probably left Brigitte wondering why he didn't get on a plane and come home. On the day he arrived, the front page of the *Salt Lake Tribune* (the non-Mormon paper) carried an article by the First Secretary of the Mormon Church, announcing that the federal government was entirely in the hands of aliens whose civil law training had put price control theories into their heads. The heavy taxes they planned to collect from Americans would all go to Josef Stalin. A few days later, there was a lunchtime discussion of the article among Edgar's new colleagues. He learned that the church "has more or less degenerated into a large property holding corporation. Present church doctrine teaches that the world will some day be destroyed and extinguished by fire, and that the New Deal was the first sign of impending doom."

Edgar heard more from the Jewish Judge Herbert M. Schiller, who taught the other section of his judicial administration course. Schiller had served as elected District Judge in Utah from 1933 to 1939 and was living proof that Mormons were ready to vote for Jewish candidates. (Utah had previously elected a Jewish governor, and Salt Lake City had had a Jewish mayor.) Taking Edgar under his wing, Judge Schiller introduced him to the rabbi of the Temple B'nai Israel and took him to Yom Kippur services. "I was such a religious Schnautzer this Yom Kippur. Lifted my paws in prayer yesterday night as well as today," Edgar reported.

Judge Schiller, a single man about town, loved to gossip. He told Edgar that Utah "Gentiles"—non-Mormons—were not allowed to own books critical of Mormonism and claimed that some doctrinally pure Mormon servant girls had removed books from his study and destroyed them. It was probably Schiller who inspired Edgar's report to Brigitte: "There is so much Hebrew mythology hovering over this area: Zion, Mount Nebo, the Jordan River, the Aaronic priesthood, the exodus of the Mormons into the '*gelobte Land*' [the Promised Land] under the leadership of 'Moses' Brigham Young." Utah, Edgar was learning, could be ultra-conservative, but the Mormons were not particularly anti-Semitic. Since they believed they had descended from one of the ten lost tribes of Israel, Mormon doctrines were often more generous to Jews than to members of other Christian faiths.

Edgar quickly found a room to rent in a widow's house and moved into his new office, which overlooked Red Butte. His "little empire," the law library, was small, but, he joked, "the acquisitions seem to be intelligently selected. For instance, they have 5 copies of my book, which is only surpassed by Vanderbilt's 'Studying Law.'" Like others trained in German universities, Edgar had some initial trouble finding the right tone for American students. Brigitte confided late in their lives that the Utah law students had laughed at Edgar's mannerisms during his first lectures.[6] His talented colleague Monrad Paulsen, who had joined the Law School a year earlier, became a sort of mentor. He sat in on Edgar's classes, discussed teaching, and reported to Dean Leary. It was not long before adjustments were made on both sides of the classroom.

Edgar envied Paulsen's brilliant teaching style, done with "a minimum of preparation and a maximum of improvisation," though he knew he could never manage it himself. The Paulsens gave Edgar dinners, invited him for Thanksgiving, and took good care of him while he was living in his solitary room. They could not imagine staying long in Utah, and they did not: Paulsen moved on a year later and would eventually become dean at the University of Virginia Law School. At the end of September Edgar told Brigitte that the place was very beautiful and the general spirit of the faculty good (with exceptions), but the Mormons were "too much convinced of their own divinity, and the Church leadership is reactionary—intolerant. *Please let me know what you think.*"

What Brigitte thought is no longer in the record. Edgar removed some of her letters from this group, leaving evidence of their existence only in his acknowledgments of receipt. Was there conflict he wanted to suppress, or was Brigitte simply focused on the final weeks of her pregnancy? After a few years of interesting work, she was back in an all-too-familiar situation. Edgar was off having new adventures and making new friends, while she was at home with the children, an imminent birth, and no idea of what was going to happen next. She had another adult in the household, her mother-in-law's cousin Kaethe Sachs, who had come to live with the family in 1945. Kaethe cooked and cleaned, doing away with the need for hired help, but she was yet another older family member who required support from Brigitte. For help with the new baby, Brigitte relied on her mother, Marie, who would come to stay for the first months.

I was born on October 11, 1946, the same day Edgar wrote, "Now Klein-Pauz III may be only a week off. I think David Ernest is a good name." They had schooled themselves for a third boy, but Brigitte was delighted to have a daughter, the "Klein-Bitz" she had anticipated when she was first pregnant with Peter. Edgar missed Kaethe's phone call announcing the birth and got the message from his excited landlady after he returned from eating dinner and seeing Ingrid Bergman in *Notorious*. Brigitte herself called him the next day, and he passed out cigars—presumably not to the Mormons—and candy to his new colleagues. "It is a *very* funny feeling to have a daughter and not to know her," Edgar wrote, and plied Brigitte with questions. "Is Klein-Bitz a very hungry animal, like Tommy? And do you have enough to eat for her? Does she look as 'wild' as Tommy first looked? What do Peter and Tommy say about her?"

Brigitte was still in the hospital a week later, enjoying the "sweet little monkey" with "sweet soft velvet skin, the little rascal," when she got a phone call from the new General Counsel for the Housing Authority. He wanted her to stay on at the agency and work for him. Not wanting to relinquish the possibility, she told him it was too early to say. Even if she had to let it go, she wrote to Edgar, she was glad to be appreciated. If they were to go to Seattle, she might be able to work at the agency's regional office there. On October 21, Edgar responded: "It was very nice of Mr. Glick to call you so soon, and it just shows what a smart little animal you are. I would remain in touch with him; it certainly can't hurt. I don't see much chance for us to stay in Washington, but Seattle might be a possibility, and it would probably be easier than anywhere else, because of Miezchen." Edgar had travelled west with a Housing Authority colleague of Brigitte's, "who said to me, 'Brix is such a smart little girl.' Smart and sweet, both," Edgar added. That was the sound of gender equality, circa 1946.

Brigitte continued to argue for Seattle, since they would be unlikely to stay in Salt Lake City for more than two or three years, and it would be hard on the boys to uproot them twice. Although he kept the Seattle ball in the air for a while, Edgar was quickly coming to his own conclusion about Salt Lake City. His star student that quarter was Spencer L. Kimball, son of a prominent Mormon family led by Spencer W. Kimball, who was one of the Twelve Apostles, and later President, of the Mormon Church. The talent and liberalism of the younger Kimball may have provided a turning point in Edgar's ideas about Mormonism. Judge Schiller had been invited to join a legal fraternity, only to be rejected by the national office because he was Jewish. Kimball wrote to headquarters, saying that Salt Lake City would resign from the national organization unless the anti-Semitic rule was dropped. (Both Judge Schiller and Edgar became members.) Kimball also initiated an invitation to Edgar from the Salt Lake County Bar Association for a lecture on the Nuremberg trials.

At the end of October, Edgar reported on his midterm grades: A's for both Miss Leary (the dean's daughter) and "the son of the apostle." Spencer Kimball would go on to win a Rhodes Scholarship to England. When he returned he joined the Utah law faculty, became its youngest dean in 1950, and brought a chapter of the ACLU to Utah. He left Salt Lake City in the mid-1950s for a career at the Universities of Michigan and Wisconsin. His "A," along with Edgar's respect for him, was well deserved.

By early November, Edgar's tune had changed. The Mormons want to control everything, he wrote, but the Gentiles (Jews and non-Jews) can come together to fight certain schemes of Mormon domination. "And the Mormons are not vicious, they just feel they built up this beautiful city and made a blooming garden out of the desert, and that they should have priority in reaping its fruits. (I suppose the Jews in Palestine feel the same way.)" The state of Israel was yet to be established, so Edgar's later fears about the consequences of Jewish nationalism had not yet been activated, and he was free to play around with comparisons between the Jewish and Mormon Zions. That Election Day he enjoyed a party of faculty from across the university, all Democrats, who turned off the radio in disgust when it became clear that Republicans were winning the midterm congressional seats. The hosts had a lovely house with a private swimming pool that was made available to Edgar and his family on summer weekends. (I remember long sunny afternoons around the pool in their steeply terraced back garden.) Edgar was also impressed by a Utah Symphony concert, and rejoiced in the vivid acoustics of the Mormon Tabernacle.

Once snow fell on the Wasatch Range, the die was cast. Edgar went skiing in Alta, which was "fantastically beautiful," with "scorching sun and marvelous snow. I feel like new born," he exclaimed. Alta was "like Switzerland"; no higher praise could be imagined. It would be wonderful to bring up the boys in these mountains; perhaps they could stay as long as five years. Tommy had been dreaming of poisonous snakes, but, Edgar assured him, they were found only in the western mountains, not the Wasatch. There was an on-campus school for faculty children run by a German Jew, Walter Hahn. Somehow, Edgar was not making arrangements to attend the Bar Association meetings in Chicago, though he was coming home for Christmas to meet his new daughter. Once she read the first Alta letter, Brigitte must have known that the family fate had been decided. Would it be all right for the baby to move so soon? Edgar wanted to know.

December brought hard times to the Washington home front. Peter came down with measles, and Brigitte followed. Nursing stopped; the household was strung out between illness and the prospect of a winter move early in 1947. Edgar came home to a sick wife who gradually recovered, but by mid-January, when he was back in Utah, everyone was sick again. Under the pressure of new courses to teach, Edgar was looking seriously at houses in the tight postwar Salt Lake City market. By January 8 he had found one at 1451 Uintah Circle, in a peaceful older neighborhood on the east bank of the city. It was a red brick house with seven rooms and a large backyard, just a block from the local elementary school we would all attend. The owner wanted to move as soon as possible to join her husband back in Washington, so the deal was quickly settled. From then on, Edgar's correspondence with Brigitte was all house business: How was he to go about buying a stove? A refrigerator? What about the mortgage on the Washington house? How would they get the car to Salt Lake City? The upstairs rooms would be a bit tighter than in Washington; where would everyone sleep? He was rushing around frantically to get ready for his family's arrival, hoping that they would approve of the choices he had made.

What Brigitte was doing and feeling as she answered those letters can only be imagined, but in mid-February 1947, the house still unsold, she packed her baby, her boys, and Kaethe Sachs into a cross-country train and set out for the promised land. The family would stay in Salt Lake City, living in the house Edgar had found, for twenty years.

# 6
# Returns

In the fall of 1945, Edgar was offered an extraordinary opportunity to witness in person the physical and moral ruins of his once-beloved homeland. The beginning of the adventure is recorded in a late August letter from Washington, DC, to the Levys in Seattle. The War Department had requested that the Office of the Alien Property Custodian loan Edgar to them for a three-month research trip on behalf of the War Crimes Commission. They wanted him to participate in the US effort to assess the evidential value of Nazi documents for Justice Robert Jackson's prosecution team at the Nuremberg war-crimes trial. The plan was to leave for Germany in two weeks; he had already passed the medical exam and was awaiting a passport, his first as a US citizen. "Brigitte and I never had any doubt that I should accept this offer," he wrote to his parents-in-law. "This is an opportunity which will never recur. But it is like a fairy tale: somewhere there pops up a witch whose mind is bent on evil." The wicked witch in this case was the head of the US Passport Division, an alleged Fascist and anti-Semite who had decided that German Jewish refugees had no business serving at the War Crimes trials. Had Edgar been commissioned by the Army, he might have gone without a passport, but he was to be a civilian employee of the War Department.

Weeks of interagency politics were to follow, as the passport question was pursued at various levels and Edgar's employers bickered over which agency was to pay his wages and per diem expenses. On October 5 he finally received a mimeographed sheet from the War Department: Invitational Travel Orders authorizing Edgar and another German Jewish American attorney, Sidney B. Jacoby, to proceed to Nuremberg via any other destination that might be necessary for the accomplishment of their mission. They were to carry American army uniforms, though they would not be required to wear them under most circumstances. On October 7 Brigitte and the boys spent most of the day waiting with Edgar at the airport as his flight was repeatedly delayed. They were used to official "timetables" by now; throughout the trip Edgar would receive last-minute orders changing his destinations. The unprecedented operation of the War Crimes Commission was being hastily improvised on a day-to-day basis in the hectic weeks leading to the official opening of the Nuremberg war-crimes trial on November 20, 1945.[1]

Edgar's excitement about returning to Europe remained consistently high through the early and middle phases of his three-month adventure. He was participating in the thick of history at a crucial postwar moment, and he intended to make the most of every visit and conversation. He was getting a trip to test his own responses to defeated Germany, sheltered under the expansive and luxurious umbrella of the US occupation forces. In the special journal he kept—in English—for this period, he marked his return with a keen memory of dates: "On Oct. 11, 1933, I arrived in the U.S. for the first time. On Oct. 11, 1945, I returned to Germany for the first time." Best of all, he was part of a principled legal team. In the absence of any previous international legal apparatus defining aggressive war as a criminal act, the highly contested Nuremberg trials were essentially based on principles of natural law in which Edgar fervently believed. What could be more satisfactory to a man of his experience than the opportunity to respond to Nazi violence against human rights through an international tribunal based on careful evidentiary judgment?

The International Military Tribunal established in Nuremberg, the site of Hitler's annual Nazi Party rallies, was to a large extent the creation of Robert L. Jackson, then an Associate Justice of the Supreme Court, who was tasked by President Truman to develop a system for the prosecution of Nazi leaders after the war. Its rationale had to be created out of virtually nothing: there were no legal precedents, and no previous modern court had attempted to prosecute war crimes. Yet to many people the ritual of a legal trial was preferable to imitating the Nazis by summarily shooting or exiling their leaders, without the benefit of a public forum in which their deeds could be publicized and punished in the eyes of German citizens and the world at large. The work of the Tribunal depended on defining the Nazi regime as a criminal conspiracy to wage aggressive war on other nations, in order to exploit, enslave, or destroy both human and natural resources in the service of the Third Reich.[2]

To the objection that such a definition constituted ex post facto law—declaring actions to be criminal only after the fact of their committal—Jackson appealed to a universal code: "What we propose is to punish acts which have been regarded as criminal ever since the time of Cain and have been so written in every civilized code."[3] In the months after Germany's surrender, on May 6, 1945, working together with Soviet, British, and French legal leaders in London, Jackson managed to piece together a Charter and a trial procedure that would hold together for the duration of the trials, despite the differing courtroom rules and procedures that divided the legal systems of the French and the Soviets from the Anglo-American common-law tradition. According to the London Charter, the Nazi defendants would be charged with aggressive war crimes, with violations of the customs of war, and with crimes against humanity.

If the legal validity of the War Crimes Tribunal remains contested to this day, the evidence it gathered and made public became its own justification. Once Jackson discovered that the Nazis had stashed away meticulous records detailing each campaign of destruction, he decided to emphasize the self-incriminatory evidence of the documents rather than basing the prosecution primarily on testimony from victims and witnesses. Setting up a Documents Division of the US Army, he needed people with expertise in European languages and law to go through the files, translate them, and prepare briefs for presentation in court. All told, his operation brought about seven hundred Americans to Germany in 1945–46, among them a number of German Jewish refugee lawyers like Edgar. In some respects, the network that supported the Nuremberg trials was like a reunion of old schoolmates or colleagues from prewar times. In that bizarre landscape of occupied, bombed-out cities, Edgar hobnobbed and exchanged information and gossip with many of his own kind. He was part of the advance guard in the American campaign to reestablish German democracy after the war, in which many formerly German émigrés would be involved.

Both in his letters home to Brigitte and in his Nuremberg journal, Edgar tried to capture the strange atmosphere of occupied Germany. His account began with the long flight to Paris, his first experience of air travel, requiring refueling stops in Bermuda and the Azores. Enchanted by the cloud formations and the play of light, he described them in ways he knew his sons would enjoy: "Some huge clouds towering on the horizon looked like mighty icebergs and became red and glowing for a while when the sun went down, like the mountains on Heidi's alm." For Brigitte's sake he always mentioned the excellent food provided at negligible prices by the Army. He was being well taken care of among the ruins of the postwar world, and he was very aware of the distressing contrast between the elegant billets and flowing liquor provided by the Army and the unspeakable rubble, poverty, and starvation that surrounded them.

In Paris, both Edgar and Sidney Jacoby visited Jewish friends who had survived the war in hiding under assumed names and false papers. Now they were freezing and scrounging for food in run-down Paris apartments on unlighted streets. "One feels like a member of a privileged nation, a master race," Edgar wrote. In the privacy of his journal, this weird joke indicated his discomfort in the new role of American occupier. That role had its uses, though: the next day he and Jacoby returned to the suffering families bearing PX rations. In Frankfurt, where the Documents Division was headquartered, Edgar sniffed happily at the familiar native air as they landed, but the destroyed streets quickly ended that moment of nostalgia. He and Jacoby wandered through the night city, "nothing but a heap of rubble. Just some fantastically formed pillars or parts of buildings are staring into the sky. . . . Everywhere broken pipes hang around; plumbing and wires lie around or dangle in the air. . . . 'My God,' we exclaimed all the time."

The Americans were based at a former I.G. Farben palace and casino, formerly owned by the chemical conglomerate that had collaborated with the Nazis in supplying the gas, Zyklon B, used for mass killings in extermination camps. Enhanced by rock gardens, an orchestra, and three dining rooms, the intact site was now the headquarters of the American occupation. "The contrast between the splendor of these surroundings and the devastation in the city did not let one sleep that night for a long time," Edgar wrote at the end of his first day in Germany. What could he feel under these circumstances? His country of origin had been destroyed in a cause he supported, and now he had returned as an agent of that powerful victor.

It all seemed *unheimlich*—unfamiliar yet weirdly familiar. "In the station, lit by one lamp, people sit on little suitcases and wait for the rare trains. . . . The station at night is like a scene from Gorki's 'Nachtasyl.'" He was referring to Maxim Gorky's 1901 play, "The Lower Depths," to sketch a picture of starving homeless people sheltering in railway stations. On a night drive to Vienna, his ears were tuned to stresses within the four-power occupation: "An English Captain in the truck fed anti-Russian propaganda into a Frenchman. It was pitch dark since the streets were not lighted." He was amazed to discover that Munich, where he had once lived and studied law, was so bombed out that he could no longer recognize streets or give directions to his driver. "Munich is an inferno. We walked through the city at night. Full moon. Sometimes it looks like a rocky Ur-landscape." Photographs could not touch the scale of the rubble, which stretched beyond the limits of any photographic frame, and often concealed decaying corpses. In Nuremberg, women cooked over small fires on top of the rubble; people lived in caves beneath it. The barter system prevailed; cigarettes were the only real medium of exchange. At times, Edgar's imagination turned Germany, the place of his *Bildung*, into a precivilized, hopelessly ruined place. From destroyed Frankfurt, he wrote to Brigitte, "It is a ghastly nightmare

Figure 16. Nuremberg in 1945

and no picture can give a clear conception of the continuity and completeness of the annihilation. I just cannot see how anything new can arise out of these ruins."

His sense of hopelessness about the German future was partly based on the physical shock of return, but it was also shaped by American attitudes to Germany in 1945. The punitive plan that emerged from the Treasury Department under the leadership of Secretary Henry Morgenthau was in place by 1944. President Roosevelt supported it, though it was opposed by State Department officials and proved largely unworkable on the ground. Morgenthau intended to prevent Germany from ever again raising its armed fist. To that end, he proposed that the country be divided and "pastoralized"—returned to an agricultural economy, with its heavy industry and military dismantled. Industrial output would be severely curtailed, German POWs would be used as forced labor to rebuild Europe, and Nazi Party leaders shot or exiled. The German population was to be reeducated through a stringent denazification campaign that would assess the extent of each citizen's collaboration with Hitler's regime and dismiss all tainted party members from positions of responsibility in German society.[4]

In fact, much of the Allied effort in the months immediately following Germany's unconditional surrender in April 1945 was required to feed and resettle huge populations of displaced persons and stateless refugees. It would soon became apparent that a working German economy was necessary to the rebuilding of Western Europe in general, especially in the face of the threat posed by an expanding Soviet Union. Denazification also proved unworkable: trained people were required to run German business and industry, and many of them, by choice or under pressure, had been members of the Nazi Party. By 1947, the Marshall Plan for the reconstruction of Europe had replaced the Morgenthau Plan, but in the fall of 1945 denazification was still a primary concern of the American sector in particular, as was the generally negative spin on Germany's future. Edgar made a grim joke about pastoralized Germany in a letter to Brigitte, after driving through pristine country villages on the way to Munich. "The AAF [Army Air Force] has in fact accomplished the Morgenthau Plan. You see it when you drive through the Bavarian villages, neat and untouched . . . and then enter that nightmarish horror that once was Munich."

Before Edgar left for Europe, he had been warned that he might end up sitting in a back room translating files for three months. Happily for him, that prediction proved to be quite wrong. Soon after arriving at the Frankfurt base, he was sent on a ten-day "top secret mission" to Austria, where he visited Vienna on his way to Linz and a nearby town that held Austrian Foreign Office files of Nazi plans for the invasion of Ukraine. Discovered in salt mines and caves, the files were a hot item: the British had tried to get hold of them before the Americans did, and, Edgar suspected, may have succeeded in covertly removing a few. He and his colleagues also travelled through Salzburg to Munich to check another cache of files at Freising before returning to Frankfurt, where Edgar worked under high pressure to prepare a brief for presentation early in the trial.

It was November 15 before he arrived in Nuremberg, where he spent another week revising the document, staying up all night for last-minute alterations required by Thomas J. Dodd, the federal prosecutor who presented the brief to the court on November 23. Dodd did not do a very good job, Edgar lamented. Still, he had had his "day in court," sitting at the American prosecution table. In the final weeks before departure, he worked on other issues alongside colleagues in Nuremberg. Altogether, Edgar listed four categories of research he had done: Germany's economic preparations for war, the spoliation of Russia, Goering and the concentration camps, and Hans Frank's horrific and well-documented reign as Governor-General of Poland.

A few stories from the files made their way into the journal. Two were Hitler's draft plans for German-occupied France and Poland, in which populations were to be diminished, intellectuals deported, and economic conditions kept at bare subsistence. Some were Edgar's expressions of outrage or disgust. "The files on [Julius] Streicher are incredible. Pornographic, vulgar, stupid." On December 11 Edgar commented directly on what had happened in court that day. Like every other Nuremberg observer, he was forced to watch the Hermann Goering show in the defendants' box: "When Goering was led into the court room this morning, he said with a loud voice, 'Nun muss ich wieder in den Afferkasten herein.' (Now I have to climb into the monkey cage again.) He shows a great effusion of emotions, and his reactions of approval, disapproval, surprise, and anger are always very marked." Goering, who made himself the star actor among the defendants, made Edgar angry; he especially disliked seeing American staff members laughing and joking with Goering.[5] He was a bit more sympathetic to Hitler's Minister of Economics Hjalmar Schacht, his father's former colleague at the Danat-Bank. "Schacht seems shocked at some of the atrocities." Few of those atrocities were mentioned in the journal, though one widely circulated story does appear. "The wife of a concentration camp commander in Buchenwald loved lamp shades made out of human skin. The skin was tattooed and afterwards the victim was killed and his skin removed." The resistance I feel to copying these words from Edgar's pages gives me some understanding of the silences he otherwise kept. Perhaps Brigitte heard more details after he returned, and after the children had gone to sleep.

When I first read the Nuremberg journal and imagined my father returning to Germany under those strange and heart-wrenching circumstances, I was rather put off. Where was Edgar's subjectivity? Why did he not say more about his reactions? Rereading the notebook years later, I can better sympathize with its intent and with its omissions. The daily writing was an attempt to capture every conversation, opinion, rumor, and wartime experience that Edgar was told, generally without adding his own comment or interpretation. There were certain questions on his mind, which can be discerned from the journal's repeated themes. What was it like to encounter ordinary Germans now? How were the Americans behaving in their sector of the divided country, as compared with the British, the French, and especially the Russians? How were Germans responding to the American occupation and to the denazification program? What was it like to walk in each city, or to cross a boundary into the Soviet zone? How did the defendants and the prosecutors conduct themselves in the daily work of the War Crimes Tribunal? He was after physical facts, political rumors, and stories he could use in his self-appointed mission to explain events in Germany to uninformed Americans at home. Along with his official tasks, adopting a research mentality was a way to find some distance from the pain he encountered both in the files and in the streets.

Most of Edgar's interlocutors were United States Army people or émigré Americans like himself. Enclosed in the American occupation bubble, he did not have to consider the Germans he encountered as his former countrymen, or to wrestle directly with problems of dual identification such encounters might have generated. Despite the Americans' attempts to "reeducate" the German population about Hitler's atrocities, the death camps were rapidly being repressed. Stunned Germans, shell shocked by the Allied bombing campaign, simply turned their faces away from the evidence, as they did from the smell of rotting corpses trapped in the rubble of their cities. In his book about the silences of postwar Germany, *On the Natural History of Destruction*, W. G. Sebald quotes the returning German writer Alfred Döblin describing Germans in 1945 who "walked down the street and past the dreadful ruins as if nothing had happened and . . . the town had always looked like that."[6] Edgar's postwar silences were widely shared by people everywhere on the spectrum of guilt, shame, survival, and suffering.

It was only as he reached the last stage of his trip in Nuremberg itself that he broached some emotional conclusions. After a walk through destroyed Nuremberg, "like finding your way through a maze of rocks in the mountains," he drew a heavily ironic moral. "There is a certain bizarre romanticism connected with ruins. But I believe the nostalgic longing of the Germans for romanticism and ruins is over-satisfied this time, and the desire of many of their intellectuals to return to the 'universalist' order of the Middle Ages may be cured by the extreme relapse into primitivism which they are experiencing." As his service neared its end, he seemed to take a grim pleasure in the notion that the Allied bombing campaign was just the right medicine for the regressive folly of Nazi thinking.

The letters to Brigitte are suffused with warmth and more personal notes about people they both knew and Edgar's activities in the American enclaves. The Grand Hotel in Nuremberg housed most of the trial delegations. Although it was partly destroyed—guests had to walk along scaffolding to get to their rooms—it retained its grandeur and its huge ballroom. "I have never had so much 'social life' as in these days here," he wrote. The ballroom of the hotel is "practically the only place you can go after dinner," and he was dancing a lot. He enjoyed tantalizing Brigitte with the mystery of what he was doing on his "very confidential mission" to Austria. During that trip he became close to his cohorts Benedict Deinard, an American lawyer from Minneapolis who served as head of the economic division at Frankfurt, and "my WAC corporal" Erna Uiberall, a Viennese American who was also returning to the scenes of her youth. She was married to Peter Uiberall, who served as a key member of the simultaneous translation team at the Nuremberg trials. Aware of Brigitte's tendency to feel uneasy about other women he met, Edgar noted, "I am travelling with a WAC (a fact that need not disturb you whatsoever), attached to me as an assistant for my special mission. She is a married woman, young and energetic, and we laugh a lot because there are always funny situations that come up." Whether or not his lines reassured Brigitte, Edgar was writing for a particular audience, a wife he did not want to upset from a distance and perhaps his young sons, who would hear excerpts from his letters.

As Edgar tried to take the temperature of postwar Germany, his fascination with things Russian continued. American harshness toward Germany was soon to be replaced by an extreme distrust of the Soviet Union, but in that immediate postwar moment Edgar remained uncertain. He recorded the stories that circulated about the Red Army's violent entry into Austria and Germany, its soldiers raping and pillaging mercilessly after a prolonged period of unbroken battle. Was it true that Stalin could simply turn off that bad behavior by pushing a button? Edgar wondered. He wrote down whatever he heard about good organization in the Soviet zone, but he also heard his colleagues' complaints about how difficult it was to work with the Russians. One officer explained that Edgar had not been cleared for a visit to Berlin because Russians were jailing Americans in their zone. Corporal Uiberall's mother, who had remained in Vienna during the war, reported six months of hell under Russian occupation: starvation, rape, and indiscriminate looting for no purpose except to throw merchandise into the streets where anyone could pick it up. Billeted in her house, Russian soldiers slept with their uniforms on, boots resting on the pillow.

In divided Vienna, Edgar's curiosity led him to wander into the Russian sector, where he observed the very young Russian soldiers, finding their faces "unrefined, a little primitive, good-natured." As they drove from Vienna to Linz, on the border of the Russian zone in Austria, the Red Army was very much in evidence: "They move along the roads in trucks, in horse carts drawn by small horses, on foot led by music bands." The Russians were utterly foreign: that seems to have been Edgar's primary impression, but he drew no conclusions. To balance the picture, he also noted stories about Americans who looted, stole Nazi documents as keepsakes, and fraternized with German girls.

Edgar's observations were tuned to another mission as well. Ernst Levy was already thinking about ending his exile in Seattle and returning to his real home, Heidelberg University. He had somehow heard that he would be recalled to his German professorship once the law faculty started up again, and he was in the throes of the questions such an invitation would raise. Perhaps Edgar and Brigitte were reminded of the agonizing and rather unrealistic process that had preceded his emigration and were not eager to see it repeated. Edgar, in any case, had a very clear agenda: to dissuade the Levys from returning to Germany in the immediate future. To that end, he travelled to Heidelberg from Frankfurt in an Army Jeep, spending a long day interviewing many of his and his father-in-law's former teachers and colleagues. Chief among them were Karl Jaspers and his Jewish wife, Trude, who had barely escaped deportation by the arrival of American troops in Heidelberg, and the legal philosopher Gustav Radbruch, who had been named dean of the law faculty. Both Jaspers and Radbruch had been dismissed by the Nazis for their liberal beliefs and were now central figures in the committee that was reconstituting the university along lines approved by the Americans.

According to Edgar, no one in Heidelberg thought it was a propitious time for Ernst Levy to return. "The advice of *everybody* was negative, at least for the time being," he wrote to Brigitte. Although Heidelberg had not been bombed, "living conditions are appalling. All the houses were ice cold. . . . It is a *ghost world* there (Radbruch actually looks like a ghost). Pale, freezing, hungry people." He repeated these opinions in a letter to Ernst, adding a few details. Ernst's former student and colleague Wolfgang Kunkel would teach Roman law at Heidelberg when classes resumed, though his appointment was only temporary. Frau Radbruch collected wood in the forest every day to feed their only source of warmth, a wood stove. People were bitter. The Germans spent much of their time complaining about mistakes Americans made in the denazification process.[7]

Ernst was not convinced, and said so in a late October letter to Edgar. Bad living conditions were surely not the real reason he had not received the expected invitation from the law faculty. After all, it was his decision as to whether returning would constitute a sacrifice. "You know how things are in regard to my research and how we are cut off from life, scholarly and otherwise," he wrote. He was suffering from a renewed sense of exclusion and exile. And he didn't like the idea that Edgar, in Heidelberg, had discussed his situation in his absence. Ernst was not yet aware that neither German universities nor the government would make a systematic effort to restore dismissed Jewish scholars to their former positions. In fact, Germans who had survived the war, the firebombing, and the hunger in their own country were not eager to reincorporate returning refugees who had escaped those horrors. To their way of thinking, it was the Germans, not the Jews, who had been the chief victims of Hitler's imperial ambitions.[8]

Edgar's campaign of persuasion only escalated in response to his father-in-law's resistance. In a letter of November 11 he went through the denazification news from Heidelberg, listing those who were no longer acceptable, and those Radbruch was attempting to save for his faculty. "I did not care for Radbruch's attitude . . . as a matter of fact the whole place is an anachronism. You should see how incredibly dirty the Schurman building looks. It used to be white, now it looks dark grey. Both of you would feel deeply unhappy there. Heidelberg is a memory of the past, but I am sure it has no future." Ten days later, writing from Nuremberg, he returned to the fray. "Nürnberg is a heap of rubble, a pathetic sight. Just like the rest of Germany. The idea that anybody could wish to go back to this country, even to an undestroyed city, is inconceivable after what I have seen. There cannot be any future. I am not authorized to speak of Jaspers' plans, but he agrees fully with me on this. The hint may suffice. I think self-respecting people would not even wish to die in Germany." His experiences had put him through a "catharsis" he was grateful for; if Ernst and Marie could be there with him, they would understand what he meant. Edgar's eagerness to consign Germany to history's dustbin was in character: anything so emotionally confusing was better thrown away.

In January 1946, Ernst Levy did receive a somewhat belated invitation to return to Heidelberg. Edgar immediately returned to his anti-German campaign in a letter of February 9. This time he let living conditions rest, and spoke more forthrightly of German anti-Semitism. Since his return, he had heard from one of Justice Jackson's officials that when Heidelberg professors were asked to bring evidence against Nazi leaders, "every one of them with the sole exception of Jaspers refused to make incriminating statements against the Nazis." Trude Jaspers distrusted the anti-Semitism of Heidelberg academics and felt that ordinary Germans were far more sympathetic to her plight as a Jew. As for Radbruch, though he was "one of the most decent men in Heidelberg," he had complained at length to Edgar about the severity of the American denazification process. He was also on record as opposing the recall of Jewish professors, giving as his reason the anti-Semitic environment in Germany. Edgar was not sure exactly why Radbruch had reversed himself in Ernst Levy's case but suggested that he may have been responding to pressure from elsewhere. "I do not think that the German people, and especially the intellectually leading groups among them, have shown any change of heart and have done any acts which prove that they want to distance themselves from their Nazi past and to repudiate it completely," Edgar wrote. "As long as this situation exists, I feel that people with our background and experience cannot consider associating again with them."

Edgar's journal entries about passing encounters with German strangers were suffused with disgust; that seems to have been the primary emotion that fed the "catharsis" he mentioned to Ernst and Marie. German waiters served as his whipping boys: time and again he commented on the extreme servility they displayed with Americans. "If you put your hand in your pocket in order to pull out a match, they rush to you: 'But please, allow me to light your cigarette.' If you only move your hand, a waiter will come: 'But please, what would you like?'" Taking up a sugar bowl would lead to the same response. "All this, although no tips are allowed in American eating places." Although he did not articulate the idea, Edgar was feeling intense discomfort at the way petty tyranny turned so nauseatingly into petty servility. To Brigitte he put it a bit differently: "The Germans are servile, co-operative, numb. The barber who cut my hair today took three times as much time as an American barber would take, and asked me over and over again whether this was the exact way I liked it. I have constantly the feeling that reality is much more unreal than fiction."

Like many of his American colleagues, Edgar recorded stories about the lies Germans told to deny their Nazi sympathies. Someone from the Quartermaster Corps told him that the Germans he was feeding all claimed to be half Jewish, which would qualify them for larger food rations. In Nuremberg, Edgar had to bribe a caretaker with cigarettes to get the heat fixed in his billet. "For 2 packs, a German will tell you he never was a Party member. For 3 packs, he will tell you he hated the Nazis. For 4 packs he will assure you the Nazis put him in a concentration camp." Whether these are his words or variants of someone else's, Edgar was getting well into the spirit of the early occupation. He passed some of it along to the Levys: "Most Germans try to prove that they had a Jewish grandmother since rations for non-Aryans are slightly higher. Everyone expresses disgust about the atrocities. One woman said to Newkirk, 'Isn't it sad, that they murdered all the Jews? Since they were so disliked, they should all have emigrated.'"

Their old neighbor Marianne Weber was against the Nuremberg trials despite her liberal beliefs, and Trude Jaspers found her unsympathetic to persecuted Jews, Edgar noted. "I think their concepts of right and wrong are completely confused." Near the end of his stay, he elaborated from Nuremberg: "The Germans must suffer from a complete atrophy of the mind, otherwise they could not have reduced their most horrible misdeeds to writing to the extent they did. If Goering reprimands Heydrich that 200 windows in Jewish stores were smashed in the face of a glass shortage, and tells him he should instead have killed 200 Jews, you will find that in an official 'memorandum of conference.' . . . But I still have to find a German who has a real feeling of shame. They are all so small-minded, even the Heidelberg professors, that their only worry is that some party member who really 'wasn't so bad' was thrown out of his job by the Americans."

His conclusions about Germany were, he thought, quite definite. What he called his "check-up on history" had not been a sentimental journey. As he wrote to Brigitte on November 29, "I think my attitude towards the U.S. is changing. My reactions to Europe were so different from what I expected, and this includes Vienna. My hatred, dislike and indifference to the fate of Europe are growing every day. We are all having the same reaction, it seems to be a natural one. I am very grateful for the experience, but don't want it to be prolonged beyond the three-month period. . . . I am not fit to live in ruins, physical or mental." Had some of that ruin invaded his own peace of mind and undermined his efforts to distance himself? He was longing to be safely at home with his family. A few days later, he added, "All of us without exception hate Germany and hope that we shall never see it again."

After taking a last walk through the ruins of Nuremberg with a German Jewish colleague, he wrote in his journal: "My feelings are devoid of any sentimentality or pity. This had to happen to the German people, after the misery and devastation it has wrought upon others. There has always been in history a collective responsibility of a people for the misdeeds of its rulers." When the Nuremberg verdicts were announced in the fall of 1946, he commented to Brigitte, "I would not have acquitted von Papen and I am doubtful about Schacht, but the gradations of the others' punishments seem fair to me. [Army Field Marshall] Keitel should be hanged twice, he was perhaps the worst of the lot, from what I saw in Nuremberg in the way of his memoranda."

Edgar's rejection of Germany and Germans was well in tune with the reactions of other Jewish and non-Jewish Americans who served in Germany during those chaotic postwar months. He was also aware of missteps and disorganization in the American mission to reeducate the Germans through the spectacle of the trials and the denazification process. Nonetheless, his pride in being part of the Nuremberg War Crimes Tribunal would never fade. Because he died in 1991, he just missed the revival of Nuremberg protocol in the United Nations International Criminal Tribunals for the former Yugoslavia in 1993, and for Rwanda in 1994. During his lifetime, the Tribunal's rebuke to Fascist Germany had stimulated a revival of natural law theory in American jurisprudence, creating a somewhat more receptive place for Edgar's work in the postwar period.[9] And he had done what he could to keep the memory of Nuremberg alive. Near the end of his life, on the fortieth anniversary of the 1946 judgments on key Nazi defendants at Nuremberg, he gave the last version of his lecture on legal aspects of the

International Military Tribunal. He began with a very brief section on his own participation, with a few examples quoted from Nazi files on preparations for war and the extermination of populations. The rest of the lecture addressed the legal status of the trials, carefully setting out each objection raised by the defense and describing the arguments used to justify the work of the tribunal. Avoiding any overt expression of emotion, refusing to dwell on the Holocaust itself, it was a late effort in Edgar's dedication to principles of international justice.

"I hope never again to set foot on German soil," Edgar declared to the Levys after his return to the United States in 1945. That determination was not fated to last, nor was his proclaimed indifference to European history. As early as 1953 and again in 1959 he would return with his family, on Fulbright-sponsored summer teaching and lecture tours. After all that he had seen and heard in 1945, he continued to respond to the call of his native land and language, in ways that other refugees and many American Jews found incomprehensible. Why? No one else on the Bodenheimer side of the family had any interest in renewing German ties; the extended New York family and the German Jewish community there were enough for them. Edgar might have said that his belief in educating the next generation of Germans, as well as his endless curiosity about developments in postwar Europe, had led him to change his mind. I would add that America never entirely won his heart, that he remained an ambivalently homesick European for the rest of his life. Because had left Hitler's Reich early on, he may have faced fewer inner obstacles than later, more desperate refugees would feel.

Some might frame my parents' decision to return in terms of forgiveness: Could one let go of hatred and bitterness about the genocide, or not? A crucial point lay in the way one imagined the *Hitlerzeit*, the years between 1933 and 1945. If those years meant that the German people had participated in a course of murderous evil beyond imagination, then one might well vow never again to set foot on German soil. If they meant that the country had gone mad for a certain length of time, after which the Nazi house of cards collapsed in on itself, one could believe that a new German democracy could emerge, and that normal life would resume after that interval of aberration. This latter approach had little to do with the emotional work of forgiveness.

As he had so often done, Edgar retreated from his absolute rejection of Germany once events in the family and the political world shifted. His returns in the 1950s were officially part of the American effort to spread democratic ideas through cultural exchanges between Germans and Americans.[10] More personally, they were determined by the decisions of his parents-in-law. Immersed with all his formidable powers of concentration in fourth-century Rome, Ernst Levy in 1945 wanted to believe in the aberration theory of Nazism. Although he was a popular teacher at the University of Washington, his life's work depended on access to German libraries, German colleagues, and German audiences familiar with Roman law.[11] Ernst had been lucky: he had continued his research under the auspices of an American university. But he had not recovered from the shock of exile.

Edgar's trip to Heidelberg in 1945 brought Ernst the welcome news that Karl and Trude Jaspers had just missed their scheduled deportation, and that Wolfgang Kunkel, Ernst's closest German colleague, had survived his army service in Hitler's *Wehrmacht*. When postal service between the United States and Germany resumed early in April 1946, Levy's first letter went to the Jaspers couple, celebrating their renewed family connection. But the resumption of his dialogue with Kunkel, expressed in a letter of September 15, 1946, is especially moving. Each of them had taken the initiative to get in touch with the other that July; their first letters had crossed in the mail. It showed, Ernst wrote, that "in all those tragic years we had kept one another in mind." Like Kunkel, he was grateful for the good luck that had kept him afloat amid general bad luck. Yet, he confessed, there were moments when gratitude did not suffice, when "the break in the line is experienced as a fresh wound." Kunkel's own struggle with adversity was not less, he surmised, though it was more national than personal. But who could really establish the boundary between personal and national? The general collapse might well be the more difficult.[12]

In the very act of writing these meditations, Ernst Levy was hoping to reconnect the broken line between pre- and postwar history. He went on to describe the work he had done in Seattle and plied Kunkel with questions about former colleagues and the state of Roman law scholarship in Germany. The urgency of his wish to fill in the gaps and link himself to the pre-Nazi past is evident. And his lifelong correspondence with Wolfgang Kunkel, preserved for posterity in Dorothee Mussgnug's 2005 edition of their letters, testifies to the notion of an interrupted but continuous line of professional trust and friendship.

Working it out in life would prove to be an altogether more complicated affair. Ernst and Marie did not return to Heidelberg and take up their former lives, nor did their personal wounds heal. Instead, they played a kind of hide-and-seek game with Germany.[13] Ernst's sabbatical in 1947–48 was spent in Basel, Switzerland, the university town that nestles closest to the German border, providing easy access to colleagues and libraries at Heidelberg and Freiburg. At that time Kunkel was serving as rector of the university at Heidelberg, and he reached out to bring his older colleague in touch with old and new faculty in the field. During these immediate postwar years the anti-Nazi old guard of Heidelberg resumed its intellectual salons. Marianne Weber and her brother-in-law Alfred Weber, among others, were active in political debate, looking forward to a unified, neutral Germany governed by Social Democratic principles, while Karl Jaspers published *Die Schuldfrage* (*The Question of German Guilt*) in 1946, calling all Germans to a truthful investigation of the degree of guilt they had incurred during the Nazi regime. Ernst Levy may have been reassured by the activities of his acquaintances, but liberal discourse peaked in the late 1940s. During the 1950s former Nazis dominated the university; even Wolfgang Kunkel and Alfred Weber were defending Heidelberg against accusations of reactionary activity. As Steven Remy writes, "By the 1950s, this culture of forgetting at Heidelberg was entrenched as it was throughout West Germany." It would not be until the 1960s that "substantial cracks in the Heidelberg myth" would begin to appear.[14]

In 1952, when he turned seventy, Ernst Levy retired from the University of Washington. Brigitte kept a news photo of her father surrounded by apparently adoring full-skirted coeds who had brought farewell gifts to his last class. It's one of the rare photos in which Ernst Levy is relaxed and smiling. Perhaps American students had worn off some of his stern Germanic edges, but he was not ready to give up on his German center. The chronology of the next four years is not entirely clear to me, but it involved frequent trips between Seattle and Germany or Switzerland. The Levys had a residence in Heidelberg for about two years between 1952 and 1954, though I am not certain they lived there continuously. The lingering shades of Nazi feeling during those years resulted in a four-year uncertainty about where to settle. In 1956, when commuting between countries became too strenuous, they moved to Basel, where Karl and Gertrud Jaspers had also established themselves. It was a compromise, Ernst explained to Max Kaser, a German colleague in Roman law. "But even now the feelings of hate have not vanished, and we cannot take it upon ourselves to confront them at our age, after all our experiences."[15] He was a European once more, but the break in the line had not been repaired.

Rector Wolfgang Kunkel's gracious invitation to Edgar, offering him summer courses at Heidelberg in the summer of 1953, was certainly prompted by the presence of Ernst and Marie Levy. If Edgar had any doubts about returning to Germany eight years after his Nuremberg experience, there were many circumstances to override them. He had a strong connection with his parents-in-law, and Heidelberg was still dear to his heart. Brigitte had not returned to Germany since 1934, and he wanted to share the experience with her. She had not participated in the fierce anti-German feeling that pervaded the American occupation in 1945, and she seemed eager to reestablish connections with the German friends she had nurtured with food packages since the end of the war. Edgar had been unable to arrange a trip to Berlin in 1945; now the two of them could revisit the city of their births together, as well as other places they had known separately before the Nazi period. The politics of divided Germany and divided Berlin fascinated Edgar, and he wanted to get some first-hand knowledge of the situation. And the Fulbright exchange program, established in 1946 as a central feature of America's cultural mission in Europe, had just begun its Program for Germany. Edgar's application was accepted, and he was flown with the first group of American Fulbright scholars to Germany, landing in Frankfurt on May 30, 1953.

Without the benefit of Fulbright funding, Brigitte and the children travelled by boat. My brothers were about to turn fifteen and thirteen; I was six. The MS *Goya*, a small freighter in the Holland-America line, took just a handful of passengers. We had a wonderful time: the captain took the boys on the bridge and showed them how the ship was steered, and we shouted our breakfast preferences from the deck down to the cook in the galley. Brigitte made friends with a Swedish Mr. Thelander whose good works for the world made him a soul mate, while I fervently admired his black beret. Our happy adventure came to an abrupt halt, however, once we all arrived in Heidelberg.

What were they to do with the children in Germany? Clearly this had been a question as Edgar and Brigitte planned the trip. They would be based in Heidelberg for the two months of summer classes, but Edgar had set up lectures at several other German universities as well, and they would frequently be on the road. Our grandparents were unprepared to take charge of us during those trips. Marie had found my parents a tiny apartment in Heidelberg, too small for comfortable family life. And surely the children should have stimulating educational experiences of their own; Brigitte was always intent on making sure that we did. If nothing else, we were expected to learn German, though—or perhaps because—our parents had never actively established a bilingual household.

The solution they arrived at was to put us into the care of German strangers. Edgar escorted Peter and Tom to a kind of boarding school in Heidelberg, while Brigitte took me to a *Kinderheim* a long train ride away, in the Black Forest above the town of Freiburg im Breisgau. German parents saw nothing amiss in placing young children in institutional "children's homes" for periods when it was inconvenient to have them around. But we were not German children, and—though I was not conscious of this at the time—we were Jewish children at a time when the existence of Jews was barely mentionable in Germany. Yet somehow, under the pressure of their own needs, our parents and grandparents went temporarily blank about issues that otherwise concerned them. Children were seen as adaptable and unencumbered by adult history, and it was supposed that we would quickly get used to our foreign surroundings, cheered on by letters from our parents. It would be part of our *Bildung*: an immersion language-learning experience like the ones both our parents had had in England during their teens. In my case, I would guess, they also banked on the argument that children learn languages much more easily when they are very young.

We were Americans of course, but our parents assumed that we would take on native colors for the duration of our European visits, and for the most part, we complied. I absorbed the idea that it was somehow better to be European, but my childhood experiences in Germany did nothing to endear that culture to my heart or my imagination. The whole question of our relationship to our parents' native country was ambiguous—as was their own. Had they decided they wanted us to know German after all, now that the Nazi horror was receding into the past in the face of Cold War politics?

In our household, the Holocaust was a powerful but rarely mentioned presence. We knew that Hitler had killed millions of Jews, including distant members of our parents' families. Every so often such a person might be named, and my mother's eyes would focus very far away as she quietly noted that he or she was *umgekommen*. Nothing more was to be said. *Umgekommen*: it was always the German word, uttered into the distance, and carrying the particular passivity of perishing, not being murdered or killed. Our families were not "survivors," yet we were somehow connected with the fates of those who were. Edgar and Brigitte did not want to burden their children with the weight of the Nazi past, but the emotional repercussions of family silences on such matters would take me a long time to figure out.

None of these questions trouble Edgar's "Diary of the European Trip, 1953," which was kept in much the same way as the Nuremberg journal, except that this one, like most of his other personal journals, was written in German. The diary does not touch on Edgar's primary activity, which was teaching at Heidelberg. Like the earlier journal, it is a record of what other people said, primarily on three topics: the state of Nazi and anti-Semitic feeling in Germany, the emerging differences between West and East Germany, and the possibility of reunification. During that summer most of Edgar's interlocutors were educated Germans he and Brigitte already knew, or people to whom they were introduced in the course of their travels. Reading the journal is like listening in on a cross-section of contradictory opinions on subjects that historians of our time can weave into a single narrative.

Tony Judt, for one, writes about the connection between forgetting and rebuilding: "The distrust of short-term memory, the search for serviceable myths of anti-Fascism—for a Germany of anti-Nazis, a France of Resisters, or a Poland of victims—was the most important invisible legacy of World War Two in Europe. . . . Without such collective amnesia, Europe's astonishing post-war recovery would not have been possible."[16] As Edgar noted when he touched down for the second time at Frankfurt, the place looked quite different after eight years, with dense traffic that made it look like an American city. He seemed encouraged by early signs of the *Wirtschaftswunder*, the German economic miracle of the 1950s. He also recorded the opinions of someone who distrusted "the American-owned Adenauer administration" and its reliance on American money. According to this man, "uttering platitudes is now the fashion" among Germans clinging to what they had and unwilling to think about politics.

When it came to collective silences about the Nazi period, Edgar seemed rather baffled about how to feel. On the one hand, he liked hearing stories about Germans who were especially sensitive to Jews because they felt a sense of responsibility for what had happened. Marie's doctor in Heidelberg was his first example, and a few others led him to conclude that the many educated and cultured Germans felt an honorable sense of collective guilt. Separating "cultured" Germans from the masses on the subject of anti-Semitism was a dangerous business, but it came naturally to a man of his class who was ready to reexperience his German roots. Edgar recorded with interest what an old friend of Brigitte's had told her about the apparent erasure of Nazi feeling in the populace: "It was amazing how the blots of Hitlerism in people's characters had been left behind. The people are exactly as they were before 1933. The militarism, arrogance, and hardness that Naziism brought out seem to have simply disappeared from people's faces. When I was here in 1945, the 'steel-hard glance' was still there to be seen." The statement touched a chord; it was what Edgar wanted to believe in 1953. He took the idea at face value, never stopping to consider what might have motivated the speaker.

At times, Edgar's journal would revert to his more cynical 1945 mood: "The Germans one meets try to reassure you how anti-Nazi they were, and how much they did for the Jews. Frau—, the landlady at the parents' house, told them she had nothing to do with the police state, and that she even had a Jewish banker (!)" In yet another counterpoint, there was the Jewish woman who hid in a forest hut outside a German village and said that all the villagers had kept her secret and hidden food parcels for her. Late in the war, one person pointed her out and she was deported. In 1953 she was back, a member of the Jewish Society in Heidelberg. "There are still three Jewish children in Heidelberg!" Edgar noted, forgetting momentarily about his own.

Like other American observers, Edgar now embraced the notion that a newly American-made Germany was a place of optimism. What he made of it after his return can be seen in brief talks he gave to members of the two synagogues in Salt Lake City. Revising his earlier private pronouncements, he argued against the concept of collective guilt, giving examples from the range of experiences he had recorded in his journal. If Germans did not rise up against the Nazis, it was because they were "motivated by fear and a feeling of helplessness, often also by opportunistic considerations. Germans are not different from other peoples." He had seen very few remnants of the Nazi spirit and very little interest in militarism. It was the military high command and the industrialists who had largely supported Hitler's imperial ambitions, not "the common man." And, he noted wryly, he had heard of little anti-Semitism, "one reason being the lack of an object." Anticipating the sentiments of American Jews in his audience, he referred to a personal struggle: "Should Jews go to Germany at all?" But if the Austrian-born Israeli philosopher Martin Buber was willing to lecture in Germany that summer, then so was he. He rested his case.

Like American policy makers in the postwar period, Edgar had turned from the Nazi past to the Soviet present: the division of Germany and the condition of Berlin, which had been transformed from the occupied capital of the Third Reich into the central touchstone of the Cold War. In June 1948, responding to the Western Allies' plan for a West German state led from Bonn, Stalin cut the rail lines linking West Berlin to West Germany. His hope that the blockade would force the Allies to quit Berlin altogether, or to abandon plans for a West German state, did not pan out. Three days later, the Berlin Airlift began: for eleven months, the Allies would fly food and supplies into West Berlin, keeping their half of the city alive until Stalin turned the electricity back on and allowed the trains to move. An officially divided state, a rearmed West Germany, and the NATO Alliance against the threat of Soviet force were soon to follow. The Americans, the Soviets, and West German Chancellor Konrad Adenauer would continue to pay lip service to German reunification while they all banked on the political advantages of the status quo.[17]

Edgar's journal recorded a variety of opinions on the questions of German reunification, though most of his German subjects expressed little hope or desire that it would occur. His Salt Lake City audiences heard something very close to the prevailing Cold War story as it was told in the United States. Citing the deprivations of life and freedom in East Germany, Edgar suggested that West Germany was now America's best friend in Europe. The dreams he had dreamed in his twenties, about the emergence of a just and homegrown German Communism, were no longer on the horizon.

The most compelling pages of Edgar's 1953 journal are devoted to the four packed days he and Brigitte spent in divided Berlin. They were fêted at the Free University, where Edgar delivered his lecture "Normativity and Realism" in legal philosophy, but their true purposes were to walk the familiar streets, find the old landmarks, and get a sense of the divided city. Edgar's nostalgia went unexpressed, but it is evident enough in the unusual concreteness of his writing. He named the streets they walked on, the routes they took, the cafés they visited, and his pleasure in the atmosphere at the Berlin Opera. Berlin was far behind western zone cities in the rebuilding process. "Rubble-women" were still at work collecting usable stones and laying them in neat piles on the edges of the street for building contractors to collect. Edgar's visit to the wrecked Bodenheimer family home on Jagowstrasse produced just this comment: "Only the back wall and back balcony remain of the house, and the rubble lies around messily. The garden is entirely overgrown and wild." But a quest for the manor house built by Brigitte's grandfather Emanuel Wolff, now located just over the line in East Berlin, brought personal memories into direct collision with a historical moment in eastern zone politics.

Traffic between the two sides of Berlin was still possible in those years before the Wall went up in 1961. Streams of eastern zone refugees were coming through West Berlin on their way to settle in the west, creating anxieties for both regimes. Brigitte and Edgar talked freely with acquaintances who had chosen to live in either the western or the Soviet zone, and who expressed strong opinions about the bad faith of those who had chosen differently. But it also happened that their days in Berlin coincided with an event that would come to be known as the East German Uprising. Stalin had died on March 5, 1953, opening the door to thoughts of change. On June 17, four hundred thousand workers in East Germany went on strike to protest unpaid increases in the official work norms. The largest and most active demonstrations occurred in East Berlin. They were violently put down by police and Red Army tanks; hundreds of protestors were killed, executed, or imprisoned.[18]

The next day, apparently unaware of the magnitude of these events, Edgar and Brigitte found that they could not walk through to Berlin's central square, the Potsdammerplatz, and were told that the West police had barred it to keep out job seekers from the East. That wasn't the real story. Located close to the dividing line, the Potsdammerplatz had been an especially violent site during the uprising of the previous day and was now roped off.

Brigitte and Edgar took a different route and persuaded a policeman to let them go to a street corner where they could catch a glimpse of her grandparents' house. No one was around, and Brigitte wanted to sneak around the corner to get a closer look, but Edgar saw that "out of the doorway of a bombed house two Russians in olive-green uniforms and a policeman were moving in our direction. So I held Brigitte back and we left. A few hours later, a German who stood at the border and went over the Potsdammerplatz was wounded by five bullets in his arm." Impressed by their brush with real-world danger, he missed the political implications of the East German repression.

Five months later, now informed about the context for their adventure, Edgar gave an account of that day during a lecture about Germany at the University of Utah. There were really three Germanys, he said; West Berlin was a political entity of its own, with an atmosphere quite different from cities in West Germany. Their walk on the morning of June 18 had been "to convince us personally that the iron curtain runs right through the middle of the city."

> We were in Berlin during the memorable days when the people of the Soviet sector of Berlin and the Soviet zone expressed their dissatisfaction with communism by riots, demonstrations, and overt acts of defiance, like hauling the red flag down from the Brandenburg gate in the center of the city. During these exciting days, East Berlin was hermetically sealed off from West Berlin, nobody could cross the zonal line, and when we reached the border between the two sectors, we were facing Russian guns and several people from West Berlin who inadvertently entered Soviet territory were killed or wounded.

He loved being close—but not too close—to the heat of history, the bearer of news direct from the European front.

The returns of 1945 and 1953 were recorded in very different keys, but there was a coda yet to come. Had I not been there myself, I might not have remembered that Edgar spent the summer of 1959 as a visiting lecturer at the University of Freiburg. Three formal letters of arrangement from the Freiburg law faculty were stuck into his professional files. Otherwise the record is nearly blank: no personal letters, no journal. The second Berlin crisis had begun on November 10, 1958, when Nikita Khrushchev demanded that the Western Allies pull their troops out of West Berlin, beginning a three-year period of tense negotiations that culminated in the erection of the Berlin Wall in 1961. Was Edgar compelled by this situation to be back on the German scene? Was he simply interested in a repetition of the energizing experience of 1953? Certainly there was no personal connection in Freiburg that could compete with his warm reception at Heidelberg six years earlier.

Edgar and Brigitte were together and the Levys were close by in Basel; that may be a reason for the absences in Edgar's letter files. But I suspect that he may have thrown out some correspondence because the third return was an unhappy one. I do not recall how Brigitte was spending her time in Freiburg, though I imagine she had been reluctant to leave her work behind. I was twelve years old and wanted desperately to be at home with my friends. My brothers were living their own lives by that time, though twenty-year-old Tom was contributing to our parents' comfort by house sitting in Salt Lake City and sending detailed accounts of work-related correspondence that arrived for them in the mail. My parents and I were living in a small pension hotel in Freiburg, as not-quite-American, not-quite-German guests. Busloads of American tourists would come through for a night or two, exacerbating the in-between status: we were most certainly not like *them*.

I was not separated from my parents this time, but Brigitte enrolled me at the nearby high school where she had spent the happiest years of her girlhood, indulging her desire that parts of my childhood might echo her own. In 1959, the appearance of an American girl was an event. My new classmates linked arms as they strolled the school courtyard during the first recess: "Are you Catholic or Lutheran?" When I said "Jewish," they said nothing. For young postwar Germans, there was no available reaction to this fact. Besides, I was small, shy, unfashionable, and therefore not really American. My best friend during that summer was a small silent refugee from East Germany who had been taken in by her West German aunt and cousins. But my main solace was the library at the *Amerika Haus*, where I could lose myself in books written in English.

Like the Fulbright grants, the America Houses were cornerstones of the postwar US cultural mission to Germany.[19] They provided open-stack libraries of English-language works, German books that had been banned by the Nazi regime, films, lectures, discussions, and children's programs intended to acquaint the populace with American democracy and culture. In a rather ghastly irony, the America Houses were themselves subject to book banning and purges of liberal personnel in 1953, during the anti-Communist reign of Senator Joseph McCarthy and the House Un-American Activities Committee. Anything remotely connected with Communism was removed from the shelves, leaving Germans and Austrians with plenty of opportunity for skeptical jokes. Yet the program survived that unfortunate interlude and continued its contribution to the Americanization of Europe. Lingering in the stacks at twelve, I had no idea about any of this. From my point of view, the Freiburg *Amerika Haus* had one function: to shelter and entertain a homesick American girl. Books in English, my childhood refuge, would later become my profession. Studying British literature was just European enough, a halfway point between America and Germany.

I finally discovered one clue that testifies to Edgar's own discomfort during the summer of 1959. On March 20, 1960, he gave another talk to members of Temple B'nai Israel in Salt Lake City, in which he outlined his three returns to Germany and his conclusions from the latest one. The prevailing attitudes in Germany, Edgar said, were economic self-satisfaction and political apathy. If Germany had made progress physically and economically since 1953, it had, in his view, deteriorated ideologically and politically. He meant that the overwhelming silence about the Nazi period threatened a return of nationalism and race prejudice. (A rash of anti-Semitic demonstrations had occurred in Germany during the winter of 1959–60, raising Nazi ghosts.) Children were not taught about the Nazi period in history classes. It was "an offense against good manners to talk about the events of 1933–1945 in respectable society. It is felt one should not dirty one's own nest." The Germans, in his view, needed "to purge themselves from the collective crimes of the past, by an unqualified rejection of the years of national shame." But the chances for such a change were slim. "Not much can be expected when 500 former Nazis sit on the benches of the German courts, some of whom have been responsible for monstrous judgments during the period of the Third Reich." The United States was not blameless: "The Germans feel that the United States has completely forgiven them for the outrages of the past. Because of this, they see no reason why they should not forgive themselves." America counted among the villains, as if the failures of the American denazification campaign now stuck in Edgar's throat.

My father's private states of mind can only be surmised from his intellectual generalities. In his renewed bitterness, did he now sense that he, too, had been too quick to forget, if not to forgive? What had happened that led him back to concepts of collective guilt and national shame? His change of mood may have been triggered by personal experiences he did not want to record. Perhaps his colleagues in Freiburg rebuffed his efforts to question them about the state of the German soul. He may have been put off by the success of American influences on German ways of life. Brigitte's feelings about the German Question would have touched him, but they cannot be recovered, though she continued to keep in touch with individual friends there. Whatever the case, Edgar did not repeat the university teaching experiment. The urge to crack the postwar silence had emerged in him—a shared desire that would grow ever stronger on the international scene during the 1960s.

The rebirth of dismay did not mean that Edgar would never visit Germany again. Warmly hosted by close colleagues of the Levys, he gave a single lecture in Hamburg on June 29, 1961, on the way home from a Swiss vacation with his parents-in-law. Later in life there would be other brief visits, following the public outpouring of Holocaust memory in the 1960s and 1970s, and official German efforts to acknowledge Nazi crimes against the Jews. In 1973, Edgar returned to Freiburg alone, as a visiting scholar in a faculty research seminar at the Max Planck Institute for Foreign and International Criminal Law. By then he was sixty-five, and his zest for personal confrontation with his German homeland had run its course.

Edgar's quite different moods in 1945, 1953, and 1959 had been largely determined by the prevailing political winds during each phase of Germany's postwar history. His appointments there had allowed him to become a minor cultural intermediary, bringing his concepts of law and justice to young Germans, and news of German developments to audiences in Salt Lake City. His shifting attitudes reflected current events, but his intellectual life remained faithful to the Enlightenment values that had initially shaped his German *Bildung*. The last article he published, at the age of eighty-two, was a defense of Hegel's philosophy of law against those who accused the philosopher of proto-Fascist or revolutionary tendencies.

# 7
# Family Law, Natural Law

On April 8, 1951, the Sunday *Salt Lake Tribune* carried a story called "Law vs. Family: A Career Doesn't Outshine Home." It featured a picture of Brigitte, Tommy (age eleven), and me (age four) dressed up and focusing with apparent pleasure and interest on a picture in a book that looks suspiciously like a collection of Swiss mountain scenes. "Occasionally you meet a woman who is endowed with the ability to do two jobs at once—raise a normal American family and successfully pursue a career of her choice," the article began. Turning us into a "normal" family seemed to be the leading message: the writer emphasized that Brigitte was no more a career woman than she was a homemaker, and that she was raising three "healthy, well-rounded children." The photo caption informed the reader that Peter, the eldest, was away at a Boy Scout powwow. The occasion for this article remains unclear, though it does mention that Brigitte had now begun to practice law in Salt Lake City.

For Edgar, as for the *Tribune*, it was a point of honor that his wife did not work during the first three years of each child's life. His support of Brigitte's profession depended on maintaining a principle of gender difference: once women had fulfilled their responsibilities to their husbands and children, they were free to pursue careers of their own. Brigitte's version, in her 1979 retirement interview, sounded quite different. "And again, I came to Utah, we had a house, there was nothing I could do. So one year later I took the bar exam. At that time it was a six-day examination. A really exhausting kind of thing. . . . It was taken in the Utah capital, in the Senate chamber, and I would take my outline in the car as my husband drove me up there, and I would read those outlines until at the very last minute I would give them to him and go in. So that was the only thing I did until our daughter was three." Oh, and perhaps Dean Leary had given her bits of work as well, though he barely paid her, and "he didn't think women knew anything anyhow . . . though now one of his daughters is a law professor."

Figure 17. The Bodenheimer children in 1951: Peter, Rosemarie, and Tom

She didn't mention that she was also helping her father by translating some chapters of his book *West Roman Vulgar Law* into English. For her, those stints of full-time motherhood were important, but her affectionate attention to her children required the relief of concentration on something else.

Set down in Utah, Brigitte gradually managed to create a career out of virtually nothing. No law firm had a position to offer, though for a while she acquired a desk in the back room of a legal firm specializing in real estate. Since she had few clients there, she ended up helping the lawyers in that firm, for little or no pay. She also took on cases for German Jewish immigrants who were applying for restitution payments from the German government. *Wiedergutmachung*—literally translated as "making good again"—was a pledge of monetary reparations to Jewish survivors of concentration and labor camps, pushed through the German Parliament by West German Chancellor Adenauer in 1953. It was later expanded to include many other categories of loss.

"There weren't that many [survivors] in Salt Lake City, and it was a very tedious kind of work, corresponding with lawyers in Germany and learning all those different laws and regulations," Brigitte said. But her clients "would talk, about all the kinds of problems they had; we became quite good friends. And some of them had really had horrible experiences, and we would try to get compensation for damage to their health, damage due to loss of earnings, and so on. Some had been in concentration camps." Many of her clients had lost the documents that could prove their claims, so Brigitte would have to take lengthy affidavits of their experiences and certify them. Although I did not hear much about their stories, my mother did convey a sense of the suffering to which she was bearing witness. Through her work, the Holocaust made its way into our household. Some clients became parts of our lives in other ways: the seamstress who sometimes made clothes for my mother and me, and the delicatessen owner who kept our family supplied with European specialty foods. Brigitte did not know how to charge for her legal services, so she "sometimes got gifts from them, because they didn't think I asked for enough." The cases dragged on for years, their sadness overshadowed by the tedium of negotiating thickets of red tape.

Meanwhile, Brigitte was keeping her eyes open for any opening in government work. One day she read in the *Salt Lake Tribune* that a lawyer in the Attorney General's office had died. He had been working on retirement benefits for public employees, which Brigitte had handled at some point during her time at the Federal Housing Authority. With the tenacity she had shown at Columbia Law School, she went to someone who knew the Attorney General and asked for a letter of recommendation. She was quickly taken on as a Special Assistant to the Attorney General, in charge of checking the constitutionality of the retirement law in question. Undaunted by the Attorney General's indifference to the outcome, Brigitte decided to go all out for constitutionality, and learned the subject cold before arguing it in both a lower trial court and, on appeal, in the Utah Supreme Court. "And I still remember that I had lunch with my husband and I said, I'm just not able to do that. I had never done such a thing—stand up in a court and argue that case, and he thought I would just collapse or something! It turned out that it was wonderful, nobody knew anything about the subject, and the judge was perfectly willing to listen, and I gave him my whole argument. . . . It must have been something like three-quarters of an hour." It was the theme of her professional life: the pleasure of knowing more about a subject than anyone else in the room. Doing the brief in the Supreme Court was "really a *lot* of fun. Because you have those five judges, they don't know about the subject, *you* know about the subject, they ask you questions."

As a result of Brigitte's arguments the law was declared constitutional, but it had other problems. Because of her performance in court, she was asked to join the Legislative Council of the state legislature to help draft a less expensive public employee retirement law. Once again, she was "so scared" to appear as an expert at the legislature's hearings, but "I was the one who had studied the most. So the people on the Legislative Council deferred to me. And that was passed in that legislative session. Then I got caught in legislation." She became the go-to person for drafting legislation in Utah. By the end of 1954 she reported to her parents that she was in the thick of legal work, busy with bill drafting, an adoption case, a divorce case, and her *Wiedergutmachung* clients.

That year, by way of another news article, Brigitte found her calling in family law. A citizen's committee interested in establishing predivorce counseling services announced their need for a volunteer lawyer. Brigitte stepped into the breach, beginning a long saga she called "a completely consuming occupation for about three years." Her actual dedication to this unpaid labor lasted longer and established the expertise on which her future work would be based. The political battle lines were intense. The idea of the law was to attach state-run marriage counseling services to divorce courts, and to require counseling during a waiting period before divorce proceedings would begin. Most lawyers were not interested in having social workers intervene with their clients to create marital reconciliations, while the Department of Public Welfare was a leading force in favor of required counseling, "because they wanted to cut down on welfare and felt that the divorce rate raised the welfare." Brigitte became familiar with every level of Utah politics, regaling her family with accounts of each loss and gain, each hero and villain. She was training herself to be an expert lobbyist in the halls of the state capitol, the outward mildness of her manner masking her shrewd assessments of the people she was trying to persuade. The Marriage Counseling Law, as it was popularly called, was passed in 1955 and promptly vetoed by the governor. Brigitte left the state for the academic year 1955–56, when Edgar took a visiting lectureship at Yale. When she returned, she rejoined the Citizen's Committee on Divorce to revise the bill, which was voted into law and signed by a new governor in 1957.[1]

Ten years after her arrival in Salt Lake City, Brigitte was committed to staying there. The idea that Utah would be a two- or three-year stopover had long faded away. As she wrote to her parents in February 1957, the skiing was good for the whole family, while the combined presence of university, legislature, and Supreme Court in the state's capital was good for her. Although the bulk of her work was unpaid, it was satisfying. She had published a useful *Manual for Justices of the Peace in the State of Utah* the previous year. She was now working with the Women's Legislative Council, and she had recently lectured about the divorce law at a County Bar Association meeting, where she had addressed about eighty people, including most of the Utah Law School faculty, from a microphone at the head table. "The lawyers don't want divorce counseling," she confided. "They're afraid that they might miss out on a couple of cases (that make up about half of the legal work here and all over the country)." Mormon Utah, with its family-centered religious community, was apparently no exception to the rule.

Her fears about the divorce reform were well founded. By 1961, most of its provisions had been repealed, leaving only a required three-month "cooling-off period" and a few other provisions. Brigitte detailed the rise and fall of the Utah Divorce Law in a long article called "The Utah Marriage Counseling Experiment: An Account of Changes in Divorce Law and Procedure," published in the *Utah Law Review* in 1961, the first of many articles she would publish in the field of family law. The centerpiece of her argument was an explanation of the practical and prejudicial circumstances that had made a full implementation of the Utah law impossible. As she wrote to her parents, the failure of the law was "all about political deals." It was a pity, she thought, because many *einfache Leute*—that rather condescending German term for simple, not highly educated people—who would not otherwise have been able to afford counseling, could have benefited. She could afford to confide in her parents, but her article displayed the even-handed diplomacy that was to mark her style. Among other things, she had learned that one could not impose a law on a judiciary that was hostile and unprepared to change its ways. She had also experienced the difficulty of creating successful collaborations among people trained in the different professional languages of psychology, psychiatry, social work, and law.

Still, she stuck to her belief that it was desirable to reform the laws of divorce in ways that responded to the actual confusion and pain of families, in the hope of reducing the divorce rate and mitigating its effect on children. Her writing was a straightforward, skillful blend of detailed legal expertise and attention to the many variations of particular human experience that she wanted the laws to address. Brigitte's sympathy for the plights of unhappy families led her to feel that the state should be responsible for creating paternalist legislation that would counteract or restrain the domestically irrational behavior of *einfache Leute*. She was in favor of updating divorce laws to eliminate the idea of fault and to make "marital breakdown" a sufficient cause, but she was indignant when anyone made light of the seriousness and disruption that divorce entailed. As she wrote in "Reflections on the Future of Grounds for Divorce," "No person in our age should be chained to another in an intolerable marriage. Those who made a serious mistake and those who experience a severe deterioration of their marital relationship, should have a way out, which is fair, dignified, and comparatively simple without being precipitous or hasty. But the law should seek to prevent divorce which is sought for reasons which are trivial, frivolous, or irresponsible."[2] Her blend of liberalism and paternalism is on full display in this statement.

Brigitte's second legislative campaign in Utah was more successful. In 1960 she was appointed chair of a Special Commission on Juvenile Courts, under the auspices of the Utah State Bar Association. Her UC Davis colleague Carol Bruch explained the work in a tribute to Brigitte's career: "Her committee prepared a complete revision of the state's Juvenile Court Law, including a proposed removal of those courts from the then-existing control and supervision of the State Welfare Department. Two stormy legislative sessions and constitutional litigation followed, but the project's eventual success brought about more than a reform of the Utah Juvenile Courts."[3] After the law passed in 1965, Brigitte heard a rumor that "some of the [Juvenile Court] judges would give their lives for you." "So now," she joked to her parents, "I have to be Mama to these judges and worry about them."

In fact, her attention was quickly turned to another arena. As Carol Bruch noted, "Governor Rampton, impressed with Brigitte's scholarship and legislative know-how, appointed her as Commissioner on Uniform State Laws for the State of Utah in 1965."[4] She would be the state's representative to the National Conference of Commissioners for Uniform State Laws, which dealt with problems arising from overlapping or conflicting state jurisdictions. Just a year later, Brigitte had to resign the position when she moved to Davis with Edgar. But the appointment signaled the beginning of her most important work, as draftsman and publicist for Uniform Codes regulating both interstate and international decisions on matters of child custody. She was particularly disturbed by disruptions in the lives of children caused by divorced parents who stole their own children across state or national boundaries in order to get custody for themselves.

Soon after her arrival in Davis, Brigitte was reconnected with the National Conference on Uniform State Laws when she was asked to serve as Reporter to draft the Uniform Child Custody Jurisdiction Act. Approved in 1968, the Act was gradually adopted by most states, though not without difficulties that Brigitte followed and described in a series of articles that outlined the full legal history of the problem, the failures of current standards, actual cases of dilemmas that needed to be fixed, and ideals toward which the legal community should strive. Sanford Katz, a family law expert from Boston College, described Brigitte's basic approach in a 1982 memorial lecture "Brigitte Bodenheimer: Protector of the Children": "Profes-

Figure 18. Brigitte in 1965

sor Bodenheimer's greatest contribution to the law and the profession is, of course, her work on the Uniform Child Custody Jurisdiction Act. To her, the Act represented the best effort to minimize the times a child's life should be upset. She thought that once a custody award was made, it should stick. Modifications should be infrequent. Decrees should be honored in sister states. By respecting custodial decrees, children's lives have the possibility of stability. 'Children, like delicate plants,' she wrote, 'should not be uprooted from their surroundings if at all avoidable.'" At least in 1982, Professor Katz shared Brigitte's resistance to the growing trend toward joint custody arrangements, which could work only if divorced couples maintained "long-continuing, amicable working relationships" in geographic proximity.

Brigitte's work differed from Edgar's in just about every conceivable way. While he theorized about an ideal social order, she advocated for practical reforms. His writing was done with a very broad brush; hers was all about brass tacks. But they shared a kind of idealism they had learned during that particular shared moment of Weimar culture in Germany. They both imagined a benevolent paternalist state that would allow individuals to develop their potential within a context of rational order and security. Brigitte was, I think, far cannier about how things were and how particular people would behave in reality. But, like Edgar, she despised cynicism and cultivated optimism about the possibility of human progress even when their experiences and feelings might well have suggested otherwise.

Brigitte began to consider teaching as early as 1957, but she didn't think she could join the faculty at the Utah School of Law because of strict nepotism rules preventing spouses from serving in the same department. Edgar's generous friend and colleague Daniel J. Dykstra had succeeded Spencer Kimball as dean of the Law School in 1954; he knew what Brigitte had to offer. When Dykstra became Academic Vice President of the University in 1961, he managed to waive the nepotism rule in her case, allowing Brigitte to teach as a lecturer in the law school. By 1964 she had been appointed Associate Professor and was whipping up new courses on a wide array of subjects including commercial and criminal law as well as family law. "Don't worry too much about preparing," Edgar would tell her—but he had done the same.[5]

There was little time to rest on her laurels as a professor. When Edgar took the UC Davis position in 1966, Brigitte had to start the whole academic process over again. Nepotism rules there consigned her to an office as an unsalaried research professor until 1971, when she became a lecturer, followed by an appointment as full professor in 1972. Through all of this she continued to work and publish articles on aspects of the Uniform Child Custody Jurisdiction Act and its successor, the Hague Convention on International Child Abduction. Whether or not she was preparing classes and reading exam blue books, she was often on the frantic verge of a deadline. As Carol Bruch fondly wrote, Brigitte was "a member of the 'Brinksmanship School of Research and Writing.' Somehow, for her the right word or the solution to a thorny problem often seems to come only long after the painstaking hours of research are completed and occasionally, indeed, after the editor's 'deadline' is past."[6] Though I saw my mother infrequently during the Davis years, I do remember the intensity that accompanied critical moments of her reform work in Utah and California.

After just seven years as a UC Davis law professor Brigitte stopped teaching, a year before she had reached the usual retirement age. As she wrote to her dean, "I wish to retire one year early because I find it increasingly difficult to devote sufficient time and energy to several projects to which I have committed myself. During the last few years I have been called upon increasingly to assist with attempts to solve some of the burning legal problems concerning child custody disputes following divorce or separation." She went on to list five different kinds of national and international drafting and consulting services she was doing without compensation, adding, "I feel a strong responsibility to do what I can to avert disastrous decisions and laws and bring about beneficial ones for the ever-increasing numbers of children of divorce." The urgency of her voice suggests the internal pressure she felt, to be Mama to all those unknown children and to worry about them.

Brigitte did not complete any of those five projects. Life had another, crueller deadline for her. The Hague Convention on International Child Abduction was adopted on October 25, 1980, in her absence: she was at home undergoing radiation treatments that failed to arrest the rapid course of her cancer. Her death at sixty-eight, on January 7, 1981, was sudden, unprepared for, and devastating to me and everyone else who knew and loved her. At that moment I was just half her age, and we were on the verge of becoming closer as adult friends. Had she lived longer, I might have come to know more about her internal landscapes. What were the costs of her drive to maintain both her strong sense of family duty and her intellectual ambitions, during a period when few women made the attempt? Because of her habitual stoicism, Brigitte's inner ways of experiencing life remain somewhat mysterious. Like the swerves into shorthand I found in some of her little diaries, her private meditations were hidden in a code that's only partly legible.

Ten years after her death I was asked by Professor Harry Krause to contribute something to a tribute he was preparing for a Symposium on German Jurists in Exile, held in Bonn in 1991.

Brigitte Bodenheimer was the only woman on the roster of the twenty-one jurists, whose careers were presented in papers written by younger colleagues. This is what I wrote for Professor Krause at the time:

> My mother possessed a strong intellectual power and drive, mixed with an extremely modest and flexible nature—a rare blend. Perhaps because of this, and the demands of a family, she really did not emerge as a recognized and decently paid professional until the age of 50, when she began teaching at the University of Utah. Before that time she did an extraordinary amount of work as an unpaid lobbyist for the Utah legislature. For a while her most visible work (to the child's eyes) was the group of *Wiedergutmachung* cases for which she acted as an attorney, and which she conducted from a desk at home. I think of her full emergence into the professional world as a kind of explosion, or release of energy that had lain half-used and almost invisible to others until her middle age.

I would not write in quite the same way now. It is certainly true that Brigitte waited for her professional time to come. But part of the invisibility I mentioned in 1991 was my own lack of vision, a child's inattention to the lives of her parents. Writing this book has shown me that Brigitte's expertise was always appreciated by those who worked with her. No one who did so failed to understand her competence and dedication, and many went further, to offer her jobs and significant public responsibilities. These, in turn, depended on her freedom to work without compensation during significant stretches of her twenty-five-year career in family law. Edgar's salary sufficed for the modest life we lived in Salt Lake City, supplemented by Siegmund Bodenheimer's college trust funds for his grandchildren.

Hovering over every aspect of Brigitte's life, there is the question of attitudes toward professional women in the middle decades of the twentieth century. Had she been a man, she would doubtless have secured jobs as an attorney in Seattle and Salt Lake City. Instead, she got her "interim periods" to bear and raise children—children she loved and worried about no less than those hypothetical children of divorce. Once I had gone off to college, she flourished professionally as never before, becoming a mentor, friend, and counselor to younger women lawyers and professors. But, as the world gradually turned toward feminist goals, she did not jump on any bandwagons. She cared about using her brain, the work, the service, and the responsibility to contribute. She didn't much like people who made a fuss—about women, about her, or about themselves. She was more interested in the shared concerns of human beings than in the differences between men and women. The tradition she served was older and less collective than American second-wave feminism. In his essay on Brigitte's work, Harry Krause cited Peter Pfund, the US State Department's attorney for private international law, who had worked with Brigitte on drafting the Hague Convention on Child Abduction. In Pfund's words, "She came out of and personified in the best sense the German-Jewish-Democratic tradition of social responsibility and activism."[7]

Edgar's attitude toward Brigitte's career mattered the most, of course, and it was not simple. They read each other's drafts and suggested revisions—but she made the indexes. He assumed that she would follow him wherever his professional life led, and she did so. Nepotism rules were only the tip of the iceberg when it came to obstacles in her path. As the daughter of a German professor, she had been raised to serve both her husband's and her father's requirements, at home and at work. She did not rebel against that role but tried to combine it with her own ambitions, fitting them in where she could and allowing them to expand once her children were old enough to take charge of their own lives. If she wrote professionally about children as delicate plants, she tended to assume that, once well rooted, her own children were rather hardy varieties. Still, we needed attention, and so did Edgar, who assumed that Brigitte was first and foremost for him. There were times when one of her commitments had to give way to another. Edgar was proud of her achievements, but he was a German man of his time, minimally available for childcare or nurturing, and sometimes impatient when his wife's deadlines pulled her away from conversation with him. Brigitte might let off a tiny puff of steam by joking about having to be Mama to those Utah judges, but she tried to play all the roles expected of her and always worried about whether she had done enough.

Like Brigitte, Edgar found Salt Lake City more congenial than he had originally expected. New law school colleagues arrived and became friends. In 1950 he was released from the librarianship and became full professor the following year. As he later summarized, "[I] taught a considerable variety of subjects, among the History of the Civil Law, History of the Common Law, Elements of Law, Jurisprudence, Constitutional Law, Equity, Modern Social Legislation, Unfair Trade Practices, and International Law. This immersion in numerous positive-law subjects was very helpful for my jurisprudential research, inasmuch as it provided me with a great deal of case law examples for buttressing general and abstract propositions." He was good at those positive law subjects and enjoyed inventing complex hypothetical situations to which his students had to apply relevant case law. As a child, I loved to read his exam questions, which were like tiny novels with amusingly named characters. I was impressed by his piles of blue books, with students' names and red-penciled grades on the front, and the variety of handwritings inside—doomed from the start, I suppose, to an academic life of my own, so long as the field could be as far as possible from my father's abstractions.

The Law School at Utah was known for its good teaching, but Edgar still yearned intermittently for a grander home, especially when he saw himself in relation to other émigré jurists who took positions at major universities. Many of them were well-established scholars in Germany or Austria before emigration and had European reputations to recommend them as he did not. Especially during the immediate postwar years, the moves of such figures from one university to another were always on Edgar's radar. His dream was to teach at Berkeley, though he knew it was a very long shot.

In 1947 Utah instituted a system that gave professors one quarter off in each academic year for "self-improvement." Edgar spent about a month doing research at Berkeley during his first quarter off in 1948, writing frequently to Brigitte. Polish-born Max Radin was about to retire, allowing Edgar to stoke his fantasies a bit, but early in February Alfred Ehrenzweig, formerly a professor at Vienna, got the appointment to what might be called the refugee position. Looking on a bit wistfully, Edgar felt that Berkeley was "really the ideal. Simply a paradise in every respect: library, landscape, excitement, climate, beauty." He concluded, "Nothing will come of it, I think." After he had established himself as a scholar, Edgar carried on a long correspondence with Ehrenzweig during the 1960s. Although

Ehrenzweig bemoaned Edgar's refusal to take psychoanalysis seriously, and Edgar swallowed his German skepticism about the "Viennese schmoozer," they exchanged ideas and friendly critiques of each other's work, agreeing to disagree in both English and German.

Berkeley was also exciting because it gave Edgar access to older scholars like Hans Kelsen, the Austrian Jewish legal philosopher Edgar had met in 1940 during his visit to the law faculty at Harvard. An important legal theorist, Kelsen now taught in the Berkeley political science department. The two men's views were quite different; in fact, much of Edgar's work was a critique of Kelsen's "pure theory of law," which separated law from external normative or ethical considerations. Nonetheless, Edgar enthused, "One can't talk in this way about jurisprudence to *anybody*. He is so clear, so rich in intellect, really goes inside the other, so it's possible to have a real exchange. . . . It's quite good to be in the larger world once in a while." It was like talking to Heidelberg professors of Ernst Levy's generation; they shared a vocabulary and European habits of mind. Kelsen's contributions to the legal background of the Nuremberg war-crimes trials may also have been a bond between the two men, though their dialogue seems to have been limited to a few encounters during Edgar's month in Berkeley.

Meanwhile, there was talk of a new law school about to open at UCLA, and Edgar wondered whether he should indicate an interest. Brigitte was skeptical. "I would hate the 'Hollywood atmosphere' for the children and high prices and unnecessary elegance and all that. Kaethe says we haven't even gotten warm here." After mentioning it to her father, however, she came around to advising that UCLA should be taken seriously. Nothing came of Edgar's 1949 application. The family put down roots in Utah, while Edgar contented himself with his cherished "good conversations" at the various legal conferences he attended. He maintained professional friendships with a number of émigré jurists scattered around the country and pursued intricate correspondences with other legal philosophers about articles and books they or he had published. Gradually the combative tone of argument he had learned from German academic life softened into a more tactful American style. As in his early conflicts with his father, he did not like sustaining an antagonistic relationship with other people even when he was convinced that their ideas were wrong.

Edgar's hunger for connection with the wider world was answered by intermittent visiting positions, seminars, and lectures. In "Returns," I have described the postwar visits to Germany. The year 1955–56 brought the family east for a visiting lectureship at the Yale Law School, supported by a Rockefeller Foundation grant. We arrived in the New Haven area just in time to drop Peter off for his first year at Harvard and to watch Hurricane Betsy

Figure 19. Edgar in his office during the 1960s

rage outside our windows. If Edgar had any private wishes about Yale, they were soon dimmed by the prevailing doctrine of legal realism he found there. From New Haven we went west for a summer term at the University of Southern California, where we rented a small house in Hollywood without great damage to our souls. During that year Edgar was working hard on revisions of the 1940 jurisprudence book; as early as 1947 he knew that a second edition would be necessary to fix its "many inadequacies."

The much revised and expanded book, now called *Jurisprudence: The Philosophy and Method of the Law*, had a rather long period of wandering in publishing wilderness before it was accepted at Harvard University Press and published in 1962. Sanford Kadish, a good friend who had taught criminal law for ten years at Utah, pulled some strings to get the manuscript read while he was in Cambridge as a visiting professor at Harvard. By then Sandy Kadish had moved on to the Michigan Law School; in 1964 he landed in Edgar's dream spot, Berkeley, where he would later serve as dean of the Boalt Hall law faculty. Some years after Edgar's death Kadish and his wife, June, established the Kadish Center for Morality, Law, and Public Affairs, meant to encourage research and discussion of moral and philosophical issues in law and public life. Edgar would certainly have approved.

The newly organized *Jurisprudence* was Edgar's central contribution to his field. Its first section provided a textbook grounding of jurisprudence in the history of European philosophy, giving American students of law or political science a condensed overview of that tradition, from the Greek playwrights to the revival of natural law thinking after World War II. Edgar's years of teaching American students had given him skills and perspective he lacked in 1940: he was now an expert synthesizer who could assess what his audience was likely to know, and not to know. As an outsider to the field, I learned a lot about the successive stages of legal philosophy by reading my father's succinct formulations, which are especially helpful when it comes to the classical natural law tradition and the German transcendental idealists. Like many of his reviewers, I found myself admiring the lucidity of his style. As he describes the historical alternations between theories of natural law and theories that separated law from values, Edgar maintains a stance of objective description. However, even I can see that his desire for objective analysis is impossible to maintain. The questions he brings to each thinker are questions that belong to his own primary concerns: How is the relation between law and justice treated? What is the role of human reason in this theory? What does this theory have to say about unjust laws perpetrated by evil forms of government? Throughout, he has a tendency to link natural law philosophies with emancipatory social policies and to assume that philosophies of law have a direct impact on the shape of civilizations.

As he brings his historical survey to an end, Edgar asks, "Is there any rational thread running through the perplexing multitude of legal theories which were reviewed in the preceding chapters? . . . Or, must we conclude that these points of view signify nothing but the subjective and irrational predilections of their authors, with the consequence that no objective validity can be attributed to them?" That, in his view, would be a "black" picture indeed. Instead, he wants to think, "These philosophies form valuable building stones in the total edifice of jurisprudence, even though each of these theories represents only a partial and limited truth" (151–52). His "edifice" image is a wish about his own work and the work of civilization in general: that philosophical discourse could shape such a building—strong, secure, integrative, and above all, rational—within which human beings might live in harmony. It's an image fired by his fear that Nazi Germany, which had disrupted his own security and brought chaos to civilized life, would appear again in new forms. "If the search for justice and reasonableness in law is abandoned by the best minds on the grounds that justice is a meaningless, chimerical, and irrational notion, then there is danger that the human race will fall back into a condition of barbarism and ignorance where unreason will prevail over rationality, and where the dark forces of prejudice may win the battle over humanitarian ideals and the forces of good will and benevolence" (156). Edgar could sound like a prophet or missionary when he touched on the quick of his fears. That sense of imminent crisis and disaster sets his work apart from anything an American legal philosopher would write and helps to explain why Bodenheimer does not figure much in the work of later American natural law scholars.

In the middle section of *Jurisprudence*, Edgar tried to build a jurisprudential "edifice" to his liking, sentence by sentence (or brick by brick). Its two supporting pillars are order and justice. Chapter 10, "The Need for Order," begins, "The institution of law is closely related to man's perennial search for order, regularity, and fixity in human social relations" (161). Edgar attempts to ground this need in the natural world, as if the law of gravity that holds the solar system together were a "natural" equivalent for human systems of orderly organization. He is aware of the uncertainty principle in contemporary physics; nonetheless "the predominantly law-governed character of at least all large-scale operations of nature must still be admitted" (164). As the analysis goes on law is defined as the mean between anarchy and despotism, providing stability and coherence in the social order. But it must constantly be checked for its responsiveness to social life and for its accommodation of fairness and justice.

The second pillar, justice, is deeply linked to natural law, while natural law is linked with rationality. Edgar writes, "The natural law is to a large extent rooted in the cognitive faculty of human beings, which recognizes the social dangers resulting from man's irrational impulses as well as the necessity for a rational control of those impulses through the agency of the law" (193). Its rules, which prevail whether or not they are embodied in actual legislation, derive from essential human needs for food, sleep, sex, children, and, of course, survival. The recognition that others have equal rights with the self is also a rational process as Edgar envisions it. Reason, rather than love, sympathy, empathy, or imagination, is responsible for overcoming self-oriented feelings and desires and recognizing the otherness of others. Edgar's reliance on an Enlightenment view of reason suggests the undimmed power of his early liberal education. The lessons of those formative years overshadowed any attempt to bring his view of the human mind and brain into significant dialogue with twentieth-century developments in psychology or neurology.

Reviewing the 1940 version of *Jurisprudence* in the *Columbia Law Review*, Lon L. Fuller, a central figure in American natural law philosophy, put his finger on an essential problem in Edgar's assumptions: "I am myself disturbed by the fact that at points the antinomy of power and law seems to be identified with the conflict of the rational and irrational forces in human life. If 'law' is viewed as a manifestation of man's rational nature, surely 'power' cannot be the opposing term. . . . The irrational side of man's being is certainly capacious enough to contain something beside a lust for domination over his fellows."[8] Edgar paid attention to a number of Fuller's specific critiques when he revised the book, but he could never let go of this antinomy. His subsequent work would return to it again and again, clothed in slightly different guises.

Whereas American legal philosophers are most likely to link natural law with the individual's rights to equality and freedom, Edgar is far more concerned to maintain a balance between (rational) social restraint and individual liberty. In his temple of jurisprudence, the potentially conflicting pulls of legal order and social justice must work together; law, in his words, is a synthesis of order and justice. His methodology is ultimately simple: set up the two sides, and then argue for a utopian mean. What's missing from that formula, and what I cannot reproduce here, is the scholarly care with which he explores every angle of each side, distinguishes each abstract term from the others, and communicates the urgency of keeping the ongoing process of normative jurisprudential thinking alive. Although few would follow in his wake, that scholarly care may have ensured that *Jurisprudence* stayed in print as an example of natural law thinking for students.

The 1962 edition of *Jurisprudence* was widely and favorably reviewed, if not by the leading scholars Edgar may have most wished to hear from. The reviews came from all over, written in English, Spanish, Portuguese, French, German, and Hungarian. As its shelf life continued, the book was particularly valued in countries that were emerging from periods of severe political repression. Translated into Spanish, it was popular in Latin American countries. In 1988, to Edgar's great excitement, it was translated into Chinese and set for a large print run in post-Maoist China, as the country prepared to open itself to the western tradition of legal thought. In his preface to the Chinese edition, Edgar named "certain basic values that transcend the relativity of any particular social and economic structure. Prominent among these values are liberty, security, and equality."[9] By this time "security" had replaced "order" as the key conservative term in his philosophy of law.

The publication of the revised *Jurisprudence* in 1962 also brought Edgar the most serious job offer to date, from the University of Texas at Austin, where he had taught a course during the summer term. Edgar and Brigitte agonized about the Texas decision for two years. I would be starting college in 1963, so it was a good time to move. Edgar would have a colleague in jurisprudence, his choice of courses, and the opportunity to teach doctoral students in law. Texas was rich, and expanding. But it had strict nepotism rules that sounded unbreachable, and Brigitte had just begun to teach in Utah. The decision was put off for a year. Then, on November 22, 1963, President Kennedy was shot in Dallas. The horror Edgar and Brigitte shared with the nation was edged by their memories of violence in Germany. Their

Utah colleague John J. Flynn later presented a memorable picture of Edgar on that day:

> I recall hearing the news on my car radio as I was leaving the law building at Utah to head home for lunch. I went back into the building and stood in a state of disbelief in the hall talking with a member of the staff and trying to make sense of it all. I recall Edgar walking quickly down the hall, his face drained of all color. I rushed over to him and we clasped hands without saying anything. For an instant, I fully appreciated what his life must have been like back in the early 1930s because I think I saw it all flash before his eyes once again in 1963. Edgar was deeply upset and unable to speak. I thought he had visions that a coup d'état was underway and he might find himself stateless once again or, even worse, being treated as less than a human being once again. It was only for an instant, but I will never forget what I saw written on Edgar's face at that instant. I saw a lifetime of fear, anger, and torment over what had happened to him as a young man and what had happened to his friends, family, and others who had not been able to escape. I understood then why jurisprudence, and a belief in the necessity for a moral content to law, if a society is to be civilized, had become not only this man's life-long academic interest, but his central intellectual conviction and passion as well.[10]

I don't know how Edgar felt about having his inner life interpreted in the pages of a professional journal, but I am grateful to John Flynn for putting the case so beautifully.

After that, the culture of Texas could not help but become a strong emotional element in my parents' thinking. In the end, Brigitte's work may also have been a deciding factor. Did her Utah appointment as Associate Professor in 1964 have anything to do with the university's desire to keep them both there? Or did Brigitte, for once, make clear her reluctance to move to Texas? I was not in on their extended dialogue, so I cannot say, but they remained in Utah until 1966. When they moved to another university with nepotism rules, they did so along with their friends Dan and Lily Dykstra, invited by another colleague, Edward L. Barrett, who served as founding dean of the new law school at UC Davis. The small collective migration west carried an implicit hope that Brigitte would regain a faculty position if it became possible. It made a difference that Edgar and Brigitte would be going to Davis with people who already knew and respected them both; it was not quite like starting over. And, unlike Texas, California had mountains and natural beauties of its own. You just had to drive a little farther.

Figure 20. Brigitte and Edgar in their Davis living room, 1978

At sixty-seven, after nine years on the UC Davis law faculty, Edgar retired from full-time teaching, but his habitual workday did not change. He continued to teach courses in the Law School and the School of Administration. He would always be a writer; the Davis years added three books and many articles to his already substantial bibliography. The books, *Treatise on Justice* (1967), *Power, Law and Society: A Study of the Will to Power and the Will to Law* (1973), and *Philosophy of Responsibility* (1980), were published by small presses and did not make much of a ripple. They expanded on certain subjects he had treated in *Jurisprudence*, fighting a rearguard action against the various liberation ideologies of the American sixties and seventies. Edgar was upset by the disrespect for law and family morality he saw in my generation of students and felt increasingly like a prophet crying in the wilderness. His political liberalism sat with some discomfort alongside his social and moral conservatism.

As I imagine them now, his books were arguments with himself and with his German heritage in all its facets. His main antagonist in *Power, Law and Society* was Friedrich Nietzsche, who had fascinated him as a young man. The threat of social chaos was never far from his mind, yet he thought he ought to be an optimist about human nature and social organization. He did not take altogether easily to the messiness of family life, but he believed in the family as an idea and did his best to play his part. He was a bit of a loner, but he insisted that the development of a civilized individual could only occur within a stable collective. As Raymond Dennehy pointed out in an essay on Bodenheimer's theory of natural law, the internal arguments of his books were also divided against themselves, wavering among intellectual allegiances of different sorts.[11] Although Edgar reached out to different fields—anthropology, physics, sociology—for help, the difficulty of grounding a secular theory of natural law in human nature remained an insoluble problem.

In Edgar's writing, a hostile representation of someone else's theory would often be revised, qualified, or later revisited. Because of that, it is sometimes tempting to see his intellectual life as a continuation by other means of his difficult relationship with his father, which alternated between resistance and the need for reconciliation. That thought would, rightly, have made Edgar angry. The emphasis belongs with the historical trauma he suffered, and with its lifelong reverberations. The "Hitler shock," as my uncle Teddy Blau once called it, had pounced when Edgar was twenty-five, just poised to enter German society as a professional with a promising future. The self-making he had so carefully cultivated was abruptly declared worthless, his membership in the state annulled. The story I have been telling here is not a particularly dramatic one in the annals of Holocaust history, but it represents one man's way of building a productive and positive life around a major disruption of habit, language, entitlement, and expectation. Writing his way back to a just society was Edgar's way of deflecting the blow.

# 8
# Gray Lady

Whenever I thread a needle I remember her. *Langes Fädchen, faules Mädchen*, she would say—long thread, lazy girl—but gently, as if murmuring a little rhyme that had floated in her head since her own childhood. She was the one who taught me to sew; watching her, I learned how to iron a shirt. Her room was at the back of our Salt Lake City house, looking over the branch that held my swing, the arbor with its sour grapes, the sweet apricot and rotten apple trees at the far back. It had a full-length mirror coming down to child height; when I made faces at myself she'd warn I'd turn into a monkey. The closet, a good hiding place, was full of old-lady shoes and rarely worn dark silk dresses. The table beside her bed held a radio, a framed photo of a man reading with a handkerchief in his breast pocket and a cigarette in his lips, and a small magnifying glass that swung neatly out of a brown leather case engraved with her initials: K.S. A few novels in English sat in the small bookcase on top of the dresser, among them a Modern Library edition of Henry James's *The Portrait of a Lady* with a red cover. The title was alluring. Years later I would write about the novel in my doctoral dissertation, making use of that very copy.

Who was she? Family member or housekeeper? It was never entirely clear, though she was occasionally referred to as my grandmother Rosi's cousin. Her name was Kaethe Mathilde Sachs, but my baby talk turned her into "Gaga." She helped with the cleaning and cooking and ate with the family; there were always six places to set at the dinner table. She didn't go on vacation with us, or appear downstairs when my mother entertained law school faculty friends. When I got home from school, she would give me milk and cookies. When my friend Toni came over to play, she would make us picnic lunches to eat under the grape arbor, pouring our milk into empty peanut butter jars with their tops on to keep out the flies. She was always around, if never entirely present. There was a grayness hanging about her, not only because her hair was gray and her housedresses colorless. Although she helped take care of me for the first fourteen years of my life, my memory of her is blurry. She was like a woman whose real life had been over for a long time.

Some years after Kaethe died, my mother sent me her dressing gown as a keepsake. Hanging in my closet, it is both familiar and exotic: a silk kimono, very soft to the touch, lined in dark maroon and printed with a garden of beautiful multicolored flowers. Its extravagantly long wide sleeves, squared off at the bottoms, would make it difficult to perform most household tasks. Where did she get it? What richness of life and taste does it recall? Once in a while I put it on and wonder, though it is a little too capacious for me to wear.

I was in my fifties before I woke up to another feminine legacy Brigitte had smuggled into a package she had sent to me, long after Kaethe's death. It is a soft black leather accordion case, the size of a small book, made in Berlin. It holds a few remnants of Kaethe's life. The man reading in the photo was the older cousin she married and lost to illness early in her adult life. The little magnifying glass was as I remembered it. There are two official documents. One is an olive-colored identity card issued by the Berlin police in 1939. Kaethe wary, dead-eyed, thin-lipped, appears in a photo stamped over twice by the imperial eagle of Nazi Germany. Her name has been changed from Kaethe Mathilde Sachs to Kaethe Sara Sachs, according to the Nazi regulation that imposed the name Sara on every Jewish woman. Next to the photo are fingerprints, both right and left forefingers, nothing left to chance. The particulars are written out in meticulous Gothic script. Occupation, *ohne*—none. Comments, *keine*—none. She had been made into a woman without qualities.

The second document is a United States Certificate of Naturalization, dated December 3, 1946. The address is my parents' house on McKinley Street, N.W., Washington, DC. Her name has been Americanized but restored: Kate Mathilde Sachs. In the photograph she looks proud, alert, and well dressed in a suit with a little black bow at her neck. When she received this certificate I was almost two months old. In February Kaethe would take the train across the country with my mother, my brothers, and the new baby, to join Edgar in Salt Lake City. In 1962 she would be buried there in B'nai Israel West cemetery, a spot she never could have imagined during her Berlin life. How did all of this come about?

Lodged in the midst of our thriving family, Kaethe Sachs was something of a mystery woman. Her story is important to this book because it offers an alternative view of German Jewish exile, one that carries the sadness and loss that were largely hidden, or turned in academic directions, in the lives of my parents and grandparents. For the length of this chapter I will restart the chronology, to narrate what I have learned about Kaethe from her Berlin origins to her life in Salt Lake City. This partial biography is based on fragments: slips of personal writing and photographs I found in the black leather case, and pieces of information I have gathered with the help of a few others who once knew her and the people around her.

Kaethe's early life was nested in an extraordinary group of cousins whose lives helped shape her own. Filled with loss and disaster, her later years were spent caring for other people's households and children. Her aspirations, her love of literature, her elegant clothing, her natural dignity, and her fierce need for love were gradually forced underground. I cared about her as a child accepts its family, without question. When I remembered her later, the memory carried a taste of sadness. In our diligent, energetic household she carried, unmentioned, the clouds of persecution and depression. Yet my attempt to track her history has opened windows onto a life among vital people who loved and were loved by her.

Born on August 6, 1883, Kaethe was the second daughter of Minna Lachmann and Immanuel Sachs. Her sister, Eva, was just sixteen months older; her brothers, Hans and Walter, two and three years younger. The Sachs siblings were especially close to two sets of first cousins in Berlin: Erich, Nina, and Vera Lachmann, and Rosi, Alfred, and Oskar Maass. (The older Lachmann generation had included ten children, so there were a number of other cousins scattered around Germany.) Rosi Maass's marriage to Siegmund Bodenheimer placed her in the most stable situation of the group, and the house on Jagowstrasse became a familiar destination for the Berlin cousins.

Among them Rosi and Alfred Maass were the only ones who produced children of their own. Suicides and early deaths put their marks on all three families. Rosi's father, Louis Maass, died at forty-four, in 1902, when she was sixteen. Her mother Henriette (Lachmann) killed herself before the First World War ended in 1918. Rosi's brother Alfred left safely for Palestine in 1933 with his wife and children, but her younger brother Oskar committed suicide to evade the death-grip of the Nazis in 1939. Both of Kaethe's parents died at fifty-five: Immanuel Sachs in 1904, when Kaethe was about twenty, and her mother, Minna, in 1912. The well-known architect Louis Lachmann killed himself at forty-nine because the misdoings of a business partner had brought his firm to bankruptcy. His daughters, Nina and Vera, were just ten and five years old. Their brother, Erich, would die four years later fighting for Germany, brought down on the French front during the first month of the war on August 29, 1914.

Hans Sachs, Eva and Kaethe's physician brother, died of cancer in May 1933. He and his cousin Nina Lachmann, who was fourteen years younger,

Figure 21. Kaethe Sachs

had loved each other for years, but he would not marry her, perhaps because he was wary about marrying within the family, perhaps because he could anticipate his own death by the time she was old enough to marry.[1] Well before Hitler threatened their lives, these families knew a good deal about personal tragedy and unfulfilled yearning. Early death for both adults and children struck frequently in all households of that period, and suicide was not uncommon in the German Jewish bourgeoisie. Still, the aftereffects of death in a particular family are not mitigated by statistics, or by the stoicism with which they are endured.

Hans Sachs's reluctance to marry his younger cousin may have been influenced by his sister Kaethe's experience. When Kaethe was about sixteen, her parents took her to visit an ailing cousin on her father's side, Eduard Sachs. She was immediately taken with him. For the next fifteen years she loved him and lived in the joy of his attentions. Finally, after the deaths of her mother and his father, they married rather inauspiciously on June 30, 1914, two days after a Serbian terrorist assassinated the Austrian Archduke Franz Ferdinand, precipitating the events that led to the First World War. Kaethe was thirty; Eduard about nine years older. Their happiness lasted less than three wartime years. Then, at forty-three, Eduard died suddenly, leaving her bereft. His health had always been precarious, and he died at home of illness, not of war wounds. Kaethe missed him for the rest of her life.

Those are the bare facts. A few surviving bits of writing, kept in the black leather case, surround them with feeling. The first is a small piece of brownish parchment filled with unrhymed lines in an exquisite small hand. The initial letter, as in an illuminated manuscript, is a large red D, drawn as if it were an organic being, with little nicks and branching pieces, twined around with delicate flowers and vines in black ink. *Du schaust bedenklich drein, ich weiss es wohl*, the verse begins:

> You look thoughtfully inwards, I know it well,
> Anxious, that I might be solemn, banal, old-fashioned.
> What do I know about what a modern couple hates and avoids?
> Yet I bring you the wreath according to the old custom,
> And I do it gladly, bring you with joy
> The old holy symbol of happiness, of faithfulness and purity.

It is Hans Sachs writing to his sister on her wedding day, asking her to accept the wreath as a symbol of her love of flowers, and of her siblings' hopes and love for her.

> So take the simple wreath as thanks from us
> To you, who have been at the center of the house,
> Who have steadily been its luck and its joy.

The holiness Hans mentions has nothing to do with Judaism; what's acceptably modern to him is ancient pagan ceremony. He gives us a glimpse of Kaethe's role in the household before and after the deaths of their parents. She was the one who nursed the dying and held things together while Eva and Hans pursued their work in classical studies and medicine. Although she was to lose most of her possessions, Kaethe held onto the little parchment tribute in remembrance of her wedding day, and of the talented, thoughtful brother who had died too early.

Kaethe's own fragmentary writings attest to her autobiographical impulse and to the intensity of her emotional life. Most of the surviving pieces seem to have been written in the late 1950s, near the end of her life in Salt Lake City, so they are pervaded by the sadness of a lost world recalled in old age. The fragments are in German, in Kaethe's large, quite legible handwriting, on assorted pieces of whatever paper came to hand. The longest, covering eleven pages of letter paper, relives early moments of love and loss as if they were, quite eerily, taking place in the immediacy of the present. I will let Kaethe's words speak for her.

> I have just torn up my diary. What does it mean to me now, if Galitz, in school, admired my embroidered belt, if Brutschke criticized my pronunciation, or Emmi Lindeman gestured with her white hands? This day, today, signifies "death." Can it be that Camilla, as the old porter at the house-door said, "lies in death"? Yesterday we spoke about Werther's sorrows, about summer journeys and her new velvet dress, and what can this mean, "dying," and he must not let anyone in? What is that, "death"? A memory comes to me; the fat woman in the white garb of a sister pointed into the children's room and said "He won't make it," and the other one just went in. And that evening in bed Aunt Tina: "Now the little twin is also dead." I didn't think about it. But now I am 16 and Camilla, my best friend, will be 17 the day after tomorrow, dead.
>
> No, the diary is useless. There are certain days when everything is unreal. But to whom can one talk, who has a youthful point of view? I hear the parents always talking about Eduard with worried faces, but one can't ask them anything, even though they are dear to me. Now I know that he's our relative, very ill, somewhere in the Black Forest, and that we are going to visit him. They must love him a great deal, otherwise they would not take this detour from our peaceful Wildbad. I gather that he has to pursue his profession *in case*, Father says, he gets better, and Mother says he is the best son, the best student in his field.
>
> Four weeks, the loveliest of my life. He *is* captivating, if he really, really means everything he says! I hope so! He will do his final exams in our town, visit us often, read with me, go to the theater and hear music. But what else do I know about him? That he treats me as an adult, asks me my opinion of Keller and Meyer and Fontane. What he *thinks*, who his friends are—nothing.

And now it is winter. E's father is seriously ill, he has been with him for weeks, apparently cares for him day and night, though he is so delicate. I worry! Never a line from him—what do I mean in his life?

The willow trees in the park have their feather-deckings. Now too we go to the Lake in the evenings—we? E with me. Often he takes my arm when it gets dark, and he talks of his father, whom he so loved, of his mother, who now tries to possess all his love. Then I must tell myself he brings out of me what's sleeping; I have no reticence, as with the parents or Toni or Lenchen or Dora. But when there are no more evenings, how empty everything is.

I am transformed, what has happened to me? Now everything pulls on me, I must, must, must—but what, I don't know.

So that's a kiss!

The park is full of magic and I know, or I intuit, how love can free the body. What will become of me? He has assured me that his love belongs to another.

I "know," now. And everything that I don't know doesn't bother me. Isn't *he* the one who has to think it over? "You have the power to become a major love"—do I understand that? No, I don't know anything and again I can't ask.

And I have not asked, not planned, not thought, but I have something of his soul. And for 14 years, *that* was life. No day without flowers, without gifts. How easily one lives in the beautiful. Sorrow and death in the immediate family—if he was there it was good, and death seemed part of life. 14 long years that seemed so short! as if strung on a pearl necklace. And then suddenly in the street came a stroke of lightning and then the question, "Why don't we marry?" Everything with him happened easily. "Yes, why not?"

The evening before the wedding the daily papers shrieked out the murder in Sarajevo. Would it have consequences?—but surely it wouldn't upset us personally? We stayed on the heights, the unimaginable heights, of the Engadine. But there was the war. Was it years, days, hours, in the lovely home, the death that came as a strangler from one day to the next, what did it leave me? Tears, tears, cold, a never-ending train of sad days, loneliness to the point of madness. But then his mother came, robbed as I was, but thinking only of me, understanding without words. She was the one who brought me back to the duties of life that became my own. And her death was blessed, her picture has often helped to give direction to my erring ways. Now I wish for a soft passing like hers, and one person who will yet bless my life.

Yes, she could write; after a youth immersed in Romantic literature, she kept the gift of vividness in her waning years. I think of her sitting alone in her room, with Bodenheimer life going on around her, thinking of death and recovering a small space for the intensities of her past. She tried another experiment in memory, creating a "Little Wishbook" that lists what she wished for at every age. At five, "never again to fall into the flowers." At six, "to have a red coat for school like Toni's." To always stay seven. She loved color and clothes: after the red coat there were patent leather shoes, long skirts, and a pink ball gown. Then more emotional wish-memories: "Camilla must not die." "The first kiss." "No fire, no coal can burn so hot." "To stay at the heights forever" recalls her honeymoon in the Swiss Engadine; from those heights, Alpine and sexual, she descended into fear, a country at war. "I will care for his mother to the point of death" (*bis zum Tode*). After that duty was concluded, the years are telescoped, marked only by gratitude to unnamed friends. The last wish, for "a new love," never came true. Only my parents were there to bless her passing, in the grip of dementia and paranoia, at seventy-nine.

Love, death, and loneliness were the themes of her life in exile. On June 24, 1957, she wrote heartbreakingly about the death of her husband forty years earlier. Fiction, memory, and fact fuse in her re-creation of painful emotions.

> Just One Night
> A soft groan now and again—the eyes closed. Does he not know me at all any more—does he not feel that I want to speak to him? Is it so bad? What did the doctor say? As under a cloud I hear his muted professional voice and I fly back to the bed, *our* bed! It cannot be—we have just begun our life. Your clear eyes, the hands that make me tremble with delight when they caress me, is there no safety? No, no God of love? The snow falls in thick flakes outside; inside nothing stirs, only the stranger nurse goes in and out, lays her finger meaningfully on her lips. But I; I lift him up, the body that no longer belongs to me. I plead for just one more look, one kiss. "You are still alive, you have slept for three days and nights"—there, a twitch, the lungs half open, looking across to her, the stranger, he calls clearly: she is the only one here in the house who tells me the truth.
>
> Can I go on living under this curse? In this house?

No one in my immediate family could, or would, have written like this. The last of her substitute children, I may have been closest to her in sensibility, though I did not think that when I knew her. From her silences

Kaethe watched people and tried to imagine their lives. The word "psychological," given little credit in my family, came naturally to her. She was a woman who left school at sixteen and read novels to experience the pleasures of identification and the wisdom of the narrative voice. Her writing aspires to rhythm, concreteness, and sensitivity to nature. When I first came across her scraps of written memory, I wept for a long time. For her, for everything I didn't know about her, for all the questions that children couldn't ask and all the pain adults couldn't express.

And then there is the story of her survival. To begin it, we must return to Weimar Germany. Rosi's cousins Kaethe and Eva Sachs were invited to Siegmund Bodenheimer's fiftieth birthday celebration on November 22, 1924. The long poem he read to his company that day made some mention of every guest. The sisters came at the end of the list, as the verse (along with my grandfather's tact) was winding down. Siegmund does not mention their shared surname, and he separated the couplets addressed to each sister. Kaethe, seven years into widowhood at forty-one, was noticed as a favorite specimen among the company of pretty women. Eva, Siegmund joked, almost rendered him mute in the face of the scholarly radiance that emanated from her presence. By the time I learned for sure that Eva and Kaethe were sisters, I had discovered an account of the brilliant, tormented Eva Sachs, a student and assistant of the eminent Greek scholar Ulrich von Wilamowitz-Moellendorf, who reigned supreme at the University of Berlin during the heyday of German classical philology.

Eva Sachs was born on April 13, 1882. Although she and Kaethe were so close in age, she does not appear in Kaethe's surviving memories. Eva was the older sister who went on with her education at the eminent Victoria Lyceum for girls, passed her *Abitur*, and matriculated at the University of Berlin in 1904, when she was twenty-two. Ten years later, after a wide range of study, she submitted her doctoral dissertation in Latin and, for publication, in German. Its title in English is "The Five Platonic Solids: On the History of Mathematics and the Theory of Elements in Plato and the Pythagoreans." The American classicist William Calder claims that it remains authoritative in its field. "Of the classical philologists of the golden age who were women," he writes, "she had only one rival—the editor of Suidas, the Danish Jewess, Ada Adler." Nonetheless, Eva Sachs disappeared from view until Calder wrote an article dedicated to collecting what was known of this forgotten life. Writing in 1988, he began, "Only three women of great age are alive today who knew Eva Sachs. The one who could say most will say nothing."[2] The unexplained comment suggests a larger silence that hangs over the subject. One of the two women who did speak testified to Eva's obsession with Wilamowitz-Moellendorf, and to her image of him as a Greek hero. She also mentioned the possibility of a sister who went to America after Eva's death—a sister about whom Calder remained in the dark.

His other informant, interviewed in 1974, was Vera Lachmann. Like her cousin Eva, Vera was drawn deeply into the German Hellenism of the period, though not into academic philology. At the time of the interview Vera was teaching classics at Brooklyn College and writing lyric poetry steeped in elegiac feeling. Calder's excerpt from their conversation mixes summary and quotation: "A brilliant Jewess, Assistentin to Wilamowitz, she helped much for the *Platon* [Wilamowitz's major book on Plato]. She was in love with Wilamowitz. Forbidden by Marie Mommsen [Wilamowitz's wife] to enter the house, she dared not even dedicate her book to him, as male students did . . . she was ugly and went mad, ending her life in an insane asylum, speaking ancient Greek and believing 'she could save Socrates if she got there in time.'"[3] It's difficult to imagine Vera saying that her cousin "was ugly and went mad," so the wording of this excerpt may derive from Calder's notes. Still, Vera may have experienced the later years of Eva Sachs, twenty-two years older than herself, as pitiable and discomforting. The reluctance to dwell on a family member who died in a mental hospital may be part of it; what remains unspoken is the suffering that Eva endured and imposed, inevitably, on those close to her. Vera was especially close to Kaethe during the years just after Eva's death in 1936; she would have known and sensed far more than these words convey. I have seen a photograph of Eva in her twenties looking scholarly over a book, and her face is far from ugly. Perhaps her hopeless idolatry of the extraordinarily handsome Prussian aristocrat who mentored her work had not yet begun to unmoor her mind.

Long-term unfulfilled love seems to have been a specialty of the Sachs siblings. Kaethe and Hans probably lived ordinary middle-class lives until his death and the Nazi takeover in 1933, but Eva's brilliant instability would have haunted their minds and made demands on their practical resources. Their younger brother Walter Theodor Immanuel Sachs, a World War I veteran, had converted to Lutheranism and married a Lutheran woman, Irma Schellhorn, in 1914, after a brief early marriage to another Christian woman from 1909 to 1910. His relationships with his siblings remain unclear.[4] After the death of their mother in 1912, Kaethe ran the household. At the time of Kaethe's marriage in 1914, Eva had her doctorate and a published book but lacked a clear path forward. She assisted Wilamowitz with his book and taught as an *privatdozentin* (instructor) at the University of Berlin but never progressed to the point of becoming a faculty member in her own right. Her gender, her Jewishness, and her personality were impediments, making her a tragic version of the hypereducated German Jewish woman with no substantial future. In 1933 she moved to Vienna. In 1935 she was admitted to a mental facility, where she died at fifty-four in September 1936.[5]

Eva's death may have been fateful for Kaethe, helping to determine the winding path of her escape from Germany. After her appearance in Siegmund Bodenheimer's birthday poem, Kaethe shows up once more in the Bodenheimer annals of the 1930s. She was the person who escorted Edgar's girlfriend Hesi into the Bodenheimer villa on Jagowstrasse in March 1934, for the meeting at which Hesi learned that the Bodenheimer parents knew nothing of her engagement to Edgar and were going to oppose it. As the Bodenheimers were packing for emigration, Kaethe talked to Hesi about the obstacles to her romantic hopes. Her role as a general intimate and helper in the extended family is apparent. Widows without children could all too easily turn into forgotten persons, so Kaethe was probably fortunate in having an extended Berlin family ready to welcome the presence of an all-purpose auntie.

When Kaethe next appears on the radar, she is engaged with another family, also apparently cousins of hers. Hermann Fränkel (1888–1977) had been a professor of classics at the University of Göttingen since the end of World War I. He may have been acquainted with Eva Sachs during the time he spent studying with Wilamowitz and others at the University of Berlin before the war, or they may have known each other through a family connection. In 1915 he married Lilli Fraenkel, the sister of a fellow classicist, Eduard Fraenkel (not a relation, for a change); the couple had three children. Soon after the Nazis took over the Fränkels and the Fraenkels emigrated to England. Eduard occupied the Chair in Latin at Corpus Christi College, Oxford, while Hermann was invited in 1935 to join the classics faculty at Stanford University. He and Lilli arrived in San Francisco on September 14, 1935, to begin a long and successful American life in California. Their two daughters, Edith (fifteen) and Brigitte (seven), joined them three months later, escorted by Kaethe Sachs, who had accompanied the girls from Southampton to New York on the SS *New York*, and from New York to San Francisco on the *Virginia*. I do not know how or when this association began. Perhaps Kaethe moved to England with the family and stayed behind to care for the girls while they finished a term at school. Perhaps she was summoned from Berlin to England to accompany the girls on their journey after their parents had settled in and established a family home in California. Whatever the details, it seems clear that Kaethe was seen, after her brother Hans's death, as a kind of free agent who was available for service to other families in her academic German Jewish milieu. Once arrived in Palo Alto, she stayed with the Fränkels, doing full-time duty as housekeeper. Her emigration from Germany would seem to have been safely settled.

In a letter of January 1936, Brigitte mentions to her parents that she had asked Kaethe to come to Seattle, so she and Edgar were already aware of her presence in this country. Many years later my mother would tell me that when she brought the Fränkel girls to the United States, Kaethe had smuggled out some illegal money at great risk to herself, passing it from hand to hand while she was being searched. In my child's mind the story floated in that vague arena of reference to "what had happened in Germany" and stayed with me as a vivid, scary image. For Kaethe, however, the real scariness was yet to come. In the fall of 1936 she returned to Germany.

Once out, why return? I entreat her when I discover this. The answer comes back: Eva dies; Kaethe has to bury her sister and pick up the family pieces. She would have gone to Vienna to close Eva's accounts, then back to Berlin. She owned a house at Bastianstrasse 6 in Dahlem, a country-like suburb of Berlin near the Free University. At some point she had professional-looking photographs taken of its interior, which survive in the black leather case. There is Kaethe, looking contentedly at home in various chairs next to conveniently arranged tables, bookcases, and lamps, dressed in a long black silk dress with white polka dots and an elaborate white collar. The ceilings are high, the floors scattered with small Oriental rugs. It's the style of frugal but cultured German Jews; there is the piano covered with its requisite fringed tapestry throw. Some pieces of furniture get photos of their own, as if Kaethe were hoping to identify and reclaim her property later in life.

Soon after her return, Kaethe had someone else to care for at Bastianstrasse. Vera's mother, Karoline Lachmann, died in 1937, and everyone knew that thirty-three-year-old Vera, her mind fixed on Greek ideals, could not take care of herself or deal with the simplest practicalities. She moved in with Kaethe. Vera's sister Nina had been helping to support the Lachmann women through her work as a musical event organizer, but she had left home to marry three years earlier. After the death of Hans Sachs, Nina had been introduced to a grieving widower, Paul Frankfurther, whose wife, like Hans, had died of cancer, leaving three children under the age of seven. Nina and Paul hit it off initially through their shared love of music. The Frankfurther household needed her; Paul's mother-in-law had been coming in daily to keep things running and care for the children until a better arrangement could be found. Nina was warmly welcomed by both of the children's grandmothers, who rejoiced when she married Paul and gave the children a loving stepmother.

Meanwhile, Vera was absorbed in running her school for Jewish children in the chauffeur's house on the Bodenheimer property in Grunewald. The cousins and others in their circle would sometimes meet at Kaethe's house, where she was happily in charge. As Nina's stepdaughter Beate Frankfurther Planskoy recalled when I visited her in London, they called her, fondly, "Katrinchen." Beate, who attended Vera's school and enjoyed visits to the Dahlem house as a child, remembered a feeling of embattled defiance among these men and women who, in the years before Kristallnacht, were holding on to their hopes for Germany's future in the face of increasingly threatening Nazi practices.

I like to imagine the three women together in Kaethe's house in 1937–38, poised there in a delicate bubble that history is about to break. All of them are rather small and dark-eyed. Kaethe is the mother figure, with short graying hair brushed back to her neck; she cooks for Vera and makes sure that she eats; she dresses well and takes care of Vera's clothes. When the weather is warm, she serves breakfast and afternoon tea in the garden. Vera, twenty years younger, can make Kaethe laugh. She comes home from her day at school full of stories about the children; she is attached to each of them in one way or other. She is attempting to create a little aesthetic Hellenic republic, where the students study languages, put on plays and Mozart operas, and hear the ancient stories Vera loves to tell: the Odyssey, and the Icelandic sagas. Her teaching voice, rich with reverence for the human spirit, gets affectionate and witty at home. The Frankfurthers live just a bus ride away, and ten-year-old Beate enjoys visiting her aunts in their comfortable household. Nina is often there, too; her dark hair, like Vera's, is pulled back into a bun at the neck, framing a lovely face. She is worried about her husband, Paul, and the three children she has taken on, but she is keeping things going, trying to figure out what's best to do in an increasingly impossible situation.

On November 9–10, 1938, there's Kristallnacht, Hitler's violent nationwide pogrom that came to be known as "the night of broken glass" because of all the smashed windows in Jewish synagogues and businesses. Suddenly the darkening world gets much darker. Jewish men are targeted for arrest and deportation. Paul is now managing to evade the Gestapo by moving surreptitiously between houses in which only women remain. He stays for a time at Bastianstrasse with Kaethe and Vera and then moves on to some other family where the Gestapo has taken the men and is not likely to return. This way, the women of each household can say they don't know where he is. The Gestapo shuts down Vera's school. She spends a few months working with a Jewish emigration organization, trying to get her precious students out of the country.

Despite the terror of this time, all three women will live long lives. Vera's

German American friend and lover, Erika Weigand, has been in Germany during the mid-1930s; she will help Vera get a visa for the United States. Nina and Paul will send their children to England on a *Kindertransport* in April 1939, arranging for them to be kept together in a holding facility rather than separated and farmed out to British families. Their parents will follow them to London on the last prewar flight out of Germany, just a day or two before Hitler invades Poland on September 1, 1939. Living in two bare rooms, the family will endure poverty, hunger, and the London Blitz. They will survive and reconstruct their middle-class family life as British citizens.

In her émigré life across the Atlantic, Vera will be pleased to discover that she can fend for herself in the practical world. She will learn to cook and get teaching jobs; she will gradually work her way into a college professorship while presiding over a bohemian household in Greenwich Village with her partner, the composer Tui St. George Tucker. As the war ends, she will recreate her small aesthetic republic in a summer camp for boys that she will run for twenty-seven years in the mountains of North Carolina. For my brothers and many other children, the camp will be a formative experience.

For Kaethe in the fall of 1939, it is almost too late. It had been arranged that she would accompany Nina and Paul on their flight to London, but she did not. Why not? Did she insist on staying with Vera? Did she dread leaving her house and what remained of her own life to become entirely dependent on other peoples' families? Was she holding out for a way to get back to the United States? Vera, finally persuaded that things were not going to get better in Germany, left for the United States by way of a transit visa through Sweden in November 1939. Kaethe stayed on. She had already sent a trunk full of her belongings with Nina to London, but she could no longer follow it. Her state of mind can only be imagined through the dead-eyed photograph on her 1939 German identity card: she had become a stateless nonperson. All around her Jews were frantically working to arrange last-minute escapes in the face of closed international borders, German confiscations of Jewish property, and the piles of documents required for emigration.

Once the war had spread across all of Western Europe, one exit route opened briefly for European Jews in desperate need of visas. It originated in Lithuania, where the Japanese vice-consul and spy Chiune Sugihara stamped thousands of Japanese transit visas, primarily for Polish and Lithuanian Jews fleeing eastward advances of the German army. Soviet officials were persuaded to allow these Jews to travel across Russia to Vladivostok via the Trans-Siberian Railway. Japan officially required entry visas that showed a final destination for those who hoped to transit through its ports, but Sugihara took it upon himself, in July and August 1940, to issue thousands of visas without that requirement.[6] I can't imagine how Kaethe got connected with this network or how she crossed the German border. But on July 3, 1940, she left Berlin for Moscow, hoping to stay with friends there for two weeks and then make her way back to the United States via Japan and Mexico. She left some money in a German bank account blocked by the Nazis that was never recovered. Kaethe was now fifty-six years old, and alone. Except for the trunk waiting in London, she had little in the world to call her own.

What I know about Kaethe's extended journey back to the United States comes from letters that Vera sent to Nina between July 1940 and March 1942, and a 1941 letter from Kaethe to Nina.[7] Both Vera and Kaethe write quite fluently in English. German would have been dangerous, since Germans were enemy aliens in England and letters to London could be intercepted. From Moscow Kaethe took the long train trip across Siberia to Vladivostok, where she could get a boat for Japan. On August 6, 1940, her birthday, she boarded a ship in Yokohama, bound for Mexico. In September Vera reports that she is in Mexico, "bored and impatient to get here but thankful to live in safety." She is worried about her trunk and wants Nina to send it to New York. In October Vera celebrates the "wonderful news" that Kaethe now has her American entry visa and will be in San Francisco to rejoin the Fränkels by the first of November. There is an immigration document on record, which indicates that she entered the United States through the port of Nogales, Arizona, on November 1, 1940. But it did not happen.

According to Vera's letters, Kaethe was stopped at the border and told that, "according to a brand new law," she had to wait another two years before she could enter the United States. For an escapee from Nazi Germany, talk of "brand new laws" could only exacerbate the fears and apprehensions of the previous years. Applications on Kaethe's behalf were made to Washington. Meanwhile, Vera writes, "Katrinchen has been very ill but had a good Jewish doctor and is better already. . . . Yesterday she wrote already in a quite controlled manner, but the first shock had a terrible effect on her." In November she reports, "One of my greatest troubles is still Katrinchen. In spite of all the applications it seems nothing can be done except perhaps to get a Cuban visa for her and have her enter from there. She spends her time waiting and writing her memories in the most striking, charming and thrilling way. A pity that we cannot send them to you." (They were written in German and could not be sent to Nina in England.) "The chapters about our mother, Hans and many others would move you to tears as they did me." So far as I know, these memoirs did not survive.

In December 1940, Kaethe is still waiting. "She is still in that ugly little village [Nogales] at the border but will probably leave for Mexico City soon," but a month later she is still there, at the end of her strength, fighting with arrogant officials in Spanish. She does not have enough clothes. Then she moves to Mexico City. Her health and mood improve along with hopes of entering through Cuba. Finally, in March 1941, Kaethe spends ten days with Vera in New York. Somehow, probably through Cuba, she has arrived, after nine months of solitary travel and maddening frustration.

For the next several months, weary and ill, she was passed around from one family to another. She was in bed for a month nursing a severe burn on her thigh, hosted by Rosi and Siegmund Bodenheimer at their summer mountain resort on Lake Placid. She stayed at Erika Weigand's parents' house, Quiddity, in the woods near New Haven. She stayed with Edith Fränkel, now in her early twenties, and had a serious heart attack that kept her in bed for three weeks. And she stayed with Vera Lachmann and Erika Weigand, at a Quaker school where Vera had a teaching job. Finally, in the late autumn of 1941, she travelled to Palo Alto and rejoined the Fränkels.

There must have been some question about her right to remain once the United States had entered the war in December 1941; would she now be treated as an enemy alien? But in March 1942 Vera wrote that she could stay. "She is busy with housekeeping. The climate is wonderful for her health. Neither cooking, nor washing and ironing is too much for her—only longer walks remind her of her heart." Getting Kaethe back into America had turned out to be a collective effort that lights up the quiet dedication of her fellow émigrés, especially the devotion and persuasiveness of Vera, who was always prone to shelter people who had nowhere to go. "Vera's stray cats," the family used to call them. This particular stray cat could be both sweet and grateful, as a surviving letter to Nina in wartime London shows. I quote again in full, both to give Kaethe more space of her own and because the letter lets us glimpse the improvised lives of all the recent émigrés.

> A.J.H. School
> Sept. 6, 41
>
> Ninettchen dear,
>
> Your sweet birthday letter was such a joy to me! Though I always had news from you through Vera, I felt so near to you, because you wrote directly. I myself wrote twice since I have been in this country, shortly after having received the trunks. In case you should not have got my letters, I have to thank you again. Everything arrived perfectly, except that four pairs of shoes were stolen out of

the sack, but the insurance company payed [sic] for them. I am so glad Mr. Fritz M took care of the freight charges. If any of my belongings are still in his keeping, I would be glad if you would take them. Do you know how our thoughts are always with you in every respect? It would be needless to talk about the details, rather let us talk about our present life. Since I am having no further difficulties with my health, I am happy at present. I am staying with Vera since Aug 1st, first with the Geers family in an old country house and at the time being at the school where she is going to teach this winter. It reminds me of the Jagowstrasse, though it is in the country, in a beautiful landscape. Teachers and pupils have not yet arrived; Vera, Erika and I are staying in a little old house by ourselves. V. and E. are just arranging things so that they are tolerably clean. The surroundings are peaceful and lovely. You know that the salary is very small, but I think Vera will have a good time here, learning new things and methods of teaching. Vera is in very good health, better than in Pough[keepsie]. We were together with Grete Sultan [a German Jewish concert pianist, recently arrived] at the Geers. We were a big family of 9 people, Grete had to teach piano to the children and did some cooking, Vera had to clean the big house, which was no easy task because the house was 100 years old and not in very good condition; she had to teach German to the little girl, 11 years old, and I was "the guest of honor" along with the grannie of 87 years!—Before this time I stayed 4 weeks with the Bodenheimers in Lake Placid, at a beautiful big mountain lake. I plan to go to the Fränkels at the end of October and though I enjoyed my stay in the East very much, I will be glad to come "home" then. —I liked this part of the country especially because nature is so much like the one you and I loved so much in many parts of our country. It is restful, green, spacious landscape, fields and forests, lakes and mountain ranges. At the horizon, not an exciting type of scenery, but peaceful, peaceful! We all hope we may be spared here, but who knows? Many sad news come from all parts of the world, Wechsler in an internment camp in Australia, the "gute Sachs" entirely untraceable for me somewhere in France,—since the beginning of the war, a young friend in Göttingen dead like some of my dearest old friends' friends which I knew well, Hajo slightly wounded, Otto's wife without passport, Grete Sultan's father died shortly after she left. I am always glad that Walter and Irma [Sachs] write kind sensible letters. I myself must say that I was one of the lucky people: although I was so often ill since my arrival, all my friends took care of me in such a loving way that I was fully free from worries. Vera not the least, and Edithlein too, and the Bodenheimers. I have in mind to spend the last weeks in N.Y. with Leni, who was not too well. She is living in the same apartment house with Margot, has the Reiche boys often with her; the flat is small, but beautifully located. Generally spoken many things are difficult here, but of course cannot be compared with your troubles. Vera continually talks about Renascenda [her name for a rebirth of her Berlin school]; will it ever come to realization? She is by the way a much more skillful housekeeper than you and I! she really is a good cook and empties 3 garbage pails in their special order pedantically. She has made many good friends. Ninettchen dear, you *are* in my heart as ever. Don't lose courage, you are so brave and be in good health. My love to Paulchen and the children. Vera is lying lazily in the grass at my side, she sends a million kisses, the second million is from your Katrinchen.

After the war ended, Kaethe needed a new family, or a new family—mine—needed her. I'm not sure how the transition from the Fränkels to the Bodenheimers came about. Kaethe stayed with Rosi and Siegmund for a few weeks in May 1945 and accompanied some New York children on the train trip to Vera's fledgling Camp Catawba in North Carolina, stopping in Washington, DC, to pick up my six- and eight-year-old brothers and another camper. She helped in the camp kitchen and stayed on the East Coast afterward. While Edgar was in Germany for the Nuremberg trials in the autumn of 1945, Kaethe was with my mother and brothers. When Edgar went to Salt Lake City for his first term of teaching at the University of Utah in September 1946, she remained in the household. Most likely she was doing housework and providing an adult presence for the boys while my mother was working or absorbed with her new infant. Once the decision to move to Salt Lake City was made, it seems to have been understood that Kaethe would stay with the family and move west.

By the time I became conscious of the world around me, Kaethe was part of the family. I wonder, now, how her presence affected the dynamics of the household, but since she and I entered the family at about the same time, on the verge of a major move, it would be difficult to sort that out. She was sixty-three when the last phase of her life began in Salt Lake City. She did not drive or have much of a social life except when she visited the Fränkels in Palo Alto or their daughter Edith Cooper in Chicago. When Kaethe appeared in the front yard, our Mormon neighbors addressed her kindly as "Mrs. Saks."

Figure 22. Kaethe, Rosemarie, Brigitte in the yard, Salt Lake City, ca. 1950

For me, Gaga was a comfortable lap, a steady presence. I see her pinning up laundry on the laundry tree in the back yard; I see myself helping her to take down the dry clothes and fold them into the wicker laundry basket. I see her rolling dough on the floured kitchen table, giving me delicious spoons to lick clean. Now she is pounding flour into a cut of meat for a dish we call Swiss steak. Under her direction I am practicing the blanket stitch in blue darning thread on a small piece of chamois cloth. She bends down from the waist like an old lady to pick up a fleck from the floor and I make a silent vow never to look so clumsy. Then, a more searing memory: I am fourteen, angry, and sullen. I am washing the kitchen floor; she can no longer do such things. She is sitting in the living room and calls to me. In one of those terrible clear-sighted moments when people with dementia understand what is happening to them, she weeps and apologizes to me for her condition; she can't help it. I have no idea how to respond. Adults, in my experience, do not apologize to children. But for all her turmoil and confusion, she knew how I was feeling.

I wonder how often that had been true, and whether she and my mother had different ideas about how to treat girls growing up. Their relationship had not been simple. A month after Kaethe joined the household in 1945, Brigitte described her early reactions to Edgar, away for the Nuremberg trials. "K is a difficult character, very much needs to be admired, and over our views in general we sometimes run head on into an argument." Just two weeks later, though, Brigitte's tune changed: "I just had a very nice talk with Kaethe, a whole long evening. Funniest thing about it is that she is quite similar to me in many respects. She is doing a lot of good around here." When I encountered the slips of paper in the black leather case, I saw that such ups and downs had been typical of their later lives as well. In a quickly penciled note dated August 6, 1952, Kaethe's sixty-ninth birthday, my mother wrote in German, "When you come to die, it will be different than it was with them. Then this strenuous everyday life will fall away, and what will always, always remain in my heart, that will be only the good and the lovely hours, and the great thankfulness. Let us still have many of these together, with all the love that is after all still there at bottom, and let us mutually drill through the rough spots that sometimes bar the way. Your Brigitte."

Who are the others whose deaths Kaethe's will not resemble? Her sister, her brother, her husband, her parents? Her tendency to despair or feel superfluous may have clashed with my mother's desire to get on with life, occasioning the note of reassurance. Brigitte claims a "great thankfulness" for Kaethe's help, though the greater, more burdensome thankfulness may well have been on Kaethe's side. In any case, her sense that her life was or should be on the verge of ending was both permanent and premature. Ten more years of dependence on our family were yet to come. During the last two, her dementia became dangerous; Brigitte could no longer care for her and put her, guiltily, in a Catholic nursing home. She visited regularly, taking me with her only once or twice. Kaethe was suffering from terrifying hallucinations: her mind was back in Nazi Germany, trapped. On May 14, 1962, she was released into death.

Like my mother and grandmother, Kaethe copied bits of wisdom culled from her eclectic reading on slips of paper, as people did more formally in commonplace books. Among them are brief passages from Plato's *Symposium*, Samuel Butler's *Erewhon*, Rilke's *Letters to a Young Poet*, Wilhelm Müller, whose poems Schubert set as *lieder*, and Hemingway in a German translation. Most of them were chosen to inspire courage and the faith to love in the midst of melancholy or loneliness. One small slip stands apart, in English, an urgent prayer: "Let not my life have been in vain."

# 9
# Family Life in Salt Lake City

The year 1966 brought several significant changes in the family, along with Edgar and Brigitte's move from Salt Lake City to Davis. Siegmund Bodenheimer died in New York City, and my parents' first grandchild, Dan Bodenheimer, was born in Princeton. Ernst and Marie Levy left Europe again, to spend the final few years of their lives near their children in California. Around this time, Edgar's archives begin to thin out considerably; fewer personal letters or significant journal entries remain in the files. The big upheavals and decisions that resulted from their expulsion from Germany had played themselves out: the shapes of their individual careers were established, their children immersed in lives of their own. In this final chapter, my story will return to the Salt Lake City years, bringing personal memory more fully into play as I try to suggest what those two decades in Utah were like. How did a family like the Bodenheimers get along in a conservative American community dominated by the Church of Jesus Christ of Latter-day Saints? Quite well, as it turns out.

Just about every Saturday morning during the Utah winter, our neighbors in the six other houses around Uintah Circle could watch a Bodenheimer ritual unfold. Edgar would come out of the house with one of his children and a ski rack. Its two parts would be fitted onto the light green Mercury, the straps tugged tight under each set of doorframes. Then the wooden skis came out, already waxed according to the day's snow report, along with a knapsack containing sandwiches, fruit, cookies, extra gloves, and a leather-covered German pocket brandy bottle. Edgar was ready, the children were ready; finally Brigitte would come out of the house in her old ski pants and climb into the passenger seat. Would it be Brighton or Alta? Brighton was a little closer, but Alta, far grander, was kept for especially good weather and longer days. Whichever canyon it was, the drive would unfold around the familiar rocky bends in the road, and the car would fill with the smell of high dry mountain air mixed with gasoline.

Once arrived, we would split up according to our levels of expertise. Each child graduated from the rope tow to the T-bar to the lower and higher chairlifts. Brigitte favored the snowplow, while her children sped ahead. When we were old enough, Edgar would take us on the fabled Alta trip through Albion Basin, giving us a taste of old school European ski touring. Albion Basin was reached by climbing up beyond the top of the highest Alta chairlift, over a pass, and down into a usually deserted snowy bowl of breathtaking beauty. There were stretches of walking and herringbone-style uphill climbing, rewarded by glorious downhill glides in deep powder. Edgar's unfettered happiness there was infectious. Later, when skiing began to be popular for teenagers, I would go with my friends, but my nostalgic memory is especially attached to the romantic sweep of wide, snowy landscapes almost bare of people.

The family would meet at the car at noon, where we would eat our sandwiches and try to keep warm. Being cold was part of the stimulation and the fun. Brigitte suffered from asthma but did not complain: complaining was rarely allowed into family conversation. Occasionally, when it was especially cold, we would go into the lodge for hot chocolate or cider. On summer hikes, similar rituals applied. Edgar and the dog were always way ahead of the pack on the trail, though my little cocker spaniel, racing madly in and out of the underbrush, would cover more miles than Edgar and return home with her silky ears knotted in burrs. Brigitte would climb slowly and steadily, encouraging the shorter legs beside her with word games when distraction was necessary. You had to get to the goal, whether it was a mountaintop or a lake, and admire the views when the trail opened up along the way.

Edgar's European habits were the guiding laws of daily life at home. At least by the time I became conscious, most days proceeded as if they ran by clockwork. Edgar would walk to the university after breakfast and return home at noon for a simple lunch. Then he would take a short nap. During this sacrosanct time everyone in the household had to be quiet, including small children. When he got up, Edgar would have a small cup of coffee left over from breakfast and a bit of Danish pastry before he drove back to his office for the rest of the day's work. Dinner was at six o'clock, preceded by the news. Summer evenings might see Edgar out watering the lawn or in his special chair with a book.

Edward R. Murrow was a household god. His quarter hour of daily news aired at 5:45 in the Intermountain West, and Edgar was always there, right beside the radio. Murrow had risen to prominence through his onsite reporting of Hitler's Austrian Anschluss in 1938, and we followed him through to the end of his radio career in 1959. Laments and speculation about the current political scene in the United States or Europe would often spill over into dinner table talk. The laments became especially intense while Senator Joseph McCarthy presided over the anti-Communist interrogations of the House Un-American Activities Committee, spooking everyone with memories of state persecution. When my grade school classes were put through air raid drills, curled up under our tiny wooden desks to await the threatened Soviet bombs, my parents refrained from commenting, though I now suspect that they understood those civic exercises as anti-Communist brainwashing.

It was only after Edward R. Murrow disappeared from the air that my parents bought a television set. The Saturday afternoon Metropolitan Opera broadcasts continued on radio, but starting in 1960 the news became a daily television ritual, changing only when an anchor retired and a new one took his place. During most of my childhood I was not allowed to watch TV programs at friends' houses, so I got used to tuning out when schoolmates chatted about the latest member of the Mickey Mouse Club or an episode of Perry Mason. True to form, Edgar and Brigitte kept us innocent of American popular culture as long as they could. I can't imagine how they would have reacted had I suddenly developed a crush on Elvis Presley, but I was so steeped in classical music that it's hard to see how that could have happened.

When it came to child rearing, my parents had landed an unexpected bonus by moving to Salt Lake City, where Mormon families brought up their many children to be respectful and responsible at early ages. Our family was a little world unto itself, but our Mormon neighbors and friends respected our differences because we were, like them, committed to a tight family structure and a disciplined way of life. The Boydens next door were actually Democrats, which made for especially friendly neighborly relations. Few other people wore "Madly for Adlai" buttons during the 1952 Eisenhower-Stevenson election campaign.

The city was safe, so Brigitte had no qualms about letting us get around by ourselves as soon as we were able to ride bikes or take buses. We played endlessly outdoors with our neighbors and friends, making free use of everyone's lawn and backyard for hiding games, marbles, jacks, and derring-do feats of sledding. My brothers were often around the block playing basketball with friends from their Unitarian scout troop. I specialized in baseball with the Uintah Circle children who were around my age, most of them boys. The lampposts in the circle served as convenient bases. When I came home from a European trip with a diabolo—two sticks and a string on which you would spin, throw, and catch a heavy rubber spool—the whole circle got involved in practicing this tricky art. Every so often a Mormon parent would interrupt our play, calling a child home to get ready to be baptized for the dead. This practice, extending the reach of Mormon salvation to the unsuspecting dead, would later be subjected to critical media attention. For me, it was just part of the normal course of things that happened in other people's families. Our own parents were glad we were doing healthy things we liked and left us alone until it was time to call us in for dinner.

In their different ways, Edgar and Brigitte imagined the family as a small entity with the same structure and goals as the benevolent paternalist state. They (which usually meant Brigitte) determined what they thought would be best for their children, and we were expected to comply. I was amused to come across a sentence in Edgar's *Jurisprudence* that was intended to make fun of a patently absurd kind of order: "A family might adopt an order according to which all family decisions are entrusted to the youngest child and are to be faithfully obeyed by all members of the family" (176). The sentence betrays an attitude shared by other émigrés who resisted the child-centered American family and were prone to imagine children "as symbols of social disorder."[1] Within the boundaries they set, however, our parents appreciated our different characters and talents, encouraged us to develop them, and fostered early independence. It was a somewhat puzzling combination of authoritarianism and laissez-faire, one that had costs as well as benefits.

We all had trouble learning to make major life decisions on our own. "Indecision is an awful thing," the punch line of a brilliant *Peanuts* comic strip, became a sort-of-funny family mantra. And, because rationality and unselfishness were the great theoretical goods of the household, we got little practice in naming, acknowledging, or working out difficult feelings. Anger, sadness, jealousy, resentment, competitiveness—of course we all felt them, but the idea was to be strong and bury them, preferably without displaying them to others. Young children were charming when they came out with expressive remarks—Brigitte and Edgar would happily quote them to each other in letters—but after a while they were expected to control their outbursts in the name of family civility. Our parents did not visibly fight or display their feelings about each other. Mormon culture, with its strong emphasis on niceness and cheerfulness, posed no outdoor challenge to such family practices.

It is easy enough to summarize the Victorian elements of our household in this way, but the exercise leaves out the essential kindness in both my parents' natures. Kindness comes up frequently in the various tributes others paid them as they reached the ends of their lives. They were free from the arrogant, brusque behavior often associated with educated German Jews. Unused to dramatizing themselves or telling stories from their pasts, they listened patiently to the elaborate stories other people told them. They loved their children and stood behind us in our adult lives even when we did things that challenged their principles. Edgar did not repeat the kind of critical, controlling behavior his own father had exercised. Brigitte, whose heroes were Albert Schweitzer and Eleanor Roosevelt, once entertained the fantasy that Tom should go to Lambaréné to work in Schweitzer's hospital, but Tom, beginning medical school, was free to decline. None of us ever gave a thought to a career in law, nor did they expect us to. I used to tease my father by singing the Lord Chancellor's song from Gilbert and Sullivan's *Iolanthe*:

> The law is the true embodiment
> Of every thing that's excellent
> It has no kind of fault nor flaw
> And I, my lords, embody the law.

He would laugh, enjoying the joke on himself. And, though we were not supposed to criticize our parents, they would put up with occasional imitations of their German accents: "Mam, don't *vorry* so much."

Practically speaking, there were two overlapping sets of parental figures in the household. Between them Brigitte and Kaethe Sachs kept the indoor things running smoothly. Having a third German Jewish adult in the house deepened its European tone, and Kaethe had strong Berlin connections with the ways of the Bodenheimer family. Her family name, Gaga, was almost on par with Mammy and Daddy. She was nearly always around, so Brigitte rarely employed babysitters; on the other hand, she suffered from heart disease and other ailments and quite often needed caretaking herself. The cooking, which she shared with Brigitte, was ordinarily the stuff of a 1950s American diet. Like everyone else, we ate peanut butter and Velveeta cheese, frozen vegetables, meat, potatoes, and canned fruit.

There were notable German variations. On Sundays we had dinner at midday, and a special supper of hot rolls (bought by Edgar at a bakery) and cold cuts, including Swiss cheese and a variety of wursts: liverwurst, German salami, or metwurst, which Edgar especially loved. Some specialty foods were kept around: *Himbeersaft* (raspberry syrup) for puddings or sweetened drinks, Tobler chocolate bars, doled out a square or two at a time, and German-style dark bread. German white wines appeared for special occasions. Our birthday cakes were chocolate and white Bundt cakes called *gefleckter Affe* (spotted monkey), sprinkled with confectioner's sugar. Somewhere along the line Brigitte learned to put up fruit and to make jam from the apricots in the backyard; she also concocted a shivery German gelatin dessert from the large sour grapes that grew over the arbor. *Kaiserschmarren*, a scrambled, baked pancake dough named for Kaiser Franz Joseph I of Austria, was, by contrast, very popular.

Christmas was German to the hilt. The tree was put up and decorated on Christmas Eve morning; then the living room was off limits to children until that evening, when it would be lighted and revealed with presents stacked under it. There were always a few Swiss mountain calendars among them. We sang Christmas carols in English, "Silent Night" in German. Each person had a decorated paper plate full of goodies, including *Lebkuchen* (a kind of German gingerbread), marzipan, nuts, tangerines, and homemade German butter cookies half-dipped in chocolate or sprinkled with colored sugars. Supper was a glorified version of Sunday suppers, with a special fruit-filled orange Jell-O. Afterward Edgar would read parts of Dickens's *A Christmas Carol* aloud. During his reading I liked to lie under the tree looking up at the lights gleaming on the carefully stranded icicles.

It was all lovely so long as it was not subjected to the gaze of people outside the family. Once or twice visiting Jewish friends were horrified. Brigitte liked to remind us that all cultures celebrate a festival of light during the darkest season of the year, though this did not explain why our festival was not Chanukah. Our parents did not seem interested in the discomfort of Jewish friends; it was up to them to show more tolerance—or, as it might be, less Jewishness. Although they tried not to let it show, they never lost their German Jewish snobbery toward those whose ancestors had fled eastern European shtetl life to assimilate and thrive in America—just as their own families had assimilated and thrived in Germany. "The children [of some acquaintance] are quite spoiled (like most Jewish children in America)," Brigitte wrote to her parents once, and she was on the alert for "selfishness" in Jewish girl- or boyfriends in her children's lives. Being a good person was a more important qualification than being Jewish, when it came to her children's marriages.

One other German Jewish family in Salt Lake became important to all of us. I met my best friend, Toni Hahn, when we were both about two years old, at a picnic in one of the Wasatch canyons. Her parents, Margot and Walter Hahn, had arrived in Utah in 1939, via England and Palestine. (Apparently they heard about Salt Lake City from a Mormon missionary.) Edgar had heard Walter Hahn's name during his first weeks in Utah; he was a native Berliner who taught in the Adult Education Division at the University of Utah, where, at the time, he ran the campus school. Brigitte was probably relieved that her daughter, seven years younger than her younger son, would have a German Jewish girlfriend her own age. Toni was to be an only child, and Margot may have felt something similar. Although we couldn't have been in on the plan at the ages of two and three, the relationship flourished, and the two families became good friends. Toni and I spent weekend days playing at each other's houses; the families skied together, mixed up German and English together, and shared Thanksgiving dinners. Although there were years when we lost touch, Toni remains my good friend to this day, the one living person who really knew my family during our Salt Lake City years. She was more interested in the Jewish part of our shared German Jewish mix than I was and felt critical of her father's unwavering love of Berlin and his research trips there. In that way and others, she offered me some alternative perspectives.

In Utah, being non-Mormon could be more important than the particular brand of non-Mormonism one espoused. Living in Salt Lake City as "Gentiles," we would occasionally be approached by a pair of young white-shirted Mormon missionaries intent on conversion. If he had time, Edgar would invite them in and give them a lecture on the Old Testament and the ethical law he thought it represented. I had a more skeptical response: when my own Mormon friends would broach the subject, I would say, or think, "Just because it's written down in a book doesn't mean it's true." Neither Edgar nor Brigitte seemed much bothered by Mormonism once they had settled into Utah life. When they gave dinner parties for their law faculty colleagues, Edgar would prepare two cocktail shakers: alcoholic for the non-Mormons, non-alcoholic for the Mormons. The University itself was a relatively cosmopolitan outpost. Edgar, who disliked "over-intellectualism," was probably happy enough that his children were schooled in a nonintellectual environment where questioning and skepticism were kept to a minimum; we would get enough of that when we went east for college. The situation may have worked better for my science-oriented brothers than for me, the family imaginist. My adolescent indignation at the unquestioning, literal-minded obedience at the heart of Mormon culture stood me in good stead, though: it gave me a substitute for rebellion against my parents.

To remind us of our non-Gentile origins, Edgar and Brigitte joined the Reform synagogue, Temple B'nai Israel, led by a thoughtful rabbi they admired. By 1950 Edgar had come to the conclusion that Jewish assimilation was desirable only up to a point. He had absorbed the idea that Jewish "people of the law" had a historical mission to work toward world freedom and justice; only when it was perfectly achieved could religious, racial, and national differences fade. In 1948, he had heard the legendary Rabbi Leo Baeck speak in San Francisco. "That was like a voice from another, higher world. He spoke of the Jews' mission for the future to be the conscience of the world," he wrote to Brigitte. It was a mission Edgar took seriously in his legal philosophy; the historical role of Judaism was indistinguishable from his ideal of natural law. Both, in his view, were meant to take up arms against all forms of moral apathy or skepticism, and to keep the flame of justice burning.

In one of Edgar's little talks about European-Jewish developments at the Temple B'nai Israel, he laid out his current thinking about assimilation. "Judaism was the first civilization which consciously recognized the primacy of certain fundamental ethical values and dedicated itself to their furtherance," he said. "If faith in the ethical ideals of Judaism becomes undermined and destroyed, the result is moral nihilism and power-worship." He meant Fascism, of course, but he also meant his younger self, the one who had briefly joined the League of Nationalist German Jews in 1933. Edgar did not confess to the folly of his personal membership; instead he used the example of Jews who joined the League as an object lesson, "a sad reminder where the policy of assimilation at any price may lead." In private, he never forgot or forgave past moments when he was seen to be guilty or wrong.

In addition to Edgar's Old Testament storytelling on Sunday mornings, the family went to High Holiday services at Temple B'nai Israel. Peter, Tom, and I briefly attended confirmation classes, to learn a few Hebrew prayers and some Jewish history. During those periods we might light Chanukah candles for a year or two, but the practice would fade rather quickly. None of it really took. When I was sent to an Episcopalian girls' school for two years of junior high school, I joined the chapel choir and sang wholeheartedly from the Episcopalian hymnal every morning. Like well-assimilated German Jews, we found our real spiritual experiences in the natural world and the worship of music.

In modern Germany, Jewish listeners, critics, musicians, conductors, and composers were central players in the process of assimilation. Loving and performing the works of German and Austrian composers, Jews became Germans in their hearts. Mere tribal differences dissolved in the transcendent beauty of Bach and Mozart, Beethoven and Schubert, Mahler and Wagner. As it happened, that tradition also led to a kind of Mormon-Jewish musical entente in Salt Lake City. The Mormon Tabernacle Choir is the most recognizable face of the church's devotion to music, but during our time there the Utah Symphony also rose to prominence under the direction of Maurice Abravanel. Born into a family of Sephardic Greek Jews, Abravanel had spent the years 1922–1933 pursuing his musical career in Germany. After he left Europe for America, he spent some years conducting the Metropolitan Opera Orchestra in New York before he took on and transformed the Utah Symphony. The New York musicians he hired to fill the first chairs of the orchestra had, in turn, a transformative influence on the young people they taught.

Studying an instrument and playing chamber music made us members of a special society that helped ease our adolescent years. The three of us took early piano lessons and then branched out: clarinet, violin, and cello, in order of birth. In a few of the Salt Lake City public high schools, string quartets were formed in addition to school bands and orchestras. Like Tom, I was lucky enough to play in one of them, and for two summers I joined a cadre of young Salt Lake musicians who accompanied Abravanel to the summer session at the Music Academy of the West in Santa Barbara. Whether they were raised in Mormon or Jewish families, my high school musical cohort revered the European musicianship exemplified by the leadership and the kindly attentiveness of Maestro Abravanel. He provided a window onto a larger world beyond the Salt Lake valley, where many of my friends would spend the rest of their lives raising Mormon families of their own. It was as if Edgar's dream of *Bildung* had materialized in that unlikely spot, so that he and Brigitte could go to symphony concerts and hear Mahler symphonies performed to a high musical standard.

When her parents moved to Basel in 1956, Brigitte was left to dismantle the Seattle house that had done so much to solace Marie during her American sojourn. (Her brother Wolfgang's family moved from Seattle to San Jose that same year.) Brigitte's old Seattle friend Claire Seltzer, "not quite so crazy any more," came into view again and took charge of the sale process once the house had been put on the market. "It's such a beautiful house. It's a shame to sell it," Brigitte wrote, taking a moment to scribble a penciled note to her nine-year-old daughter in the midst of packing and cleaning. For the next ten years she would make time to visit her parents, often sharing vacations with them in Swiss mountain or lake resorts. After her father began to suffer from dementia, she moved them back to America in 1966, installing them in a nearby Davis apartment where she could manage their affairs and provide household help.

Ernst Levy died quietly of his illness on September 14, 1968. In a eulogy for his father-in-law, Edgar emphasized his courage: "Ernst Levy walked through the valley of the shadow of death for four years during the First World War. . . . But, in the words of the psalm which I have just read in part, he 'feared no evil,' although there was plenty of it around him during those four years. All who knew him well will confirm that he was a man without fears." Marie stayed in their Davis apartment near her children, gradually losing her sight, until she died at the end of 1974. I remember reading to her in German from Klaus Mann's autobiography while my parents were abroad one summer. She knew how to savor the small things. "Dass muss man mit Verstand essen," she would smile, holding one of the wafer-thin Lindt chocolate squares she favored: this has to be eaten with understanding. When I looked through the English and German quotations Marie had transcribed into her commonplace book, I found this rogue sentence from 1961: "Dear Lord, be good enough to explain to me why I don't like brains." Her intuitive style had not made her life among strenuously Germanic academics any easier. In the memories of others, however, she was the parent and grandparent most loved and missed.

Letters and visits flowed regularly to and from the New York Bodenheimer parents as well, though Edgar kept none of their correspondence after the 1940s. Siegmund and Rosi Bodenheimer were presences in our lives, though—presences I dimly recall from childhood visits and vacations and glimpse again in Edgar and Brigitte's letters to each other. As the Jagowstrasse villa in Grunewald had once been, the apartment on the eleventh floor of 315 Central Park West was the acknowledged center of the New York–New Jersey Bodenheimer clan. For a child visiting from a practical western household, it was like a stage set for another, more luxurious era. I can still see the heavy red velvet curtain draped between the foyer and the living room, the gilt-framed chairs and inlaid bridge tables, the tapestries on the wall, and the fascinating bell under the carpet in the dining room, which would summon Hattie Mae from the kitchen bearing a platter of Southern fried chicken. The dining room also contained a huge inlaid chest in which Rosi kept a full supply of European sweets, from candied fruit slices to marzipan. The chocolate *Katzenzungen* (cat's tongues) were favorites for children, and Rosi delighted in handing them around to us. Her life seemed to be a round of shopping in elegant department stores, ordering delicious food, and being a radiantly smiling hostess to the many family members and bridge friends who came through the apartment. Her large bedroom lay at the other end of a long central corridor, with a view over the lake in Central Park and the lights glimmering beyond its shore. The off-white furnishings, the little round cabinet of jewelry and silk scarves, and the large oil portraits of my aunts Bebs and Helga as young teenagers combined to make it the most feminine room I knew. When Brigitte was in town, Rosi would take her to Fifth Avenue and buy her a new dress. Stylishness was not in my mother's repertoire, but she appreciated a well-made piece of clothing.

Siegmund and Rosi's generosity included invitations to summer resorts my parents would not otherwise have been able to afford during the early Salt Lake City years. In August 1949 Brigitte, Kaethe, and the children enjoyed Laguna Beach in a house Siegmund had rented for several weeks while Edgar finished up his summer courses in Utah. "It's hard to figure out what day this is," Brigitte wrote to Edgar. "I only know it must be Tuesday because the laundry men just brought Pap's shirts. It is amazingly restorative, this seabathing and being lazy." The waves were rough, so no one would swim beyond the surf with her, but the boys were allowed to rent a surf rider for forty-five minutes a day, and they yelled with content as the rubber mattress took them out. Still a bit frightened of the waves, my two-year-old self was happy on the beach with a bucket of water and a shovel.

Brigitte was never comfortable with the idea that Siegmund was paying for everything. When Edgar got free of teaching, she wrote, they would need a place to stay together. "*We* have to pay for it. At least I beg you that. I write down everything I pay for Pap; I've spent almost nothing myself." Financial dependence made her nervous, partly because it seemed to come with implicit pressure to bend to her father-in-law's wishes. Nonetheless, there would be a few more summers enjoyed together at the Grand Tetons and other western vacation spots before Rosi and Siegmund retreated to the Mohonk Mountain House in the Hudson Valley for their summer getaways.

Peter and Tom were connected with the New York circle because they attended cousin Vera Lachmann's Camp Catawba in North Carolina. In the spring of 1947, soon after arriving in Salt Lake City, Brigitte wrote to her own parents: "The Bodenheimer parents are horrified that we want to send the children to camp, partly because it is so far, and partly that it is a great financial burden for Vera," who apparently waived the camp fees for my brothers. "They are also especially against the return trip home by themselves, and Edgar and Kaethe agree with them. They believe it's a danger, that something ugly could happen. Now the whole trip is put into question." The boys were about to turn ten and eight at the time, so it is easy to wonder about Brigitte's apparent lack of concern. The camp had been "a second home" for her sons during the Washington years, and she was not eager to give up the freedom their absence provided. Peter assures me that they did attend camp in 1947, so I assume that some acceptable kind of chaperoning was arranged. After that the boys did not return to Catawba until they were old enough to serve as camp helpers and counselors.

In January 1950 Edgar spent a few weeks of winter quarter staying with his parents in New York as he prepared a lecture for the Riccobono Seminar of Roman Law at Catholic University. The extended visit gave him an opportunity to catch up with all the members of the Bodenheimer circle, so his letters to Brigitte provide some glimpses of life on Central Park West. Throughout his stay family and close friends streamed into the apartment for dinner; "there is something going on every night." Edgar put up with the parade of *Tantes* and *Onkels*, but he was most interested in his two sisters. Bebs remained the well-beloved friend and counselor of their youth together. The handsome and headstrong Helga, twelve years younger than

Edgar, tended to evoke a comical or skeptical tone in her older brother. She had been just thirteen when Hitler came to power, and sixteen when she moved to New York with her parents. Her attempts at careers in music and the fashion industry had not taken hold.

In 1950 Helga's first marriage to the older Hungarian pianist Arpád Sándor was literally going to the dogs (as would her second marriage to the American oboist Whitney Tustin, some years later.) At thirty, she had acquired the first of many English spaniels to whom she would eventually dedicate a life of dog breeding and showing. "Helga and Derry appeared at 5:30, and you should see those two together," Edgar wrote on New Year's Day. "All the sweet names which used to be reserved for Arpád are now profusely showered on Derry." Sándor, looking "old, a little sad," arrived half an hour later. "[Rosi] says he often does not speak a single word when he is there. He considers Derry a great nuisance." As time went on and Helga's dog obsession grew, Edgar began to distance himself further from this sister, whose temperamental nature had, he thought, been spoiled by their father's early doting on his pretty youngest child.

Among the extended family in New York, there were other signs of more difficult passages from Germany to America. Our favorite Tante Else, married to Siegmund's brother Louis Bodenheimer, had arrived in 1940 after a last-minute flight from Germany via the Trans-Siberian Railway and a stay in Japan. In New York, she worked for a company that made cheap artificial flower pins to be worn on coats or dresses. For years I kept a light blue one she gave me, quite unconscious of the menial work this wife and daughter of successful Berlin businessmen had accepted. Like other wives in émigré couples, she was the one who found employment; many middle-class German Jewish women worked as maids or secretaries to keep their families going after emigration. For men in my parents' generation, the import-export business seemed to be the norm. Bebs's husband Teddy Blau had been a somewhat reluctant apprentice lawyer in Germany, with a strong interest in engineering. He did not want to repeat law school in America, and—like the majority of his émigré cohort—struggled for years to find satisfactory jobs. Most of his working life was spent as a machinist, though he was also a talented photographer.[2]

Bebs and Teddy and their sons, Fred and Ron, were the Bodenheimer relatives closest to our family; we were most at home in their easy-going house on Ely Place in East Orange. Bebs's warmth and human savvy had the charm of a healing power in our more austere family life, while Teddy's many interests made him a comfortable and observant companion. Unlike Edgar and Brigitte, the Blaus (or, as we sometimes called them, "the bears") had stayed within the family orbit and kept mostly to German Jewish circles. When Edgar was visiting in 1950, Teddy was recovering from a surgery that had gone badly. "Teddy is better but may not be able to work for 8 weeks and may never again be able to do the manual work he has been doing," Edgar wrote, conveying the family's sense of anxiety. Out in Salt Lake City, Brigitte was probably reminded that their own decision to maintain a considerable distance from New York family headquarters left them more freedom from immediate scrutiny. Yet Siegmund's judgments were still a force to reckon with. In his late-life interview with Ron, Teddy recalled that Siegmund had despaired of Edgar when he decided to become a law professor, pronouncing that line of work a "beggar's profession," the lowest-paying job a lawyer could choose.[3] I do not know whether that sentiment was conveyed so directly to Edgar himself, but Teddy's memory suggests that the tensions between Siegmund and Edgar were not easily resolved, even after Edgar began paying for his own life.

My parents were certainly not free to bypass the elaborate celebrations that marked Siegmund's seventieth, eightieth, and ninetieth birthdays, or Siegmund and Rosi's fiftieth wedding anniversary. Such occasions required serious preparation: unusually fancy clothes, dinner table remarks for Edgar, and sometimes a poem or musical piece to be memorized by a grandchild. For me, forever the youngest person on the scene, the memorable aspects of those New York visits had more to do with the wonders of the city. I would sit at the window of Helga's old room above the street and try to keep count of the yellow taxis as they passed the corner of 91st Street and Central Park West. I would linger in my grandmother's bedroom, staring at the portraits of my aunts, looking out at the city lights, or playing with the pretty scarves. I would go on walks to Central Park with my grandfather, he with his cane and I with my little bag of bread to feed the pigeons. I would be taken to the Natural History Museum down the street. Once when I was older, a kind second cousin escorted me to a Broadway musical as if we were on a date. Best of all, we could take a bus from Port Authority that left us at the corner of Bebs and Teddy's block in East Orange. In their kitchen, friends and relatives sat around and talked for hours. Meals happened as if by accident. Up in the attic, there were fascinating things to explore. It was all wonderfully informal and *gemütlich*.

In 1960, Rosi Bodenheimer suffered a heart attack and died. I was not taken to her funeral, and I never knew how his mother's death affected Edgar; mourning was not a process much spoken of in the family. Rosi was twelve years younger than Siegmund, who outlived her by six years and died at ninety-one. During the interval the widowed Tante Else came to Central Park West to care for her brother-in-law; it could not be supposed that the patriarch would carry on alone. Tante Else also kept an independent space, her little apartment in the German Jewish colony of Washington Heights. But she and Bebs made sure that Siegmund would continue the pleasant, habitual way of life he preferred, watching the stock market, walking in the park, reading, and attending the Metropolitan Opera on Friday nights.

At his father-in-law's funeral on February 9, 1966, Teddy Blau began his eulogy with these words: "The tall tree in the center of the family has fallen. For close to a century it had been standing, erect and powerful, not just in the center but being the center." Not just *in* the center but *being* the center: Teddy's distinction may be hard to parse, but it captured something essential about Siegmund Bodenheimer. Soon afterward, the Central Park West apartment was dissolved, marking in substantial and symbolic ways the end of an era of German Jewish life.

# Afterword

Around the time this story ends, the word "holocaust" was undergoing a transformation. In modern times, it had come to mean any large-scale mass slaughter, especially those caused by fire or explosives. The firebombing of Germany by Allied forces and the atom bomb attacks on Hiroshima and Nagasaki could serve as examples. Beginning in the late 1960s, however, the word acquired a capital letter and a definite article, "the Holocaust," and came to mean one thing. That thing, the mass destruction of Jews and other European groups in concentration and death camps, was often symbolized by one site, Auschwitz. At the same time, the postwar cloud of silence and forgetting began to dissipate, and representations of the Holocaust cropped up everywhere.

Exactly how this shift occurred lies beyond the scope of this narrative, but the trial of Adolf Eichmann in 1961 is a notable historical marker. Captured in Argentina and brought to Israel in 1960, Eichmann was tried in Jerusalem under the glare of international attention. The prosecution brought victim after victim to the witness stand, and their stories, instantly broadcast around the world, broke through the public silences of the postwar period. The trial recemented the connection between Hitler's Final Solution and the founding of Israel, a connection that helped to define the meaning of Jewish identity for many Jewish Americans of the twentieth century. The German Jewish philosopher Hannah Arendt sustained the world's attention when she published her controversial assessment of the trial, *Eichmann in Jerusalem: A Report on the Banality of Evil* (1963). Arendt was interested in using Eichmann as an example of the way evil overtakes ordinary people in a totalitarian regime, and her argument implicated Jews along with Nazis as agents of destruction. For many readers, that idea was simply intolerable in the face of Eichmann's crimes and what had happened to their relatives, their friends, and their lives.[1]

Wherever you stood on the Arendt question, the postwar ice had been broken. Memoirs, testimonials, novels, poems, films, histories, psychoanalytic theories, and philosophical meditations on the meanings of the Holocaust began to appear, the pace only quickening into the present. A history of organized evil that's so mind-boggling creates an unending need for retrospective reimagining and rewriting. Building Holocaust memorials was something to do, and many cities did it. The Jewish Museum Berlin, which opened in 2001, took a further step by celebrating two hundred years of Jewish life in Germany. *Stolpersteine* (stumble stones) on the pavements of several German cities now mark residences that were formerly owned or inhabited by Jews. Increasing numbers of Jews, including young Israelis, are going to live in Germany, as if they are compelled to experience the mixed feelings raised by the German Jewish history of mutual love and hatred.

How did Brigitte and Edgar respond to such developments? Did they follow the Eichmann trial or read Arendt's book? I am sure that they did, though there is no evidence, either in my memory or in the letters and journals Edgar left. I am left to wonder how they experienced the trial in light of Edgar's participation at Nuremberg, and how they felt about Arendt, whose name I can dimly recall floating around the house in parental conversation. I do not think that they used the term "Holocaust" to refer to Hitler's extermination camps. Perhaps they maintained their reserve as that term acquired its powerful meaning, especially because it refers to a history they and their immediate families had so fortunately escaped before it turned murderous.

As for Israel, Brigitte and Edgar shared with Hannah Arendt a dilemma described by Anthony Heilbut: "For those émigrés who had kept faith in a larger international vision, whether socialist or humanist, the postwar transformation of the Wandering Jew into the rooted Israeli was profoundly disturbing. They discovered themselves despised by other Jews for confiding their suspicions of Jewish nationalism in public."[2] I remember how agitated Edgar became as he listened to news reports about the Six-Day War of June 1967 and subsequent Arab-Israeli conflicts. The alarm he felt was palpable: Jews must not become aggressive nationalists or seize territory as the Germans had; such behavior would reignite worldwide anti-Semitism. He would always be wary of American Jews who supported Israel no matter what its government did, though he and Brigitte maintained a low public profile on this subject.

After my mother's death in 1981, Edgar lived on for a decade, marrying another German Jewish, Berlin-born woman who was also called Brigitte.[3] Her story is not mine to tell, but I cannot imagine Edgar marrying anyone with a different background, even after living in America for fifty years. He continued to enjoy "good conversations" with his children when we met.

I remember walking with him around a beautiful salt marsh on Cape Cod when he was in his early eighties. He told me about Hegel's phrase, "The owl of Minerva flies at dusk." It was only when a historical period was on the verge of passing, he explained, that we begin to understand it. I loved the image and will always associate it with my father. Not many months after his article on Hegel appeared in the *American Journal of Jurisprudence*, Edgar died. He was still a healthy man, or so it had seemed until his collapse, but his death came rather quickly on May 30, 1991. Perhaps he was ready; he knew that his writing career had come to an end. In Hegel's owl of Minerva his work had found a fitting epitaph.

Before his death, Edgar had been planning to attend the Symposium on German Jurists in Exile, held in Bonn that September, where both his and my mother's work were to be honored. In his absence W. Cole Durham Jr., a Mormon professor of law and religion at Brigham Young University, talked about Edgar's work. Durham had some experience of the differences between German and American legal reasoning and placed Edgar's philosophical methods largely in the German camp. He knew that Edgar had influenced some Brigham Young University colleagues who had taken Bodenheimer's courses at the University of Utah, so he was in a good position to weave various pieces of Edgar's past together. His talk was called "Edgar Bodenheimer: Conservator of Civilized Legal Culture."

Other discussions, tributes, and memorials for Edgar and Brigitte were published closer to home, in issues of the *UC Davis Law Review*. After Brigitte retired, the summer 1979 issue, "A Symposium on Children and the Law," was dedicated to her and opened with the celebratory poem/memoir by her family law colleague Carol S. Bruch. After her death, Davis instituted the annual Brigitte M. Bodenheimer Memorial Lecture on the Family, with its inaugural lecture presented by Sanford Katz in the fall of 1982.[4] The spring 1988 issue was a Festschrift in honor of Edgar's eightieth birthday. After his death, "A Symposium in Honor of Professor Edgar Bodenheimer" (Spring 1993) collected ten articles about the nature and meaning of his work, Cole Durham's among them.

This book, my own contribution to the memory of my parents, has a very different purpose. In its family stories the German Jewish culture destroyed by Hitler's regime finds a brief American afterlife. By the 1970s, as Steven Lowenstein writes, "the German-Jewish immigrant lifestyle was entering eclipse. . . . The culture of German-speaking Jewry was being transformed from a personal into a historical memory."[5] As a member of the second generation these words make sense to me, though they do not tell the whole story. As I complete the work on this project, I find myself increasingly conscious that my parents' ways of being inhabit my own, and

Figure 23. Edgar in 1985

more attuned to an inner landscape that has always been there, shaped by a heritage of forced migration.

In that private landscape, I have always feared that my peaceful life could be suddenly and violently disrupted, that at a moment's notice I might be persecuted as a Jew. Although I participated in one or two demonstrations to protest the Vietnam War, I am uncomfortable with mass movements of any kind. When I was thirteen, I declared myself an atheist: between the Mormon environment and the off-and-on Judaism of my household, I suppose I wanted to avoid the whole question of organized religion and its potential for inciting hatred. Was it a related impulse of defiance that prompted Edgar, at about the same age, to declare his religion as "Prussian"? I no longer lay claim to the definitive position of the atheist, but I have lived an entirely secular life, Jewish in heritage but not in practice.

Most other Jewish families I knew would not have dreamed of going back to Germany after the war. The reasons for my parents' willingness to spend a few summers there were not discussed with their children, though we were expected to understand that harboring hatred or resentment against an entire people was not on the agenda for our family. This may have been high-minded, but its effects on us were not very carefully imagined. My brief experiences in 1950s Germany were lonely and unhappy. I suffered from the brusque manners, the kowtowing to authority expected of children, and the feeling—akin to that of the recent émigré—that my abilities counted for nothing in a different language and culture. As a young woman I fiercely—if internally—reacted against my father's Germanic habits, some of which I share. I owe him a life's worth of pleasure in reading and writing, as well as my love for activity in the outdoors and my enthusiasm for classical music. I also owe him an inability to be late, the almost embarrassing neatness of my office, and a growing sense of compulsion about details of everyday life. I have retained my resistance to Edgar's love of abstract thought, which generally strikes me as a kind of fiction making rather than an approach to truth. As American literary studies grew more enamored of European theory, I turned aside to practice textual and biographical criticism.

If my descriptions of Edgar mix love and admiration with some skepticism, my attempt to bring Brigitte into focus mixes love and admiration with wistfulness. That is primarily because she died too soon, but also because she did not indulge her children's feelings. She was German in her no-nonsense approach to mothering, but I never thought of her as a particularly Germanic person. It is difficult to convey her particular blend of sweetness, toughness, and attentiveness in words. As a professional, my mother was awesome in her intelligence and persistence, and very human in her scrambles to get things done. For a daughter who preferred the world of books, Brigitte was a hard act to follow, but she was an experienced, inventive coach during my efforts to establish a career she did not live to see unfold.

Where did we belong in this world? That question comes with the territory of emigration and exile and is not easily answered. My parents conveyed an unspoken sense that real life was going on elsewhere, though it was not clear where elsewhere was. Their intimates were elsewhere, kept close by correspondence. The German Jewish paper *Aufbau* came through the mail slot monthly, bringing news from elsewhere in uninviting, closely printed German. We were Jewish, but not American Jewish; we were American, with Europe mixed in. We were cosmopolitan, living in Utah. We were unlike other Jewish refugees whose escapes from the later stages of Hitler's genocidal program had put their lives and livelihoods in great danger. Perhaps because "German," "Jewish," and "American" were all terms associated with puzzling mixtures of pride and shame, I never felt that "identity," even the hyphenated kind, was a helpful concept. Wasn't everyone's life full of mixtures and contradictions?

What was most familiar, what belonged to us, was a sense of not quite belonging. In our household, the prevailing spirit suggested that there was no need to be quite like other people, or to conform to whatever was fashionable. For me, this meant occasional feelings of envy or estrangement, but overall it has proven to be a strangely liberating inheritance. Once I had found my place in marriage, academics, friendships, musical groups, and my adopted hometown of Boston, questions of belonging were largely put to rest. Writing this book has taken me a step further, to confront the particularities of my parents' part in twentieth-century German Jewish history. In the end, the writing has widened my sense of belonging, both to a family lineage and to a human history of disruption and displacement that continues somewhere in the world, every day.

# Notes

## Chapter 1

1. I have drawn from the memoir of Rudolf Zipkes, a Swiss Jew who attended the Grunewald Gymnasium from 1921 to 1930 and describes the school in *Gelebtes Leben: Jude sein in einer weltoffenen Zeit*, 70–76.

2. George L. Mosse, *German Jews Beyond Judaism*, 3, 12–15.

3. Ron Blau, 1979 ms. interview with his mother, "Why I Refuse to Make this Film." Ron Blau's film *Our Time in the Garden* is based on footage from the Grunewald family home.

4. Eric D. Weitz gives an account of the devastating 1922–23 inflation and its social consequences in *Weimar Germany: Promise and Tragedy*, 131–45.

5. Jacob Katz emphasizes the distinctive character of the German Jewish subgroup within the German middle class, noting its disproportionate support of the arts. Katz, "German Culture and the Jews," 85–91.

6. For conservative attacks on Jews in the 1870s and early 1890s, see Donald L. Niewyk, *The Jews in Weimar Germany*, 6–7.

7. Katz notes that marriage with other German Jews was the rule; in cases of intermarriage, the Jewish partner "almost always dropped out of the Jewish community." Katz, "German Culture and the Jews," 86.

8. For a description of Rathenau's end, see Shulamit Volkov's *Walther Rathenau: Weimar's Fallen Statesman*, 205–10. Weitz discusses Rathenau and the resurgence of the Right after 1923 in *Weimar Germany*, 100–111.

9. The cultural critic Walter Benjamin is an eminent example. His difficult financial relations with his father are recounted in Howard Eiland and Michael W. Jennings, *Walter Benjamin: A Critical Life*, 17, 113–14.

10. Avraham Barkai and Paul Mendes-Flohr describe "the excruciating paradox of the Weimar experience for Jewry: while the Jews at long last became full participants in German culture and public life, their right to do so was questioned with ever greater intensity." Michael A. Meyer, ed., *German-Jewish History in Modern Times*, 4:171.

11. On German Jewish identity and Leo Baeck, see Niewyk, *The Jews in Weimar Germany*, 100–101.

12. Paul Mendes-Flohr, *German Jews: A Dual Identity*, 41. Mendes-Flohr explores the impossible contradictions within German Jewish identity.

13. Richard Wagner, "Judaism in Music," 80. Subsequent page numbers cited in text.

14. Katz, "German Culture and the Jews," 88–90.

15. Amos Elon's *The Pity of It All: A History of Jews in Germany, 1743–1933* charts the periodic alternations in German Jewish relations through two centuries.

## Chapter 2

1. Detlev J. K. Peukert, *The Weimar Republic: The Crisis of Classical Modernity*, 256–57.

2. I have drawn from Weitz's account in *Weimar Germany*, 350–58.

3. For Hitler's rapid actions in 1933, see Saul Friedländer, *Nazi Germany and the Jews: The Years of Persecution, 1933–1939*, 17–40.

4. Ibid., 27.

5. The boycott and its partial failure are described by Friedländer, *Nazi Germany and the Jews*, 19–24, and by Avraham Barkai and Paul Mendes-Flohr in *German-Jewish History in Modern Times*, ed. Michael A. Meyer, 4:198–201.

6. My information about the League of National German Jews comes from Carl J. Rheins, "The Verband Nationaldeutscher Juden 1921–1933," 243–68, and Donald Niewyk, *The Jews in Weimar Germany*, 165–77.

7. I have drawn broadly from two detailed studies of Eastern Jews in Germany: Steven E. Aschheim's *Brothers and Strangers: The East European Jew in German and German Jewish Consciousness, 1800–1923*, and Jack Wertheimer's *Unwelcome Strangers: East European Jews in Imperial Germany*.

8. For the language of the Right, see Weitz, *Weimar Germany*, 332–42.

9. Had Edgar been born just a few years later, he would have faced similar dilemmas at the Grunewald Gymnasium. Reinhard Bendix, who was seventeen in 1933, was required to give the Hitler salute in class there. After his father, Ludwig, was imprisoned by the Nazis, he refused and was forced to leave the school. Bendix, *From Berlin to Berkeley: German-Jewish Identities*, 145–47.

10. In 1933, the United States had an annual German immigration quota of 25,957. Little of it was used because the State Department instructed consuls to deny visas to people who might become burdens on the state (United States Holocaust Memorial Museum, "U.S. Quotas and Visas"). Debórah Dwork and Robert Jan van Pelt discuss the variability in visa decisions made by American consuls in *Flight from the Reich*, 44–47.

11. In *Exiled in Paradise*, Anthony Heilbut writes, "Émigrés would always appear politically eccentric to Americans, despite their normally centrist positions and their fanatical devotion to the Roosevelts, by virtue of both their assumption that welfare was a citizen's right and their intense concern with public events" (68).

12. Edgar's bluntly prejudicial reactions to the American scene were shared by many other German Jewish intellectuals who landed in New York and may have been especially pronounced during his early days of association with the other émigrés. Their attitudes were recorded by Donald Peterson Kent in his 1953 sociological study, *The Refugee Intellectual: Americanization of the Immigrants of 1933–1941*, and by Heilbut throughout *Exiled in Paradise*.

13. Blau, "Why I Refuse to Make this Film."

## Chapter 3

1. My information about Ernst Levy's family and career comes largely from Wolfgang Kunkel's 1969 memorial article, "Ernst Levy zum Gedächtnis."

2. Marie's journal was translated by her son, Wolfgang, during the 1980s. I am grateful to my cousin Edna Levy Lowe for sending me a copy.

3. For discussions of the 1916 *Judenzahl*, see Amos Elon, *The Pity of It All*, 338–40. Werner Angress gives a detailed account of the genesis and consequences of the census in "The German Army's Judenzahlung of 1916."

4. Brigitte's memories are quoted from a taped interview made April 10, 1979, on the occasion of her retirement from the UC Davis Law School.

5. Ulrich Simon, *Sitting in Judgement, 1913–1963*, 17.

6. Ruprecht-Karls-Universität Heidelberg, "Levys Ruf an die Universität Bonn."

7. The Levys had a copy of the third in a series of five prints, published together as The Concert.

8. Max Weber is best known to English-speaking audiences as the author of *The Protestant Ethic and the Spirit of Capitalism* (1904). I am indebted to sociologist Guenter Roth for information about the Max Weber House, now owned by the University of Heidelberg. One seminar room bears a plaque in honor of Ernst Levy. In this section I draw on Guenter Roth's article "Marianne Weber and Her Circle."

9. Much of the information here is drawn from Marianne Weber, *Max Weber: A Biography*.

10. The story of the von Richthofen sisters is told at length by Martin Green in *The von Richthofen Sisters: The Triumphant and the Tragic Modes of Love*.

11. Information about Jaspers comes from Suzanne Kirkbright's *Karl Jaspers: A Biography: Navigations in Truth*.

12. A good part of the interview was published in a special women's edition of the UC Davis Law School student paper, *The Advocate*, 12:13 (April 17, 1979). Years later I was sent a tape of the interview; quotations are based on my transcription of the tape.

13. Noting the struggle for acceptance that women faced in Weimar-era universities, Detlev Peukert writes, "The struggle against such discrimination in universities and in the workplace in general was made more difficult because women themselves were very much influenced by the traditional argument of the German women's movement that 'female' virtues had a distinctive part to play in culture and society" (Peukert, *The Weimar Republic*, 98).

14. For the academic response to Hitler's decrees, see Friedländer, *Nazi Germany and the Jews*, 49–52.

15. Ruprecht-Karls-Universität Heidelberg, "Ernst Levy stellt seine Vorlesungen ein."

16. Dorothee Mussgnug, ed., *Ernst Levy und Wolfgang Kunkel: Briefwechsel, 1922–1968*, 73. My translation.

17. Ernst Levy was one of just ten *Ordinarius* (full professor) historians dismissed from German universities after 1933. Catherine Epstein, *A Past Renewed*, 2n.

18. I thank Guenter Roth for sending me a copy of this letter from the Marianne Weber archives.

19. Mussgnug, ed., *Ernst Levy und Wolfgang Kunkel*, 75, 77. My translations.
20. Wolfgang Kunkel, "Ernst Levy zum Gedächtnis," xviii. My translation.

## Chapter 4

1. Edgar's reaction to New York seems to have been a necessary part of his leftward turn. Anthony Heilbut notes, "For émigré Marxists, America was everything about European capitalism, enlarged." Heilbut, *Exiled in Paradise*, 49.

2. This is the central thesis of David Nirenberg's magisterial survey, *Anti-Judaism: The Western Tradition.*

3. Such attitudes, familiar to me from my own upbringing, were noted by Donald Peterson Kent in his 1953 sociological study, *The Refugee Intellectual: Americanization of the Immigrants of 1933–1941*. Thirty years later, Heilbut would elaborate on them throughout *Exiled in Paradise* (1983).

4. Henry Pachter "On Being an Exile: An Old-Timer's Personal and Political Memoir," in *Hitler's Exiles*, ed. Mark M. Anderson, 340.

5. See Kent, *The Refugee Intellectual*, 23, 172–73, and Heilbut, *Exiled in Paradise*, 53–54.

6. Catherine Epstein writes, "Despite their arduous experiences in finding positions in the United States, the [refugee] historians of Roman law helped make the field known in the United States." Epstein, *A Past Renewed*, 11.

7. Although he traces the decline of Levy's influence after his death, Detlev Liebs writes, "The scholar who made Roman vulgar law into a basic idea of Late Antique law and who caused a vivid discussion lasting for decades, was Ernst Levy." See Liebs, "Roman Vulgar Law in Late Antiquity," 39. Reviewing Levy's collected essays, A. Arthur Schiller says, "Solely through Ernst Levy's efforts a new field has been added to the study of Roman law, an area internationally recognized as most fertile for future research." Review of *Ernst Levy: Gesammelte Schriften*, 1313.

8. Katz, "German Culture and the Jews," 96–97.

9. For Einstein's skepticism about quantum theory, see Walter Isaacson, *Einstein: His Life and Universe*, 448–70.

10. Xeroxes of the photographs were passed down to me, but they do not include the date for that issue of the *Seattle Times*.

## Chapter 5

1. For these paragraphs, I have relied on Susan Dunn, *1940: FDR, Willkie, Lindbergh, Hitler—The Election amid the Storm.*

2. Max Horkheimer and Theodor W. Adorno, *Dialectic of Enlightenment*, 126, 138, 139.

3. Timothy Snyder's *Bloodlands: Europe Between Hitler and Stalin* is a stunning history of the overlapping mass murders of the two regimes.

4. In December 1934, the German-Jewish Club of New York launched its monthly newsletter *Aufbau* (Reconstruction). In its early years the paper was primarily aimed at easing the entry of new immigrants: it announced teas, lectures, and English classes, and published ads from German Jewish businesses in German and/or English. After the Austrian Anschluss and Kristallnacht in 1938, it became

an international anti-Nazi newspaper to which my parents subscribed, wherever they lived.

5. Biographical information about Leary comes from "Dean William H. Leary," published at his retirement in 1950, *Utah Law Review* 2, 5–11.

6. Donald Peterson Kent reported in 1953 that American students tended to resist the "dogmatic positiveness" and the "intense intellectualism" of their German-trained professors, who concentrated more on their subjects than on their students. Kent, *The Refugee Intellectual*, 120–21.

## Chapter 6

1. The rushed atmosphere during the run-up to the trial is well described by Joseph Persico, *Nuremberg: Infamy on Trial*, 7–128.

2. My sources for the rationale of the Nuremberg trials include Persico's *Nuremberg* and two chapters from *Perspectives on the Nuremberg Trials*, ed. Guénaël Mettraux: Robert H. Jackson, "Nuremberg in Retrospect: Legal Answer to International Lawlessness," 354–71, and Telford Taylor, "The Nuremberg Trials," 372–407.

3. Robert H. Jackson, "Justice Jackson's Report to the President on Atrocities and War Crimes" of June 7, 1945, section III.

4. For the Morgenthau and Marshall Plans, I have relied on Tony Judt, *Postwar*, 90–99, 105–6. Carolyn Eisenberg discusses the failure of the denazification campaign in *Drawing the Line: The American Decision to Divide Germany, 1944–1949*, 122–35.

5. For a deliberately entertaining account of Goering close up, see Richard Sonnenfeldt, *Witness to Nuremberg: The Many Lives of the Man Who Translated at the Nazi War Trials*, ch. 1.

6. W. G. Sebald, *On the Natural History of Destruction*, 5. Sebald's narrative is an eloquent meditation on the situation Edgar witnessed in 1945.

7. For a study of Heidelberg's resistance to denazification, see Steven Remy, *The Heidelberg Myth*, 152–60. Remy shows in detail how the Nazi past would live on through the 1950s at Heidelberg, despite the university's reputation for liberalism.

8. Judt, *Postwar*, 57.

9. Rodger D. Citron, "The Nuremberg Trials and American Jurisprudence: The Decline of Legal Realism, the Revival of Natural Law, and the Development of Legal Process Theory."

10. Frank Trommler notes the crucial role of émigrés in US missions to Germany, whether as political spies or cultural mediators. *The United States and Germany in the Era of the Cold War, 1945–1990*, ed. Detlev Junker, 1:376–77.

11. Jessica Gienow-Hecht began a 1991 newspaper article on exiled German Jewish jurists with an anecdote about Ernst Levy ("Im Irrgarten der Stimmen. Ein Symposium zum Einfluss emigrierter Juristen in Amerika"). Levy, she claimed, had sent an article on Roman law to the *Columbia Law Review* in the late 1930s. "A thousand thanks for this fantastic article," the editor replied. "Unfortunately we can't publish it, because none of our readers would understand it."

12. Mussgnug, ed. *Ernst Levy und Wolfgang Kunkel*, 86, 86n. My translation.

13. The Levys' ambivalence about remigrating to Germany was shared by other academics who experienced both resistance on the German side and doubts about

returning after serving in American universities. Claus Dieter-Krohn, "Remigrants and Reconstruction," *The United States and Germany in the Era of the Cold War, 1945–1990*, ed. Junker, 1:528–35.

14. Remy, *The Heidelberg Myth*, 245, 231.

15. Mussgnug, ed. *Ernst Levy und Wolfgang Kunkel*, 14. My translation.

16. Judt, *Postwar*, 61.

17. Judt, *Postwar*, 146–49, and essays by Thomas A. Schwartz and Frank A. Ninkovich in *The United States and Germany in the Era of the Cold War, 1945–1990*, ed. Junker, 1:30–31, 118.

18. Judt, *Postwar*, 176–77.

19. These key components of the US cultural mission to Germany are described by Frank A. Trommler and Rebecca Boehling in *The United States and Germany in the Era of the Cold War, 1945–1990*, ed. Junker, 1:374–77, 390–412. See also Judt, *Postwar*, 224–25.

## Chapter 7

1. For a survey of Brigitte's legislative work, see Carol Bruch's footnotes to "Poem in Tribute."

2. Brigitte Bodenheimer, "Reflections on the Future of Grounds for Divorce," 192.

3. Bruch, "Poem in Tribute," note 12.

4. Ibid.

5. According to Harriet Friedenreich and Marion Rowekamp, just "Three European Jewish women became professors of law after World War II: Helen Silying-Ryu in Puerto Rico, Brigitte Levy Bodenheimer in Utah, and Kate Wallach in Louisiana." Jewish Women's Archive, "Lawyers in Germany and Austria."

6. Bruch, "Poem in Tribute," note 4.

7. Harry D. Krause, "American Family Law and Brigitte Marianne Bodenheimer," 320.

8. Lon L. Fuller, review of *Jurisprudence* (1940), 967.

9. Ms. in English, "Author's Preface to the Chinese Edition," 1–2.

10. John J. Flynn, "Edgar Bodenheimer and the Search for the Good," 474–75.

11. Raymond Dennehy, "Bodenheimer's Theory of Natural Law: The Conflict of a Divided Intellectual Allegiance."

## Chapter 8

1. Here and throughout the chapter I am indebted to Beate Frankfurther Planskoy, for her memories of the Sachs-Lachmann-Frankfurther connections.

2. William M. Calder III, "Eva Sachs on Ulrich von Wilamowitz-Moellendorf," 203. Professor Calder spent much of his writing career on the life and work of Wilamowitz-Moellendorf.

3. Ibid., 207.

4. Although the name of Walter Sachs had come up occasionally over the years, I could not be sure that he was Kaethe's brother until my nephew Dan Bodenheimer came up with documents that support these facts.

5. Calder, "Eva Sachs on Ulrich von Wilamowitz-Moellendorf," 208–10.

6. I learned about Sugihara's heroism from Joanna Olczak-Ronikier, *In the*

*Garden of Memory*, 274–75, and Snyder, *Bloodlands*, 143. His effort to save fleeing Jews was an unusual by-product of intelligence connections between Poland and Japan.

7. I am grateful to Beate Planskoy for allowing me to copy these letters.

## Chapter 9

1. Anthony Heilbut, *Exiled in Paradise*, 208.

2. Ron Blau, "On the Deck a Man Dances," ms. interview with Teddy Blau. The difficulty of finding American work commensurate with one's German training and the special resilience of the women are common themes in the literature of German Jewish emigration.

3. Ibid.

## Afterword

1. For a helpful assessment of Arendt's positions, see Deborah Lipstadt, *The Eichmann Trial.*

2. Heilbut, *Exiled in Paradise*, 349.

3. Brigitte (Schoenberg) Hirschfeld Bodenheimer.

4. Katz's lecture and subsequent lectures by other family law scholars were published in the *UC Davis Law Review.*

5. Steven M. Lowenstein, "Epilogue" to *German-Jewish History in Modern Times*, ed. Meyer, 4:402.

# Works Cited


Anderson, Mark M., ed. *Hitler's Exiles: Personal Stories of the Flight from Nazi Germany to America*. New York: New Press, 1998.

Angress, Werner. "The German Army's Judenzahlung of 1916." *Leo Baeck Institute Year Book* 23, no. 1 (1978): 117–38.

Arendt, Hannah. *Eichmann in Jerusalem: A Report on the Banality of Evil*. New York: Penguin Books, 1964.

Aschheim, Steven. E. *Brother and Strangers: The East European Jew in German and German Jewish Consciousness, 1800–1923*. Madison: University of Wisconsin Press, 1982.

*Aufbau* (New York, 1934–2004). https://archive.org/details/aufbau. Accessed April 9, 2015.

Bendix, Reinhard. *From Berlin to Berkeley: German-Jewish Identities*. New Brunswick and Oxford: Transaction Books, 1986.

Blau, Ron. "On the Deck a Man Dances." Ms. transcript of interview with Teddy Blau, 1980.

———. *Our Time in the Garden*. The National Center for Jewish Film.

———. "Why I Refuse to Make this Film." Ms. transcript of interview with Gerda Blau, 1979.

Bodenheimer, Brigitte M. "Law and Family: One Woman's Dialectic." Interview with Stella Levy. Martin Luther King, Jr., Hall. University of California, Davis. *The Advocate* 12, no. 13 (April 17, 1979): 1–2.

———. Ms. transcript of interview with Stella Levy, 1979.

———. "Reflections on the Future of Grounds for Divorce." *Journal of Family Law* 8, no. 2 (Summer 1968): 179–218.

———. "The Uniform Child Custody Jurisdiction Act: A Legislative Remedy for Children Caught in the Conflict of Laws." *Vanderbilt Law Review* 22, no. 6 (November 1969): 1207–52.

———. "The Utah Marriage Counseling Experiment: An Account of Changes in Divorce Law and Procedure." *Utah Law Review* 7, no. 4 (Fall 1961): 443–77.

Bodenheimer, Edgar. "Author's Preface to the Chinese Edition" of *Jurisprudence*. Ms. 1987.

———. "Hegel's Politico-Legal Philosophy: A Reevaluation." *The American Journal of Jurisprudence* 35 (1990): 217–46.

———. *Jurisprudence*. New York: McGraw-Hill, 1940.

———. *Jurisprudence: The Philosophy and Method of the Law*. Cambridge, Mass.: Harvard University Press, 1962.

———. *Philosophy of Responsibility*. Little, Colorado: Fred B. Rothman & Co., 1980.

———. *Power, Law, and Society: A Study of the Will to Power and the Will to Law*. New York: Crane, Russak and Company, 1973.

———. *Treatise on Justice*. New York: Philosophical Library, 1967.

Bruch, Carol S. "Poem in Tribute" to Brigitte M. Bodenheimer. *UC Davis Law Review* 12, no. 2 (Summer 1979): i–vi.

Calder, William M., III. "Eva Sachs on Ulrich von Wilamowitz-Moellendorf." *Illinois Classical Studies* 13, no. 1 (1988): 203–16.

Citron, Rodger D. "The Nuremberg Trials and American Jurisprudence: The Decline of Legal Realism, the Revival of Natural Law, and the Development of Legal Process Theory." In *The Nuremberg War Crimes Trial and its Policy Consequences Today*, ed. Beth A. Griech-Polelle, 77–96. Baden-Baden: Nomos, 2009.

"Dean William H. Leary." *Utah Law Review* 2 (1950): 5–11.

Dennehy, Raymond. "Bodenheimer's Theory of Natural Law: The Conflict of a Divided Intellectual Allegiance." *UC Davis Law Review* 26, no. 3 (Spring 1993): 619–52.

Dunn, Susan. *1940: FDR, Willkie, Lindbergh, Hitler—The Election amid the Storm*. New Haven and London: Yale University Press, 2013.

Durham, W. Cole, Jr. "Edgar Bodenheimer: Conservator of Civilized Legal Culture." In *Der Einfluss deutscher Emigranten auf die Rechtsentwicklung in den USA und in Deutschland*, ed. Marcus Lutter, Ernst C. Stiefel, and Michael H Hoeflich, 127–43. Tübingen: J.C.B. Mohr, 1993.

Dwork, Debórah, and Robert Jan van Pelt. *Flight from the Reich: Refugee Jews, 1933–1946*. New York and London: W. W. Norton, 2009.

Eiland, Howard, and Michael W. Jennings. *Walter Benjamin: A Critical Life*. Cambridge, Mass., and London: Belknap Press, 2014.

Eisenberg, Carolyn Woods. *Drawing the Line: The American Decision to Divide Germany, 1944–1949*. Cambridge: Cambridge University Press, 1996.

Elon, Amos. *The Pity of It All: A History of Jews in Germany, 1743–1933*. New York: Henry Holt, 2002.

Epstein, Catherine. *A Past Renewed: A Catalogue of German-Speaking Refugee Historians in the United States after 1933*. Cambridge: Cambridge University Press, 1993.

Flynn, John J. "Edgar Bodenheimer and the Search for the Good." *UC Davis Law Review* 21, no. 3 (Spring 1988): 471–76.

Friedenreich, Harriet, and Marion Rowekamp. "Lawyers in Germany and Austria." *Jewish Women's Archive*. http://jwa.org/encyclopedia/article/lawyers-in-germany-and-austria. Accessed April 18, 2015.

Friedländer, Saul. *Nazi Germany and the Jews: The Years of Persecution, 1933–1939*. New York: HarperCollins, 1997.

Fuller, Lon L. Review of Edgar Bodenheimer, *Jurisprudence* (1940). *Columbia Law Review* 41, no. 5 (May 1941): 965–67.

Gienow-Hecht, Jessica. "Im Irrgarten der Stimmen. Ein Symposium zum Einfluss emigrierter Juristen in Amerika." *Frankfurter Allgemeine Zeitung*, September 25, 1991.

Green, Martin. *The von Richthofen Sisters: The Triumphant and the Tragic Modes of Love*. New York: Basic Books, 1974.
Heilbut, Anthony. *Exiled in Paradise: German Refugee Artists and Intellectuals in America from the 1930s to the Present*. Berkeley: University of California Press, 1983.
Horkheimer, Max, and Theodor W. Adorno. *Dialectic of Enlightenment*. Trans. John Cumming. New York: Continuum, 1944.
Isaacson, Walter. *Einstein: His Life and Universe*. New York: Simon and Schuster, 2008.
Jackson, Robert H. "Justice Jackson's Report to the President on Atrocities and War Crimes" of June 7, 1945. Yale Law School Avalon Project: Documents in Law, History and Diplomacy. *http://avalon.law.yale.edu/imt/imt_jack01.asp*. Accessed April 16, 2015.
Judt, Tony. *Postwar: A History of Europe Since 1945*. New York: Penguin Group, 2005.
Junker, Detlef, ed. *The United States and Germany in the Era of the Cold War, 1945–1990*. Vol. 1. Cambridge: Cambridge University Press, 2004.
Katz, Jacob. "German Culture and the Jews." In *The Jewish Response to German Culture*, ed. Yehuda Reinhartz and Walter Schatzberg, 85–99. Lebanon, N.H.: University Press of New England, 1985.
Katz, Sanford N. "Brigitte Bodenheimer—Protector of Children." *UC Davis Law Review* 16, no. 1 (Fall 1982): vii–xi.
Kent, Donald Peterson. *The Refugee Intellectual: The Americanization of the Immigrants of 1933–41*. New York: Columbia University Press, 1953.
Kirkbright, Suzanne. *Karl Jaspers, A Biography: Navigations in Truth*. New Haven and London: Yale University Press, 2004.
Krause, Harry D. "American Family Law and Brigitte Marianne Bodenheimer." In *Der Einfluss deutscher Emigranten auf die Rechtsentwicklung in den USA und in Deutschland*, ed. Marcus Lutter, Ernst C. Stiefel, and Michael H Hoeflich, 309–20. Tübingen: J.C.B. Mohr, 1993.
Kunkel, Wolfgang. "Ernst Levy zum Gedächtnis." *Zeitung der Savigny-Stiftung für Rechtsgeschichte (SZ)*. Romanistische Abteiling 86 (1969): xxiii–xxxii.
Levy, Ernst. *West Roman Vulgar Law: The Law of Property*. Philadelphia: American Philosophical Society, 1951.
Liebs, Detlef. "Roman Vulgar Law in Late Antiquity." In *Aspects of Law in Late Antiquity*, ed. Boudewijn Sirks, 35–53. Oxford: All Souls College, 2008.
Lipstadt, Deborah E. *The Eichmann Trial*. New York: Schocken Books, 2011.
Mendes-Flohr, Paul. *German Jews: A Dual Identity*. New Haven and London: Yale University Press, 1999.
Mettraux, Guénaël, ed. *Perspectives on the Nuremberg Trial*. Oxford: Oxford University Press, 2008.
Meyer, Michael A., ed. *German-Jewish History in Modern Times*. Vol. 4. New York: Columbia University Press, 1998.
Mosse, George L. *German Jews Beyond Judaism*. Bloomington: Indiana University Press, 1985.
Mussgnug, Dorothee, ed. *Ernst Levy und Wolfgang Kunkel: Briefwechsel, 1922–1968*. Heidelberg: Universitätsverlag, 2005.
Niewyk, Donald L. *The Jews in Weimar Germany*. Baton Rouge and London: Louisiana State University Press, 1980.

Nirenberg, David. *Anti-Judaism: The Western Tradition*. New York and London: W. W. Norton, 2013.

Olczak-Ronikier, Joanna. *In the Garden of Memory: A Family Memoir*. Tr. Antonia Lloyd-Jones. London: Weidenfeld and Nicolson, 2004.

Persico, Joseph E. *Nuremberg: Infamy on Trial*. New York: Penguin Books, 1994.

Peukert, Detlev J. K. *The Weimar Republic: The Crisis of Classical Modernity*. Tr. Richard Deveson. New York: Hill and Wang, 1989.

Remy, Steven P. *The Heidelberg Myth: The Nazification and Denazification of a German University*. Cambridge, Mass., and London: Harvard University Press, 2002.

Rheins, Carl J. "The Verband Nationaldeutscher Juden, 1921–1933." *Leo Baeck Institute Yearbook* 25, no. 1 (1980): 243–68.

Roth, Guenter. "Marianne Weber and Her Circle." *Society* 27, no. 2 (January 1990): 63–69.

Ruprecht-Karls-Universität Heidelberg. Special Exhibition: "Jews at Heidelberg University." "Levys Ruf an die Universität Bonn." *Universitätsarchiv Heidelberg*. http://wwwnp.tphys.uni-heidelberg.de/Ausstellung/show.cgi?de&D&24&169. Accessed January 8, 2003.

———. "Levy Stellt seine Vorlesungen ein." *Universitätsarchiv Heidelberg*. http://wwwnp.tphys.uni-heidelberg.de/Ausstellung/show.cgi?de&D&24&170. Accessed January 6, 2003.

Schiller, A. Arthur. Review of *Ernst Levy, Gesammelte Schriften*. *Columbia Law Review* 65, no. 7 (1965): 1311–15.

Sebald, W. G. *On the Natural History of Destruction*. Trans. Anthea Bell. New York: Random House, 2003.

Simon, Ulrich. *Sitting in Judgement, 1913–1963*. London: SPCK, 1978.

Snyder, Timothy. *Bloodlands: Europe Between Hitler and Stalin*. New York: Basic Books, 2010.

Sonnenfeldt, Richard W. *Witness to Nuremberg: The Many Lives of the Man Who Translated at the Nazi War Trials*. New York: Arcade Publishing, 2002.

United States Holocaust Memorial Museum. "U.S. Quotas and Visas." *Resources for Teachers*. http://www.ushmm.org/exhibition/st-louis/teach/supread2.htm. Accessed April 4, 2015.

———. "Voyage of the St. Louis." *Holocaust Encyclopedia*. http://www.ushmm.org/wlc/en/article.php?ModuleId=10005267. Accessed April 6, 2015.

Volkov, Shulamit. *Walther Rathenau: Weimar's Fallen Statesman*. New Haven and London: Yale University Press, 2012.

Wagner, Richard. "Judaism in Music." *Judaism in Music and Other Essays*. Trans. William Acton Ellis. Lincoln and London: University of Nebraska Press, 1995.

Weber, Marianne. *Max Weber: A Biography*. Trans. Harry Zohn. New York: John Wiley and Sons, 1975.

Weitz, Eric D. *Weimar Germany: Promise and Tragedy*. Princeton: Princeton University Press, 2007.

Wertheimer, Jack. *Unwelcome Strangers: East European Jews in Imperial Germany*. New York and Oxford: Oxford University Press, 1987.

Zipkes, Rudolf G. *Gelebtes Leben: Jude sein in einer weltoffenen Zeit 70–76*. Zurich: Orell Fuessli Verlag, 2005.

# Index

*Page numbers in italics refer to illustrations*


Abravanel, Maurice, 183, 184
Adenauer, Konrad, 131, 138
Adler, Ada, 164
Adler, Mortimer, 106
Adorno, Theodor, 74, 103
America First Movement, 94
America Houses, 134–35
anti-Semitism: in America, 41, 77, 94, 112; in Germany postwar, 122–23, 125, 127, 129, 131; in Germany prewar, xiii, 8, 9, 21–22, 60, 81, 101
Arab-Israeli conflicts, 191
Arendt, Hannah, 190–91
Aristotle, 106
*Aufbau*, 105, 194, 200n4
Auschwitz, 79, 190
Austrian Anschluss, 87, 177, 200n4

Baeck, Rabbi Leo, 21, 182
Barkai, Avraham, 197n10
Barrett, Edward L., 153
Beer Hall Putsch, trial of Hitler after, 12
Bendix, Reinhard, 198n9
Benjamin, Walter, 197n9
Berlin Airlift, 131
Berlin Wall, 132, 133
*Bildung*, xiii xiv, 2, 4, 27, 84, 129
Bismarck, Otto von, 10
Blau, Bebs and Teddy (Edgar's sister and brother-in-law), 44, 98, 186–88
Blau, Fred (son of Bebs and Teddy), 85, 187
Blau, Ron (son of Bebs and Teddy), 187–88; "On the Deck a Man Dances" (interview with Teddy Blau), 203n2; *Our Time in the Garden* (film), 197n3
Blau, Teddy (brother-in-law of Edgar), 187–88, 189, 203n2
Bodenheimer, Brigitte Hirschfeld née Schoenberg (second wife of Edgar), 191
Bodenheimer, Brigitte Marianne Levy, early life and educaton in Germany: acquaintance with Marianne Weber and Else von Richthofen Jaffé, 55–56; birth in 1912, 46; childhood hardships, 51–52; correspondence preserved from childhood and youth, 45–46; denied admission to German state examinations, 59; emigration to United States at age of twenty, xiii–xiv, 59; entered university in 1930, 57; in family portrait, 1924, *52*; friendship with Erika Heyd, 53–54; invitations to social events hosted by German professoriate, 57–58; with mother and brother in 1915, *51*; with mother in 1931, *54*; return to Germany in 1934 to complete degree of Juris Doktor, magna cum laude, 62–63; summer in England to practice English, 46; years of school in Freiburg, 52–53; youthful obliviousness to Nazi threat, 59–60
Bodenheimer, Brigitte Marianne Levy, education and career in America: assistance to Ernst Levy in translation of his book into English, 138; autobiographical interview at retirement from UC Davis Law School, xv, 59–62, 199n12; bar ex-

ams in Washington and Utah, 86, 91, 137; became US citizen in 1939, 86; break from career for first three years of each child's life, 137; chair of Special Committee on Juvenile Courts, Utah Bar Association, 142; at Columbia and University of Washington law schools, 44, 60–62, 71, 75–76; Commissioner on Uniform State Laws for the State of Utah, 142; drafting of legislation in Utah, 139–40; effect of attitudes toward professional women on career, 86–87, 146; on faculty of UC Davis School of Law, 144; on faculty of Utah School of Law, 144, 153; with Federal Housing Authority, 95–96, 104; publication of articles about family law, 141; publication of *Manual for Justices of the Peace in the State of Utah*, 140; "Reflections on the Future of Grounds for Divorce," 141–42; resistance to growing trend toward joint custody of children, 143; sacrifice of career for Edgar's career moves, 75, 142, 144, 146–47; *Salt Lake Tribune* story on her ability to raise a family and pursue a career, 137; as Special Assistant to the Attorney General of Utah, 139; tribute to at Symposium on German Jurists in Exile, 1991, 145; US delegate to Hague Conference on Private International Law, xv; "The Utah Marriage Counseling Experiment: An Account of Changes in Divorce Law and Procedure," 141; *Wiedergutmachung* clients, 138–40, 145; work on divorce reform laws in Utah, 140–41; work on Uniform Child Custody Jurisdiction Act and Hague Convention on International Child Abduction, xv, 142–44, 146; work with Women's Legislative Council, 140

Bodenheimer, Brigitte Marianne Levy, family and personal life in America: in 1965, *143*; approach to mothering, 186, 194; assistance to Jewish refugees in Seattle, 92; death in 1981 at age sixty-eight, xv, 145; description of newlywed state, 69; efforts to persuade parents to leave Germany, 63–64; household settlement in Seattle, 75–76; journal of children's development, 85–86, 104; letters from and to Edgar in summer of 1935, 64–67; move of parents from Switzerland to Davis, California in 1966, 75–76; postwar reestablishment of connections with friends in Germany, 70–71; relationship with Kaethe Sachs, 174–75; research for Edgar's book, 80, 86; search for acceptable childcare, 95–97; summer in Germany in 1934, 62–66; view of Americans, 76–77. *See also* Bodenheimer, Edgar and Brigitte, family life

Bodenheimer, Edgar and Brigitte, family life: affectionate family life, 84–85; birth of Peter on June 29, 1937, 77, 85; birth of Rosemarie on October 11, 1946, 105, 109; birth of Thomas on June 13, 1939, 77, 85; celebration of Passover, 102; child rearing, 178–79; children's study of instruments and playing of chamber music, 184; Edgar and Brigitte in Davis living room, 1978, *154*; family ski and hiking trips in Salt Lake City, 176–77; friendships with Americans in Seattle, 77; German Christmas celebration, 102, 181; home life guided by European habits of Edgar, 177–78; joined Reform synagogue, Temple B'nai Israel, 182–83; move from Salt Lake City to Davis, California, 153; move from Seattle to Washington DC, 91–93; move to from Washington DC to Salt Lake City, 110–11; presentation of Judaism to children, 101–2; rare mention of Holocaust in household, 104–5, 129; summer in Germany in 1953, 125–26, 127–33; summer in Germany in 1959, 125–26, 133–36; summer resort vacations at invitation of Siegmund and Rosi, 185–86; trip to Switzerland in August 1935, 67; wedding on June 6, 1935, xv, 67, *68*. *See also* Bodenheimer, Edgar

Bodenheimer, Dan (grandson of Edgar and Brigitte), 176

Bodenheimer, Edgar, early life and education in Germany: assumption that father's wealth should be used to support aims of his children, 18; beginning of political awareness, 9–12; dedication to sports and physical training, 3; devotion to music and cultivation of musical taste, 2–4; difficulties with father over engagement to Brigitte, 41–44; difficulties with father over relationship with Hesi, 36–39; dislike of *einseitig* (one-sided), 4; dismissal from state legal apprenticeship system because of "non-Aryan" extraction, 27–29; first mention of *Judentum* as a subject, 20–21; grand tour after completion of *Abitur*, 15–16; at Grunewald Gymnasium, 1, 12–13; at Joachim Friedrich Gymnasium, 1; membership in League of Nationalist German Jews, 29, 31–33; photograph of at age of eighteen, *3*; pranks played with Hilde and other friends, 11–15; production of verse dramas imitating Schiller or Goethe, 9; record of reading and intellectual life in journals, 4, 16–18; relationship between Judaism and nationalism as intellectual problem, 21, 29, 31–33; relationship with Hilde, 19–20; romantic and political turbulence during early 1930s, 26–27; with Rosi and Siegmund, c. 1911, *6*; sense of superiority, 18–19; skating with sister Bebs, c. 1919, *10*; study of law and award of degree of Juris Doktor, magna cum laude, 17–18, 25, 26; summer in England to practice English, 17; taken with degeneration theories, 16, 17

Bodenheimer, Edgar, education and career in America: degree in law librarianship from University of Washington, 88; desire to teach at UC Berkeley and interest in UCLA, 147–48; East Coast job search in 1940, 89–91; first job at New York law firm of Rosenberg, Goldmark and Colin, 35, 41; in his office during 1960s, *149*; in Labor Department Solicitor's Office, 91, 94–95, 98; mission as writer and teacher, 83–84; offer of professorship from University of Texas at Austin, 152–53; professor at UC Davis School of Law, 153–54; professor at University of Utah School of Law, xv, 105–11, 147; push for academic recognition, 81–82; search for government position, 90–91; seminars for Riccobono Seminar of Roman Law in America, 99–100, 186; Senior Attorney at Office of the Alien Property Custodian, 98–99; study of law New York University and University of Washington, 41, 44, 46; visiting positions, seminars, and lectures around the US, 80–81, 148–49, 186; writings, 154–55

Bodenheimer, Edgar, family and personal life in America: in 1985, *193*; alternation between German and English in journal writing, xvi; became US citizen in 1939, 86; courting of Brigitte Levy, 35, 40, 64–67; death in 1991, xiv, 192; difficulties with father over his decision to marry Brigitte Levy, 41–44; disgust for New York City and United States, 40–41, 72, 200n1; emigration toUnited Statesin 1933, 35; letters to Ernst and Marie Levy, 97–98; love of mountains, 75; preservation of lifetime of written materials, xv; relationship with father, 98; renewed correspondence with Hilde in late life, 14–15, 20; second marriage, 191; speech of thanksgiving and apology at father's seventieth birthday celebration, 34–35; study of American speech, xvi; weekly "Sunday school" for children, 76, 101–2, 183. *See also* Bodenheimer, Edgar and Brigitte, family life

Bodenheimer, Edgar, postwar trips to Germany: on attitudes in Germany in 1959, 135; description of atmosphere of occupied Germany, 114–16; description of attitudes and behavior of German people, 122–24, 130–31; "Diary of the European Trip, 1953," 129–33; efforts to dissuade Ernst Levy from returning to Germany, 121–22; Nuremberg journal, 114–19, 123–25; research trip to Germany to help prepare for Nuremberg trials, xvi, 105, 112–36; on returns to Germany, 193; trip to Berlin with Brigitte in 1953, 132–33; visiting lecturer at University of Freiburg in 1959, 133–36; visiting scholar at Max Planck Institute for Foreign and International Criminal Law in 1973, 136; visits in later years, 136

Bodenheimer, Edgar, beliefs, philosophy, and writings: belief that Jews would join Communist revolution, 73; Catholic affinities, 90, 100; defense of Hegel's philosophy of law, 136, 192; diatribes against evils of Disney cartoons, 102–4; distrust of democratic process, 102–4; fear of reappearance of Nazi Germany in other forms, 150–53; on forced asceticism of Jews through anti-Semitism, 102; idealized Soviet socialism, 72–74, 81, 83, 102, 104; on Jewish cynicism and intellectualism, 81, 101; lifelong belief in Enlightenment values, 136, 151; on Mormons, 107–8, 110; natural law philosophy, 29, 83–84, 88, 90, 150–52, 155, 182–83; order and justice as pillars of jurisprudence, 151–52; *Philosophy of Responsibility*, 154; *Power, Law and Society*, 16, 154; Prussian belief in discipline and self-restraint, 102; publication and revision of *Jurisprudence: The Philosophy and Method of the Law*, 80, 88, 100, 149–52; and question of Jewish identity, 74, 100–102; and reading of Einstein, 83; rejection of permissive American culture, 102; *Treatise on Justice*, 154

Bodenheimer, Else (wife of Louis), 187, 188–89

Bodenheimer, Gerda (Bebs) (sister of Edgar), 4, 9, *10*, 33, 43, 44. *See also* Blau, Bebs and Teddy

Bodenheimer, Helga (sister of Edgar), 4, 90, 98, 186–87

Bodenheimer, Louis (brother of Siegmund), 187

Bodenheimer, Peter (son of Edgar and Brigitte), 77, 85–86, 101, 105, 111, 128–29, *138*, 148

Bodenheimer, Rosa (Rosi) Maass (mother of Edgar), 5–6, 18–19, 34–35, 39–40, *40*, 67, *68*, 185. *See also* Bodenheimer, Siegmund and Rosa

Bodenheimer, Rosemarie (daughter of Edgar and Brigitte), 105, 109, 128–29, 134–35, *138*, 173–75, 184, 192–95

Bodenheimer, Siegmund and Rosa: apartment at 315 Central Park West, 44, 185–86; celebration of fiftieth wedding anniversary, 188; emigration to United States in 1936, xvii, 44; frequent travel in 1934-35, 40, 44; impressions of Palestine, 40; Jagowstrasse villa in Grunewald, 1, 7 (*See also* Jagowstrasse villa); marriage in 1907, 5; summers at Mohonk Mountain House in Hudson Valley, 186; tour of United States in 1935, 44, 67; at wedding of Edgar and Brigitte, 1935, *68*

Bodenheimer, Siegmund (father of Edgar), life and career in Germany: acknowledgment of German anti-Semitism and scapegoating of Jews, 8; acquisition of Impressionist landscape paintings, 55; and Danat-Bank, 7; and Darmstädter Bank für Handel und Industrie, 5; as demanding father, 4; despair of future due to mismanaged business and financial institutions, 24–25; disapproval of *einseitige* devotion to stock speculation in banking practices, 4–5; end of connection with Dresdner Bank, 25, 33; fiftieth birthday celebration in 1924, 8–9; letter welcoming Brigitte into family, 44; member of *Gesellschaft der Freunde* (Society of Friends), 8; patron and financier for siblings, 7–8; release from WWI duty through efforts of Darmstädter Bank, 7; with Rosi and Edgar, c. 1911, *6*; struggle with Edgar over his engagement to Brigitte, 42–44; struggle with Edgar over relationship with Hesi, 36–39; unpublished *Mein Leben* as detailed record of banking career, 5, 24–25; verses on family occasions, 9, 94; view of WWI as death of era, 6–7

Bodenheimer, Siegmund (father of Edgar), life in America: in 1944, *34*; celebrations of seventieth, eightieth, and ninetieth birthdays, 34–35, 188; death in 1966, 188;

disagreement with Edgar's decision to become a law professor, 88, 188; requests for emigration help from family members left in Germany, 87–88; requirement that Edgar not speak of his Communist sympathies, 82; at wedding of Edgar and Brigitte, 1935, *68*
Bodenheimer, Thomas (son of Edgar and Brigitte), 77, 85–86, 97, 101, 105, 128–29, 134, *138*, 180, 184, 186
Bodenheimer family tree, *xix*
Boeing plant, Seattle, 94
Braun, Otto, 10–11
Bruch, Carol, 142, 192
Brüning, Heinrich (German Chancellor), 24, 25
Buber, Martin, 131

Calder, William, 164–65, 202n2 (Chapter 8)
Camp Catawba, North Carolina, 97, 169, 173, 186
Central Union of German Citizens of the Jewish Faith, 30
Chamberlain, Neville, 87
Cold War, 131
Communism, 28, 31, 73–74, 82–83, 101
Cooper, Edith (née Fränkel), 173
Craven, Josephine (Brigitte's landlady in England), 46
"The Culture Industry: Enlightenment as Mass Deception" (Horkheimer and Adorno), 103

Danat-Bank, 7, 24–25, 33
Darmstädter Bank, 5, 7
Deinard, Benedict, 119–20
denazification, 117, 122, 124
Dennehy, Raymond, 155
Disraeli, Benjamin, 73, 74
Döblin, Alfred, 119
Dodd, Thomas J., 117
Dresdner Bank, 25, 33
Durham, W. Cole, Jr., 192
Dykstra, Dan and Lily, 144, 153

East German Uprising, 132–33
Ehrenzweig, Alfred, 147–48
Eichmann, Adolf, trial of, 190–91
*einseitig* (one-sided), 4, 5, 17, 84
Einstein, Albert, 83

Fair Labor Standards Act of 1938, 95
Flynn, John J., 153
Fraenkel, Eduard, 166
Fraenkel, Lilli, 166
Frank, Robert, 96
Fränkel, Brigitte, 166–67
Fränkel, Edith, 166–67, 171, 173
Fränkel, Hermann and Lilli, née Fraenkel, 166–67, 171, 173
Frankfurt School, Institute of Social Research, 81–82, 103
Friedenreich, Harriet, 202n5
Fulbright exchange program, 128, 134
Fuller, Lon L., 89, 151–52

German Enlightenment ideals, held by Jewish Germans, xiii, 21, 136, 151
German handwriting, debate between Gothic and Roman, xvi
German Hellenism, 2, 19, 164–65
German Jews. *See* Jewish German émigrés to United States; Jewish Germans in Germany
German National League of Women's Associations, 55
German women's movement, 199n13
Germany, post-WWII: anti-Semitism, 122–23, 135; Berlin Airlift, 131; cities in ruins, 114–16; division of, 131–33; repression of Nazi atrocities, 119, 130; unwelcoming to returning refugees, 121; *Wiedergutmachung*, 138
Germany, pre-WWII: election of 107 members of Nazi Party to Reichstag, 25, 34; emphasis on sport and physical training, 2–3; post-WWI inflation, 7, 52; shift from embrace of *Bildung* to nationalism and conformity, 2; stock market crash of 1873, 8. *See also* Germany, under Nazi rule; Hitler, Adolf
Germany, under Nazi rule: beginning of actions against Jews in early 1933, 28; campaign to appropriate Jewish property, 39; concentration camps, 104–5; Enabling Act of 1933, 28; *Gleichschaltung* (synchro-

nization) policy, 28; Kristallnacht, 87, 168, 200n4; last remaining window of escape from, 92; Law for the Restoration of the Professional Civil Service, definition of "non-Aryan," 28–29; Nuremberg Citizenship Law, stripping Jews of civil rights, 69; Reich Flight Tax and *Sperrmark*, 39; Reichstag fire of February 27, 1933, 28; student boycotts of Jewish professors, 63, 68. *See also* Hitler, Adolf
Gestapo, 168
Gienow-Hecht, Jessica, 201n11
*Gleichschaltung* (synchronization) policy, 28
Goering, Hermann, 117–18, 123, 201n5 (Chapter 6)
Goethe, Johann Wolfgang von, xiii, 2, 4, 5, 9, 26–27
Goldschmidt, Jakob, 24
Gorky, Maxim, "The Lower Depths," 115
Gross, Otto, and erotic liberation movement, 57
Grunewald, Berlin, 1, 7, 8, 10, 47
Grunewald Gymnasium, Berlin, 1–3, 10, 198n9
Gutswiller, Max, 58

Hague Conference on Private International Law, xv
Hague Convention on International Child Abduction, 144–45
Hahn, Margot, 181
Hahn, Toni, 181–82
Hahn, Walter, 111, 181
*Hakenkreuz* (swastika), 11
Heidelberg University: Brigitte's studies at, 57, 60, 62–64; domination by former Nazis in 1950s, 127, 201n7; Edgar's studies at, 17–18, 25–26; Ernst Levy's position at, 53–54, 58–59, 62–63, 68, 120–24, 126–27
Heilbut, Anthony, 191, 198n11, 200n1
Hesi (girlfriend of Edgar), 26, 36–39
Heyd, Erika, 53–55, 70–71
Heydrich, Reinhard, 123
Hilde (school friend of Edgar), 2; letters to Edgar between 1928 and 1933, 19–20; meeting with Edgar in New York, 35; pranks played with Edgar and other school friends, 11–15; renewed correspondence with Edgar in late life, 14–15, 20; study of law, 19
Hindenburg, Paul von, 11, 27–28
Hitler, Adolf: annexation of Czech Sudetenland, 87; annual Nazi Party rallies in Nuremberg, 113; appointment as Chancellor on January 30, 1933, 27–28; and Austrian Anschluss, 87, 177, 200n4; and Battle of Britain, 94; and Beer Hall Putsch, 12; draft plans for German-occupied France and Poland, 117–18; final solution, 104–5; French and English appeasement policy toward, 87; invasion and occupation of Denmark, Norway, Holland, Belgium, Luxembourg, and France, 94; invasion of Poland, 169; *Mein Kampf*, 12, 33, 63; Nazi Party flag with swastika emblem, 11; purge of Reichstag Communists and mass arrests of Communists, 28; 1933 seizure of power *(Machtergreifung)*, 25, 33. *See also* Germany, under Nazi rule
*Hitlerzeit*, 125
Holdsworth, William S.: *History of English Law*, 80
Holocaust, xviii, 129, 190–91
Horkheimer, Max, 74, 81–82, 103
House Un-American Activities Committee, 134, 178
Humboldt, Wilhelm von, 2

I. G. Farben, 115
Institute of Medieval Canon Law, 100
International Match Company, 41
International Military Tribunal, Nuremberg, 112–14, 124–25
Israel, 110, 190–91

Jackson, Justice Robert L., 112–1143, 122
Jacobs, Edward and Rose, 67
Jacoby, Sidney B., 112, 114–15
Jaffé, Edgar, 56
Jagowstrasse villa: destroyed by Allied bombing of Berlin, 40, 132; family home of Bodenheimers, 7; gathering place for Berlin cousins of Rosi, 158; renaming of street address as Richard Strauss Strasse, 40; used by Vera Lachmann as

school for Jewish children until Nazi closure of, 39–40
Jaspers, Gertrud Mayer, 58, 121–23, 126–27
Jaspers, Karl: intellectual life, 58–59; postwar, 121–22, 126; *The Question of German Guilt*, 127; taught Edgar and Brigitte in Heidelberg, 26, 59
Jellinek, Walter, 58
Jewish German émigrés to United States: correspondence in English to avoid suspicion, 97; eclipse of lifestyle by 1970s, 192; labeled as "enemy aliens" until gaining citizenship, 97; view of Americans as ignorant, crude, and permissive with children, 74, 198n12
Jewish Germans in Germany: assimilation efforts, xiii, 2, 22–23; emigration of 37,000 in 1933, xiv; Enlightenment ideals of, xiii, 21; experience of in Weimar Republic, 197n10; forced from professorate, 63, 68–69; middle-class disassociation from *Ostjuden*, 30; numbered 525,000 in January of 1933, xiv; scapegoating of during World War I, 48–49; support of the arts, 22, 197n5; welcomed into German army under "civic truce" of 1914, 48–49
Jewish Museum, Berlin, 191
Joachim Friedrich Gymnasium, Berlin-Wilmersdorf, 1, 47
*Judenzahl* (Jewish census) of number of Jews who served in World War I, 48–49
Judt, Tony, 130, 201n4

Kadish, Sanford, 149
Kadish Center for Morality, Law, and Public Affairs, 149
Kaser, Max, 127
Katz, Jacob, 195n7, 197n5
Katz, Sanford, 142–43, 192
Kaufmann, Ruth Neustadt (niece of Marie Levy), 79
Keitel, Wilhelm, 124
Kelsen, Hans, 89, 148
Kennedy assassination, 152–53
Khrushchev, Nikita, 133
Kimball, Spencer W., 110
Kokoschka, Oskar, 55
Korsch, Karl, 81
Kosterlitz, Hanna, 77, 92
Kranz, Walther, 2, 12–15
Krause, Harry, 145, 146
Kreuger, Ivar, 41
Kristallnacht, 87, 168, 200n4
Kunkel, Wolfgang, 69, 71, 80, 121, 126–27; "Ernst Levy zum Gedächtnis," 199n1
Kuttner, Eva, 100
Kuttner, Stephan, 99–100

Lachmann, Erich, death in 1914 at French front, 158
Lachmann, Karoline (mother of Vera and Nina), 158, 167
Lachmann, Louis, suicide of, 158
Lachmann, Nina, 158–59; marriage to Paul Frankfurther, 167–68
Lachmann, Vera: devotion to those who had nowhere to go, 171; embrace of German Hellenism, 165; emigration late in 1939 via transport visa through Sweden, 23, 169; first cousin to Kaethe Sachs, 158; letters with news of Kaethe's flight from Germany, 170–71; receipt of money from Edgar for emigration help, 87; school for Jewish children in Jagowstrasse villa, 22–23, 39–40, 167–68; summer camp for boys in North Carolina, 97, 169, 173, 186; visit to Bodenheimers at Villars in 1934, 66
Landis, James, 89
Landsberger, Joseph (uncle of Ernst Levy), 47
Lawrence, D. H., 57
League of Nationalist German Jews, 29–31, 183
Leary, William H., 106
legal training, German versus American system, 62
Levy, Betty Landsberger (mother of Ernst Levy), 47
Levy, Brigitte Marianne. *See* Bodenheimer, Brigitte Marianne Levy
Levy, Edna (daughter of Wolfgang and Ruth), 93
Levy, Ernst and Marie (parents of Brigitte): art legacy, 55; emigration to United

States in March of 1936, xviii, 69–70; family portrait, 1924, *52*; frequent trips to Germany between 1952 and 1956, 127; lifelong ties to liberal Heidelberg figures, 58; marriage in 1909, 46, 51; modest lifestyle, 54–55; move from Europe to Davis, California in 1966, 176, 184; move to Basel, Switzerland in 1956, 127; residence with Brigitte and Edgar in Seattle, 70, 77. *See also* Levy, Ernst; Levy, Zerline Marie Wolff
Levy, Ernst (father of Brigitte), life and career in Germany: attendance at Friedrich-Gymnasium and study at Stern Conservatory, 47; chair in Roman law at Heidelberg, 53–54; in family portrait, 1924, *52*; as father, 48; forced from teaching position at Heidelberg, 68–69; with his unit in World War I, *48*; law professor of Edgar in Heidelberg, 26, 35; positions at Universities of Frankfurt and Freiburg, 52; rigidly disciplined household, 50; teaching of law at University of Berlin and work toward *Habilitation*, 46; wartime letters to Marie, 49–50
Levy, Ernst (father of Brigitte), life and career in America: belief in aberration theory of Nazism, 126; death in 1968, 69–70; desire to return to Heidelberg, 120–22; Edgar's eulogy for, 184; influence on scholarship of Roman vulgar law, 200n7, 201n11; postwar attitudes toward Germany, 71; postwar resumption of communication with the Jaspers and Kunkel, 126; publication of *West Roman Vulgar Law*, 78; sabbatical of 1947-48 in Basel, Switzerland, 126–27; skepticism toward Soviet socialism, 104; teaching career at University of Washington, 77–78, 127
Levy, Ralph (son of Wolfgang and Ruth), 93
Levy, Reuben (son of Wolfgang and Ruth), 85, 92–93
Levy, Robert (father of Ernst Levy), 45–47
Levy, Ruth Jacobs (wife of Wolfgang Levy), 57, 63–64, 79, 85, 92
Levy, Stella, 59
Levy, Wolfgang (brother of Brigitte Levy), 47; in family portrait, 1924, *52*; left Germany for medical school in Vienna in 1928, 57; marriage to Ruth Jacobs, 57, 63–64; medical career, 51; with mother and sister in 1915, *51*; move of family from New York to Seattle, 92–93; move of family from Seattle to San Jose, 184; residency in radiology at Montefiore Hospital, New York, 64; tended to Marie during time she spent in New York, 79–80
Levy, Zerline Marie Wolff (mother of Brigitte Levy), life in Germany: awareness of Nazi danger, 59, 63; with Brigitte in 1931, *54*; with children in 1915, *51*; in family portrait, 1924, *52*; frustration at being deprived of attending medical school, 51; journal about her children, 47–48, 50–51
Levy, Zerline Marie Wolff (mother of Brigitte Levy), life in America: in 1942, *79*; commonplace book, 185; death in 1974, 70; depression over exile from Germany, 78–79; design of distinctive home in Seattle, 93, 184; help for Brigitte with baby Rosemarie, 109; move to Washington to care for children of Edgar and Brigitte, 96; relationship with Edgar, 97–98
Levy family tree, *xx*
Liebs, Detlev, 200n7
Lindbergh, Charles, 94
Llewellyn, Karl, 75, 87
London Blitz, 94
Lowenstein, Steven, 192

Maass, Alfred, 40, 158
Maass, Henrietta Lachmann (mother of Rosi), suicide of, 158
Maass, Louis (father of Rosi), 158
Maass, Oskar, suicide of, 158
Maass, Rosa (Rosi). *See* Bodenheimer, Rosa (Rosi) Maass
Mann, Thomas: *Buddenbrooks,* 16; Edgar and Brigitte's meeting with, 82; *The Magic Mountain,* 14
Marshall Plan, 117
Martini, Simone, 53
Marx, Karl, 74

Marxism, 81–83
*mauscheln* (contemptuous German verb for Jewish speech intonation), 22–23
Max Weber House, University of Heidelberg, 199n8
Mayer, Ernst, 58
Mayer, Flora Wolff (sister of Marie Levy), 47, 79
Mayer, Gustav, 47, 58, 79
McCarthy, Joseph, 134, 178
Mendes-Flohr, Paul, 197n10
Mommsen, Marie, 165
Morgenthau, Henry, plan for Germany in 1945, 116–17
Mormonism, 105, 107–8, 110, 176, 178–79, 182
Mosse, George, 2
Munich agreement of 1938, 87
Murrow, Edward R., 177–78
music, xiii, 2–4, 21–22, 47, 183–84
Mussgnug, Dorothee, 126, 201n12

National Socialist Party, 30
NATO Alliance, 131
natural law theory: of Edgar Bodenheimer, 29, 83–84, 88, 90, 150–52, 155, 182–83; Nuremberg trials based on principles of, 113; revival of in American jurisprudence as result of Nuremberg trials, 124, 150; of St. Thomas Aquinas, 106
Naumann, Max, 29–31
Neustadt, Georg and Elwina (sister of Marie), 79
New Deal, 95
Nietzsche, Friedrich, 16–17, 154–55
Nirenberg, David, 74
Nuremberg, postwar conditions, 115, *116*, 119–20
Nuremberg Grand Hotel, 119
Nuremberg war crimes trial, preparations for, 112–14, 117–18; Edgar Bodenheimer's Nuremberg journal, 112–20, 123–25

*Ostjuden*, 30

Pachter, Henry, 74
Papen, Franz von, 124
Parsons, Talcott, 89
Paulsen, Monrad, 108
Pearl Harbor, Japanese attack on, 95
Peukert, Detlev, 199n13
Pfund, Peter, 146
Planskoy, Beate Frankfurther, 168, 203n7
Potsdammerplatz, Berlin, 132
Pound, Roscoe, 89

Radbruch, Gustav, 26, 58, 121–22
Radin, Max, 147
Rathenau, Walter, 10
Recasens Siches, Luis, 100
Red Army, 120
Reich Flight Tax, 39
Remy, Steven, 127, 201n7
Richthofen, Frieda von, 56–57
Richthofen Jaffé, Else von, 55–57, 58, 76
Roosevelt, Franklin D.: acceptance of Democratic nomination for third term, 94; careful steps toward support for Allies, 94; death of, 105; declaration of war on Germany, 97; Fair Labor Standards Act of 1938, 95; institution of Daylight Savings Time, 86; national draft lottery, 94; peacetime draft law, 91; Selective Training and Service Act of 1940, 94; support for Morgenthau Plan, 116
Roosevelt-Willkie campaign, 90–91
Rosenberg, James, 35, 41
Rowekamp, Marion, 202n5
Russia, Edgar's interest in, 17, 73, 104, 120

Sachs, Eva (sister of Kaethe), 158, 160; classical philologist, 164–65; death in mental hospital in 1936, 165–66; student and assistant of Ulrich von Wilamowitz-Moellendorf, 164–65
Sachs, Hans (brother of Kaethe), 158–61
Sachs, Immanuel (father of Kaethe), 158
Sachs, Irma (wife of Walter), 172
Sachs, Kaethe, 156–75; autobiographical writings, 161–64; born in 1883 to Minna and Immanuel Sachs, 158; death in 1962 and burial in B'nai Israel West cemetery, Salt Lake City, 157, 175; escorted Hesi into Bodenheimer villa in 1934, 36, 166; first cousins of, 158; house at Bastianstrasse 6 in suburb of Berlin, 167; as housekeeper and helper to Fränkel family, 166–67, 171; identity card issued by Berlin police in 1939, 157, 169;

journey toUnited Statesthrough Siberia, Japan, and Mexico, 170–71; letter to Nina in wartime London, 171–73; life as alternative view of German Jewish exile, 157; "Little Wishbook," 163; marriage to Eduard Sachs in 1914, 160, 165; part of Edgar and Brigitte's household from 1945, xviii, 109, 111, 148, 173, 180; photo of, *159*; provision of home for Vera Lachmann in 1937-38, 167–68; return to Germany in 1936, 167; role as intimate and helper in extended Bodenheimer family, 166; with Rosemarie and Brigitte in 1950, *174*; Rosemarie's memories of, 173–75; at Siegmund Bodenheimer's fiftieth birthday celebration in 1924, 164; themes of love, death, and loneliness in life, 163; United States Certificate of Naturalization, 157; verse from brother Hans on her wedding day, 160–61; writing of the death of her husband, 163

Sachs, Lachmann, and Maass cousins: long-term unfulfilled love, 165; suicides and early deaths, 158–60

Sachs, Minna Lachmann (wife of Immanuel), 158

Sachs, Walter (brother of Kaethe), 158, 165, 172

Sachs family tree, *xxi*

Sándor, Arpád, 98, 187

Schacht, Hjalmar, 118, 124

Schellhorn, Irma, 165

Schiller, Friedrich, 2, 9

Schiller, Herbert M., 107–8, 110

Sebald, W. G., *On the Natural History of Destruction*, 119

Seckel, Emil, 46

Seltzer, Claire Wheeler, 77, 81, 184

Seltzer, Lawrence, 77, 81

Silying-Ryu, Helen, 202n5

Simon, Anna (sister of Ernst Levy), 50, 79

Simon, James, 50, 79

Simon, Jörn Martin (cousin of Brigitte), 73, 79

Simon, Ulrich Ernst (cousin of Brigitte), 53, 79

Somme, Battle of, 49

Sorokin, Pitirim, 89

Soviet Union, threat of expansion, 117

Spengler, Oswald, *The Decline of the West*, 16, 31

*Sperrmark*, 39

Spinoza, 74

*St. Louis*, German vessel carrying Jews fleeing Hitler in 1939, xiii

St. Thomas Aquinas, 106

Stalin, Josef, 83, 104, 131, 132

*Stolpersteine* (stumble stones), 191

Stone, Harlan, 95

Strauss, Richard, 4

Streicher, Julius, 118

Sugihara, Chiune, issued Japanese transit visas for Jews, 169–70, 202n6 (Chapter 8)

Sultan, Grete, 172

Swoboda, Camilla and Karl, 55

Symposium on German Jurists in Exile, 1991, 145, 192

Treaty of Versailles of 1919, 12

Truman, Harry, 105, 113

Tucker, Tui St. George, 169

Tustin, Whitney, 187

*UC Davis Law Review*, tributes to Edgar and Brigitte Bodenheimer, 192

Uiberall, Erna and Peter, 120

Uniform Child Custody Jurisdiction Act, 144

United Nations International Criminal Tribunals for former Yugoslavia and Rwanda, 124

United States: denial of visas in 1930 to people who might become burdens on the state, 198n10; isolationist and anti-Semitic attitudes of public, 94; stock market crash of 1929, 24

Utah Symphony, 183

Wagner, Richard, 19, 25; "Das Judentum in der Musik" ("Judaism in Music"), 21–22

Wallach, Kate, 202n5

War Crimes Commission, 112–13, 124

Weber, Alfred, 57, 127

Weber, Marianne: feminist sociologist, 55–56; intellectual salon in Heidelberg,

55, 58, 127; marriage to Max Weber, 56; opposition to Nuremberg trials, 123; response to Brigitte's outreach in 1946, 70; wedding gift to Brigitte and Edgar, 69
Weber, Max, 55–56, 199n8
Weigand, Erika, 169, 171–72
Weimar Republic, xv, 7; ceased to function as democracy by 1932, 25; height of Jewish participation in German public life, 21, 197n10
*Wiedergutmachung*, 138–40, 145
Wilamowitz-Moellendorf, Ulrich von, 164–66
Wilhelm II, Kaiser, 6, 7
Willkie, Wendell, 90–91, 94
Wolff, Emanuel (father of Marie Levy), 47, 51, 132
Wolff, Fritz (brother of Marie Levy), 47, 79
Wolff, Hedwig (mother of Marie Levy), 45, 50–51
World War I: Ernst Levy in, 48–50; Jewish Germans and, 48–49; and Siegmund Bodenheimer, 6–7
Wunderlich, Helen, 77, 85

Zionism, 31, 41
Zyklon B, 115